Desertion in the Early Modern World

Desertion in the Early Modern World
A Comparative History

Edited by Matthias van Rossum and Jeannette Kamp

Bloomsbury Academic
An imprint of Bloomsbury Publishing Plc

BLOOMSBURY
LONDON • OXFORD • NEW YORK • NEW DELHI • SYDNEY

Bloomsbury Academic
An imprint of Bloomsbury Publishing Plc

50 Bedford Square	1385 Broadway
London	New York
WC1B 3DP	NY 10018
UK	USA

www.bloomsbury.com

BLOOMSBURY and the Diana logo are trademarks of Bloomsbury Publishing Plc

First published 2016

© Matthias van Rossum, Jeannette Kamp and Contributors, 2016

All rights reserved. No part of this publication may be reproduced or transmitted in any form or by any means, electronic or mechanical, including photocopying, recording, or any information storage or retrieval system, without prior permission in writing from the publishers.

No responsibility for loss caused to any individual or organization acting on or refraining from action as a result of the material in this publication can be accepted by Bloomsbury or the authors.

British Library Cataloguing-in-Publication Data
A catalogue record for this book is available from the British Library.

ISBN: HB: 978-1-4742-1600-5
PB: 978-1-4742-1599-2
ePDF: 978-1-4742-1601-2
ePub: 978-1-4742-1602-9

Library of Congress Cataloging-in-Publication Data
Desertion in the early modern world : a comparative history / edited by Matthias van Rossum and Jeannette Kamp.
pages cm
1. Desertion, Military—History. 2. Military deserters—History. I. Rossum, Matthias van, 1984– editor. II. Kamp, Jeannette editor.
UB788.D48 2015
355.1'334—dc23
2015018603

Typeset by RefineCatch Limited, Bungay, Suffolk

CONTENTS

Figures and Illustrations vii
Tables viii
Notes on Contributors ix

Desertion in Global History

Introduction: Leaving Work Across the World *Jeannette Kamp and Matthias van Rossum* 3

1   Runaways: A Global History *Alessandro Stanziani* 15

2   Mass Exits: Who, Why, How? *Marcel van der Linden* 31

Europe

3   Between Agency and Force: The Dynamics of Desertion in a Military Labour Market, Frankfurt am Main 1650–1800 *Jeannette Kamp* 49

4   'The Privilege of Using Their Legs': Leaving the Dutch Army in the Eighteenth Century *Pepijn Brandon* 73

Atlantic and Maritime Asia

5   Desertion by Sailors, Slaves and Soldiers in the Dutch Atlantic, c. 1600–1800 *Karwan Fatah-Black* 97

6   'Working for the Devil': Desertion in the Eurasian Empire of the VOC *Matthias van Rossum* 127

Between Worlds

7 Just Deserters: Runaway Slaves from the VOC Cape, c. 1700–1800 *Kate J. Ekama* 161

8 From Contracts to Labour Camps? Desertion and Control in South Asia *Matthias van Rossum* 187

Selected Bibliography 203
Index of Places 209
Subject Index 211

FIGURES AND ILLUSTRATIONS

Figures

4.1 Frequency (in numbers) of first-term soldiers with a fixed-term contract leaving the army through desertion or permits as a function of the percentage of the contractual term served   85

4.2 Frequency (in numbers) of peacetime and wartime exits from the army, 1771–94 (based on sample group)   87

6.1 Absence of VOC workers at departure from Republic (percentages, five-year averages)   138

6.2 VOC employees recruited in the Dutch Republic, deserted and missing, 1680–1788   141

6.3 Desertion rate of VOC workers per departure cohort from Republic (five-year averages)   143

7.1 Convicted runaways, Court of Justice Cape Town, 1700–1800   166

Illustrations

Front cover image Deserter on the run, Van der Vinne, 1714. Collection Rijksmuseum Amsterdam, RP-P-OB-62.334

1 Soldiers in front of the firing squad, anonymous, after Jacques Callot, 1677–90. Collection Rijksmuseum Amsterdam, RP-P-1911-3672   12

2 Map of Northwest Europe   48

3 Two soldiers near a river, Romeyn de Hooghe, 1655–67. Collection Rijksmuseum Amsterdam, RP-P-1933-294   66

4 Map of North and Middle Atlantic   96

5 Slaves working in the fields (Suriname), anonymous, circa 1850. Collection Rijksmuseum Amsterdam, NG-2013-22-19   110

6 Map of Southeast Asia   126

7 Singalese soldiers in the service of the VOC and representatives of the King of Kandy, Jan Brandes, 1785. Collection Rijksmuseum Amsterdam, NG-1985-7-1-8   131

8 Map of South Africa   160

9 Map of South Asia   186

TABLES

4.1 Ways of ending service, final decades of the eighteenth century   85
5.1 Death and desertion of seamen in the service of the MCC (incl. non-Atlantic voyages)   100
5.2 Desertion by MCC seamen in the Atlantic, 1721–98   101
5.3 Seamen who did not desert Atlantic voyages of the MCC ordered by rank   102
5.4 Deaths, desertions and dismissals of military personnel on St Eustatius, 1769–74   104
5.5 Recruitment and desertion by soldiers in Suriname and Curacao, 1700–55   105
5.6 Resistance on plantations in Suriname, 1750–99   106
5.7 Size of groups of escaping slaves in Suriname, 1767–1802   107
5.8 Desertion of MCC seamen related to their place of birth   118
6.1 Revised estimates of the number of workers directly employed by the VOC   133
6.2 Share of VOC employees with *transportbrief*, but without *maandbrief* (percentage)   139
8.1 Desertion rates of European workers, within first six months after arrival (1755–75)   190

NOTES ON CONTRIBUTORS

Pepijn Brandon obtained his PhD (2013) from the University of Amsterdam. His thesis won the 2014 D.J.Veegens award of the Royal Holland Society of the Sciences (KHMW), and will be published by Brill as *War, Capital, and the Dutch State (1588–1795)*. At the moment Brandon is involved in two complementary research projects on slavery and wage labour in the Dutch Atlantic, one at the Vrije Universiteit and the International Institute of Social History in Amsterdam, and one at the University of Pittsburgh where he is currently based.

Kate J. Ekama is a researcher at Leiden University where she is undertaking doctoral research in the NWO-funded project *Challenging Monopolies, Building Global Empires in the Early Modern Period*. Kate completed her BA (Honours) at the University of Cape Town in 2010. She then moved to Leiden University where she graduated with an MA (Cum Laude) in European Expansion and Globalization in 2012. Her thesis examined slavery under the Dutch East India Company in eighteenth-century Colombo. Kate's research interests include Dutch overseas expansion, chartered companies for long-distance trade, early modern slavery in the Indian Ocean World, and legal history.

Karwan Fatah-Black defended his doctoral thesis in October 2013. He lectures at Leiden University College and the Leiden Institute for History. Slavery, smuggling and informality are at the core of his research. As postdoctoral researcher he is presently engaged in the research project *Challenging Monopolies* led by Catia Antunes, investigating the informal empire of free agents operating outside, alongside and against the colonial chartered companies of the Dutch overseas expansion. His monograph *White Lies and Black Markets: Evading Metropolitan Authority in Colonial Suriname, 1650–1800* was published in 2015 by Brill Academic Publishers.

Jeannette Kamp (1986) is a researcher at Leiden University as part of the NWO-funded research project *Crime and Gender 1600–1900: a comparative perspective* (www.crimeandgender.nl). Jeannette studied at Bern University and at VU University Amsterdam, where she completed her MA (Cum Laude) in 2012 with a study on the migration and integration patterns of Swiss soldiers in the eighteenth-century Dutch Republic. Her current doctoral research on crime and gender in Frankfurt am Main in the early modern period deals with questions related to poverty and crime as a survival strategy, the importance of social control and the influence of household authority.

Marcel van der Linden is Professor of Social Movement History at the University of Amsterdam and senior research fellow at the International Institute of Social History (Amsterdam). His recent books include *Workers of the World: Essays toward Global Labor History* (Leiden: Brill, 2008; Brazilian edition, 2013), and *Beyond Marx: Theorising the Global Labour Relations of the Twenty-first Century* (Leiden: Brill, 2013; paperback: Chicago: Haymarket, 2014).

Matthias van Rossum is senior researcher at the International Institute of Social History (Amsterdam) and lecturer at Leiden University. He received his PhD from the VU University Amsterdam (2013) for his thesis on European and Asian sailors working for the VOC, published as *Werkers van de wereld* (Verloren: Hilversum, 2014). His study into the dynamics of race and class in maritime labour markets *Hand aan hand (Blank en Bruin)* (Aksant: Amsterdam, 2009) was awarded the J.R. Bruijn-prijs (2009). He has published various international and Dutch articles on topics related to global labour history, maritime history and the histories of slavery and revolt.

Alessandro Stanziani is Professor at the EHESS and senior researcher at the CNRS, Paris. He teaches Global History and is the author of seven individual books, eight collective books and more than one hundred articles in peer review journals. His recent books include *Rules of Exchange: French Capitalism in Comparative Perspective* (Cambridge: Cambridge University Press, 2012); *Bondage: Labor and Rights in Eurasia from the Sixteenth to the Early Twentieth Centuries* (New York: Berghahn, 2014); *After Oriental Despotism: Eurasian Growth in Global Perspective* (London: Bloomsbury, 2014); and *Slaves, Migrants and Seamen in the Indian Ocean, 1750–1914* (New York: Palgrave, 2014).

Desertion in Global History

Introduction:

Leaving Work Across the World

Jeannette Kamp and Matthias van Rossum

Not unlike desertion, history is a festival of alternatives. It is about being confronted with different realities; to transgress the boundaries and limitations of what seemed static or fixed. It is about understanding these alternatives and possibilities – by studying the information preserved in fragments of the past, but also by reasoning, explaining and imagining.

This is what deserters did. They assessed their situations, and they weighed information about other opportunities. This meant puzzling together fragments of information on the possibilities of life and work outside the walls of their workplaces and cities. In this process, runaways often had to rely on fellow workers, working outside and coming back, on *go-betweens*, such as translators, message runners and carriers, or on networks of former deserters, recruiters and intermediaries. Perhaps most importantly, deserters – or anyone exploring the opportunities of running away from work – must have envisioned the possibility of a better life.

The history of desertion has often been written in isolation, studying specific groups in their respective fields of study, such as desertion of soldiers in military history or maroons and slave runaways in the history of slavery. Most of these studies did touch upon the notion of desertion as an integral part of workers' lives and strategies. Nevertheless, most studies have not applied their notion of desertion outside their field of study or compared strategies of various groups of workers. This volume aims to collect and study the experiences of various groups and type of workers across the world from a global and comparative perspective.

The histories of desertion that are central to this study are histories of work, histories of migration and, more in general, histories of the lives of working people that were often extremely global.[1] Mobility and desertion must be seen as integral parts of workers' strategies, part of repertoires of individual and collective acts, ranging from obedience and career making to strikes and mutinies.[2] Desertion is crucial in this respect as it was not only a rejection of one's work and working conditions, but was also related to finding a better future, lying either in new and better employment elsewhere, or in alternative ways of livelihood. This could mean escape leading to casual forms of livelihood in which runaways sustained themselves with daily wage work within the same economic environment, but also escape leading to forms of robbery and violence, and even more independent forms of existence in maroons.

Their histories are important because they shed new light on the worlds they ran from: they often provide detailed information on the physical and economic alternatives and opportunities of the early modern era. As running from work was often illegal, the sources remaining from these cases provide statements and traces of the imaginations of runaway workers that would otherwise have withered away.

This history of work and defiance is connected to the history of globalization, economic development and social relations in several ways. In the early modern period, millions of workers operated the ships, ports, storehouses, forts, plantations and factories that were crucial to local and global exchanges. Globalization was built on a highly labour-intensive infrastructure. The workers that were crucial to this process of early globalization, such as sailors, soldiers, craftsmen and slaves, were directly confronted with the effects of globalization themselves. Most of these workers were migrants and trading companies, merchants and states tried to discipline and control this extremely mobile workforce. Although often perceived as 'free' labour, contracts were employed as part of the strategy to bind them to their work. These contracts could last for years, criminalizing mobility and all kinds of 'defiant' behaviour.

Workers were not only crucial to global transportation and infrastructure, but also to globalized production. Labour-intensive paths to economic development were dominant throughout Eurasia in this period.[3] These trajectories are seen more and more as pivotal in the global diffusion of economic development.[4] Labour-intensive paths not only increased the *demand for* labour, but also the *constraints on* labour. The large demand for skilled and unskilled labour could create heavy competition between employers. The early modern period witnessed expanding labour markets and monetization around the globe.[5] This did not necessarily lead to the emergence of what one might think of as 'free' labour markets. On the contrary, labour-intensive paths to economic development strengthened the use of coercive labour relations as well as of coercive mechanisms in what could be seen as more or technically 'free' labour relations. Especially in the context of economic production, the early modern period was not so much characterized by the strong rise of contract labour, but much more by the remarkable expansion of the slave trade and slavery, serfdom and systems of corvée.

These developments were not isolated or distinctly 'Asian', 'African' or 'American' phenomena. The different phases of production, transport and consumption of the various important early modern global commodities were linked through worldwide systems of trade and power. As still seems the case today, coercive mechanisms were crucial in much of the labour-intensive work needed in the early or primary production stages of global commodity chains. The products concerned, such as spices, sugar, coffee, textiles, gunpowder, silver, gold, etc., immediately remind us of the workplaces involved, being plantations, mines, factories, forts and so on.

Workers were bound in various ways. The relations between workers, employers or entrepreneurs, and authorities were different in each situation, varying per labour relation, region and period. Control over the workforce did not only come from formal rules, laid down in laws and regulations related to labour, but was situated especially in a whole range of practical and physical arrangements, touching upon working environments, public space and daily life. Workers that broke through these formal and informal constraints on their mobility and life became subject to the repressive apparatuses set up by early modern corporations, institutions and states. Many of these initiatives entailed (international) contacts and contracts between different cities, states and empires. The constant flow of desertion of the early modern world directly affected the implementation and refinement of mechanisms of control and discipline. This entailed systems of identification, distinction and segregation that must have had a crucial impact on social and intercultural relations, aggravating tensions between occupational, rural–urban and ethnic divides, especially in imperial and later colonial contexts.

This project on the history of desertion has set out to study the dynamics and impact of desertion from a global and comparative perspective. The first step was taken at the conference session *Leaving work across the world: Comparing desertion in early modern globalization, 1600–1800* held as part of the European Conference of Global History in Paris (ENIUGH, September 2014).[6] The aim was to trace and compare acts and patterns of desertion across empires, economic systems, regions and types of workers. Defining 'desertion' as unpermitted absence from work sheds light on the broadness of the phenomenon, being a breach of labour obligations to authorities and employers, and a strategic act to workers. This has taken the history of desertion beyond the field of military history and right into the centre of the global histories of labour and migration.

In our perspective, it was important to relate desertion not only to the workplace, labour conditions and workers' strategies, but also to the surrounding environments and the opportunities offered. These could vary from 'open' and 'empty' landscapes offering opportunities for settlement and freedom, to 'urban' areas providing anonymity and shelter. Bringing these different sides together, the contributions to the session aimed to collect and study information on workers' perception of economic opportunity, conditions of work, strategies of revolt and, finally, how these practices among workers shaped the (much larger) history of imperial and economic expansion in the early modern period.

Studying desertion from a comparative perspective, the contributions addressed a common set of six research variables, covering: the quantification of occurrence of desertion, the definitions of desertion, the patterns of desertion, the mechanisms of control, desertion as an economic act, and desertion as a socio-political act. The studies presented at the session provide the core of the case studies in this volume. Two contextualizing contributions have been added afterwards. As academic work is marked by pressure, not all intended contributions made it to the volume. A book on desertion, of course, is not complete without its own runaways.[7]

This book brings together in-depth studies investigating desertion, control and workers' strategies throughout the early modern period in different parts of the world.[8] The two contextualizing contributions by Alessandro Stanziani and Marcel van der Linden provide a more theoretical framework to the chapters with historical case studies, covering a wide range of examples from world history (Van der Linden) and long-lasting historical developments from different imperial contexts connecting the early modern period to the nineteenth and twentieth centuries (Stanziani). The chapters with historical case studies collectively deal with groups of workers that stood at the core of the early modern Dutch global imperial sphere. Spanning the globe, these cases involve soldiers recruited in the Dutch Republic and the German hinterland, the large numbers of workers in the service of trading companies, especially sailors, soldiers and artisans (both European and non-European), corvée workers in South Asia, and – to conclude – enslaved workers transported and employed in the Dutch Atlantic world, but also in South Africa and South and Southeast Asia. After the chapters on desertion in global history (introduction; Stanziani; Van der Linden), the volume will take the reader from European case studies (Kamp; Brandon), to overviews of desertion in and around the Dutch Atlantic and Asian empires (Fatah-Black; Van Rossum) and then again to specific (African and Asian) case studies of the dynamics of desertion in regions playing an important role in early modern global (economic and cultural) exchange (Ekama; Van Rossum).

The numbers of workers involved are incredible. Over the course of the seventeenth and eighteenth centuries, it is estimated that some two million soldiers were recruited for the Dutch State Army – of whom half came from outside the Dutch Republic. The Dutch East India Company (VOC) sent out almost one million sailors, soldiers, artisans and other workers from the Dutch Republic to Asia. Simultaneously, the VOC recruited thousands and thousands of Asian, Eurasian and sometimes European workers in Asia – mainly soldiers, sailors and artisans. Thousands of workers in South Asia, especially in coastal Sri Lanka, performed obligated corvée labour for the Company. In the Atlantic world, some hundred thousand sailors and soldiers were sent out by the Middelburgsche Commercie Compagnie (MCC), the Dutch West Indian Company (WIC) and many other merchants. The Dutch Navy employed hundreds of thousands of sailors and soldiers. And of the estimated 12.5 million enslaved Africans transported by European powers to the Americas, more than 600,000 slaves were shipped by Dutch merchants. Furthermore, it is now estimated that no less than several hundred thousand, perhaps a million, Asian and African slaves must have been shipped to Dutch-controlled Asian territories, mainly by private traders and VOC personnel.[9] These numbers are intimidating, especially considering these are only the numbers of workers centring on the early modern Dutch global imperial nexus.

Millions of soldiers and sailors were employed around the world, moving significant distances as part of their occupation. For Europe the total average annual maritime workforce in Europe is estimated at some 240,000 sailors towards the end of the sixteenth century, rising to 400,000 sailors in the second half of the eighteenth century.[10] For other parts of the world, such as maritime Asia, estimates of the maritime workforce engaged by navies and merchant marines are scarce, but the size of shipping activity seems to indicate that large numbers of sailors must have been employed.[11] For the total number of troops employed in Europe at one single moment estimates range from 1.3 million (around 1710) to two million on the eve of the French Revolution.[12] It has been estimated that this involved some eight million individuals around the middle of the seventeenth century, rising to some thirteen million individuals in the second half of the eighteenth century.[13] In South Asia, millions of soldiers were employed in standing and irregular or campaign armies, engaged through slavery, corvée or wage labour.[14] In China, the Ming dynasty upheld an army of some three million soldiers in the early fifteenth century, engaged in military, agricultural and transport work. Soldiers were drafted from (hereditary) systems of corvée and garrison labour, but increasingly from the fifteenth century onwards also from hired labour. Both types of soldiers were reported to desert in large numbers. While soldiers in the hereditary garrison system ran from their corvée duties, hired soldiers often 'signed up, received their bonuses, and fled as soon as possible'. It was claimed by officials 'that some men did this on a serial basis'.[15]

Around the globe, many more millions of workers were employed in such a way that they were in some degree bound to their work, ranging from contract labourers to servants, and from corvée labourers to slaves. One striking aspect seems to be the high level of men among these workers. Indeed, some occupations involved were almost exclusively male, such as maritime and military labour. At the same time, most of the armies involved were accompanied by (predominantly female populated) 'army trains', although it is uncertain whether (or how) they were themselves bound to their work or situation. In Europe, several female occupations figure prominently among the population of workers and migrants bound to their work. Female servants especially were often bound through various regulations via contract and domestic law, making departure without permission an offence with serious legal and practical consequences. In similar fashion, it must be noted, running from marriage by men and women was also perceived as a form of desertion well into the twentieth century. The bonds of slavery also affected both men and women, although men often did make up the majority of the population of enslaved workers and deserters, as we will encounter in the contributions of this volume. The role of domestic law in enforcing regulatory regimes (based on contracts, the authority of heads of households, etc.) might be an important factor in explaining the under-representation of women in legal and administrative (state) sources on work and desertion.

The contributions in this volume show that desertion was a widespread phenomenon throughout the early modern world and that its dynamics can (and must) be studied in a comparative way. All contributions stress the importance of employing an inclusive definition. Van der Linden distinguishes between six groups of mass deserters: soldiers and navy personnel, sailors on merchant fleets, slaves, peasants, indentured labourers, and, finally, convicts and inmates. Stanziani adds that the history of runaways is 'a global history in the sense that it concerned all working people'. Due to the widespread notion of work as a service, Stanziani explains, leaving work – i.e. desertion – became criminalized. All these people did indeed run from their work. The case studies indicate, however, that definitions were not as clear-cut as one might expect. The lines between temporary absence and more permanent forms of desertion were often fuzzy. Especially for contract workers some degree of absence was tolerated (Fatah-Black; Brandon; Van Rossum). Absence could lead to desertion if one remained absent too long (Kamp). For slaves similar distinctions were employed, such as *petit marronage* (temporary absenteeism) and the permanent *grand marronage* (Fatah-Black). Under the VOC, temporary absence by slaves was dealt with through domestic law, and desertion through criminal courts (Ekama). Authorities actively struggled with employing these definitions and legal distinctions (Van Rossum).

Desertion took on considerable proportions. A number of methods can be employed to measure the incidence of desertion. First, desertion rates calculated via the number of desertions in a short period of time (often one year) from one specific place or regional workforce. Second, desertion rates calculated via the number of desertions in a short period of time (often one year) from one specific cohort of workers. Third, desertion rates calculated over a longer period taking the share of desertions relative to other ways of exit. The type of desertion rate used often depends on the sources available. This leads to different ways to assess the occurrence of desertion. The first two types of desertion rates (per place and per cohort) can be compared without too much distortion. The third rate provides a fairly different measurement.

Desertion rates were not constant. Of course, they rose in times of war and political instability, but even in normal conditions the number of desertions was considerable. In eighteenth-century Germany armies were characterized by an annual desertion rate of around 5 per cent in peacetime. In Prussia, in total some 20 to 30 per cent of its troops left through desertion; in other German regions this was between 40 and 50 per cent (Kamp). In the Dutch Republic, desertion seems to have been the most important way of exit: more than 40 per cent of the soldiers ended their service through desertion (Brandon). The VOC faced a general annual desertion rate of 5 per cent in settlements such as Surat and Bengal, but here too desertion rates could peak. The Portuguese fleet at Goa lost 14 per cent of its workers in 1759, while 10 per cent ran within the first half year from the VOC fleet in Bengal in 1770 (Van Rossum). Slaves in Suriname were less inclined to run. The desertion rate was estimated at 0.5 per cent. Roughly the same number of slaves ran away, but returned later (Fatah-Black).

The dynamics of desertion in highly urbanized regions or large cities, and in economically developed areas, were distinctly different from the dynamics in small settlements and frontier regions. This seems to have created rather comparable patterns of desertion and labour market mobility in Europe, South and Southeast Asia, especially when considering military and maritime labour markets. Although regions were marked by specific differences, for example the presence of systems of slavery or corvée, dynamics in frontier societies seem to have evolved mainly around escaping the smaller settler communities and crossing imperial borders. Bands of runaways posed threats to public order all around the globe, with former soldiers running amok in Europe and Brazil, and runaway slaves marooning in Suriname, at the Cape, Ambon and around Batavia.[16]

The socio-economic and geographical characteristics of a region determined to a large extent the opportunities provided and the strategies employed. Individual desertions occurred everywhere, but almost nowhere was desertion a completely individualized act. Runaways acquired the help of friends, relatives, intermediaries and strangers. Often individual runaways relied on (temporary) alliances – they ran alone, collaborated with others for a while and joined a different group. Running together did provide specific advantages over being on the run alone (see, for example, in the chapters of Ekama and Van der Linden).

For group desertion two important distinctions must be made. First, the size of the group, varying from pairs, small groups to larger groups. Second, carefully planned versus accidentally created groups. The interesting function of couples or pairs is noted by Fatah-Black. Desertion in small numbers – from pairs to roughly four to six runaways – seems to have been very functional in providing sufficient support while still minimizing the risks of plans leaking out. Planned desertions by groups were more often the case in situations where breaking out proved more challenging, for example in the case of slaves trying to get out of Cape Town (Ekama) or soldiers running from forts (Fatah-Black; Van Rossum). This type of desertion especially gave rise to enforcing group loyalty through bonds and rituals, such as blood oaths and lists of participants signed in circles, so-called 'round robins'. The agreements made were not without consequences as they could be enforced through peer pressure and violence (Ekama; Fatah-Black).

It is important to note that individual or paired desertions could quickly succeed another, gradually leading to desertion of small groups or turning into larger waves of desertion. This brings to mind another type of desertion in which group formation occurred after the desertion. The case of Batavia indicates that large crowded cities provided more opportunities and shelter, making individual escape more feasible and leaving more space for survival via casual alliances or post-desertion group formation. European urbanized areas may have had similar characteristics.

Intermediaries played a crucial and intriguing role in desertion. Of course, recruitment intermediaries sometimes lured workers into contract labour or other coercive arrangements. Intermediaries also facilitated desertion, providing ways from contract to contract, from slavery to contract labour, or even completely out of coercive labour systems. As such, various kinds of intermediaries were crucial in entering, bridging and exiting these labour relations. It must be noted here that desertion and coerced recruitment sometimes overlapped. Systems of 'free' and 'coerced' labour mobilization were closely intertwined, both in Europe and in Asia (Kamp; Van Rossum). Labour markets, in that sense, had a double effect, or as Stanziani reminds us: 'there was no opposition between market and coercion, or between public and private control of labour'.

So why did people desert? Or – taking into account the coercive elements in the labour relations involved – why did not simply everyone run? In general, regardless of the type of desertion and the type of labour relation, running away was a means of improving one's situation. Van der Linden points to two criteria for the occurrence of desertion: issues and triggers. If we consider the issues involved, it is possible to distinguish between negative and positive features – perhaps roughly coinciding with push and pull factors.

First and foremost, desertion was stimulated by work-related grievances: violence; harsh conditions resulting from food, accommodation, treatment; fear of deterioration of conditions in the (near) future. Almost all case studies point out that there was a shared sense of what was considered as acceptable – and what not – among different groups of workers. This included shared notions of justice related to working conditions, privileges and rights. The examples are quite telling. Crews of sailors refusing to sail ships in bad conditions, or walking away after refusing an order to unload the ship before getting their food (Fatah-Black). Corvée workers using absence as a collective means against the banishment of four locals (Van Rossum). Soldiers demanding the right to complain against maltreatment (Brandon; Kamp).

Slaves expressed their notions of justice with regard to small allowances (Van Rossum) or treatment (Ekama; Fatah-Black).

Many of the workers on the run had some level of experience or some kind of developed or specific skill they could employ elsewhere. This seems to be the case for soldiers running at the beginning of their contract (Brandon; Kamp), but also for the (experienced) sailors running in Atlantic and Asian regions with high demand for maritime labour (Fatah-Black; Van Rossum). This brings to our attention the relations between skill, desertion and career. Skills and careers could be an incentive to run, especially in the case of vibrant labour markets. At the same time, they could also be an important incentive to stay, for example, in the case of workers hoping to climb the career ladders of their current employer. The places of origin of workers were a factor of importance in these dynamics as they influenced networks of patronage, access to career opportunities and thus a sense of loyalty. In the case of the MCC, workers in the direct proximity of the Zeeland headquarters, especially from the island of Walcheren, were not likely to desert, while the desertion rate of the workers originating from places from a couple of days' walking was extremely high (Fatah-Black). Skilled workers from longer distances, especially Scandinavians, were more loyal as they found it easier to make careers on Dutch ships (Van Rossum). The dynamics of desertion were intimately linked to payment, social mobility, but also to other domains of life such as family ties and social bonds.

The structural levels of desertion stimulated the development of countermeasures. Pragmatism seemed one of the crucial features of the attitudes of authorities and employers towards desertion. Measures varied between extremely harsh punishments and pardons, depending on the need for manpower. In many cases, authorities dealt with desertion via a 'pardon' in 'punishment', for example by making deserters run the gauntlet instead of sentencing them to death. Although this might seem to indicate developments towards 'free' labour relations at first sight, this was actually a way to spare much needed labour power. At the same time, it can't be ignored that such punishments were in fact extremely brutal and could entail enduring physical consequences for workers. These punishments were feared broadly (Kamp).

Authorities mostly relied on mechanisms of control that were more refined than either punishments or pardons. First, financial and administrative mechanisms of control were created to ensure the loyalty of workers via the regulation of payment. Debts were also strongly regulated, on the one hand trying to retain control of the worker through debt, on the other hand attempting to limit the level of indebtedness, especially to civilian populations or other third parties (Kamp). Second, employers, cities and states pushed for increasing social control. They launched public assaults on the honour of the deserter, marked retrieved runaways physically, and ensured the involvement of citizens through the use of domestic law. Third, physical and public measures of control closed off working environments, creating situations that sometimes started to resemble total institutions or labour camps – forts, ships, plantations, mines, etc. Authorities employed mechanisms that created varied regimes of access to public and corporate spaces, keeping people in and out, through passes, guards and even 'hunting systems' (Fatah-Black; Van der Linden; Van Rossum). The display of power against deserters was overwhelming – and it seems that the violent and public character of control and punishment was even stronger – and remained longer – in contexts where authorities needed to establish their control. Several contributions indicate the impact of these dynamics in the context of European expansion into non-European worlds on intercultural relations and racialization (Fatah-Black; Van Rossum; Stanziani).

All these insights – and much more – are studied in detail in the chapters of this volume. But before setting off on this runaways' journey across the world, it seems fruitful to briefly reflect on the interesting routes meriting exploration in future research. After this world historical comparison, many important questions remain. Noting the structural and recurrent dynamics of desertion, it must be asked what the impact of these structural and sometimes virulent flows of deserters around the globe was on states, employers and communities. The cases presented here indicate that the mechanisms of coercion and control encountered in the histories of runaways were not at the margins of the early modern world system, and its colonial successor, but right at its core. How does that shift our perspective on the history of globalization, labour, migration and economic development? If markets have been part of human history for a much longer time than the Eurocentric thinkers of the nineteenth century have instructed us – and if markets and coercion can be closely intertwined – many new historical horizons are to be explored. These new questions not only relate to the global roots of capitalism and inequality, but also to the global roots of workers' strategies, resistance and alternatives.

ILLUSTRATION 1 *Soldiers in front of the firing squad, anonymous, after Jacques Callot, 1677–90. Collection Rijksmuseum Amsterdam, RP-P-1911-3672.*

Notes

1 Clare Anderson, *Subaltern Lives: Biographies of Colonialism in the Indian Ocean World, 1790–1920* (Cambridge: Cambridge University Press, 2012); Peter Linebaugh and Marcus Rediker, *The Many-headed Hydra: Sailors, Slaves, Commoners, and the Hidden History of the Revolutionary Atlantic* (Boston: Beacon Press, 2000); Miles Ogborn, *Global Lives: Britain and the World 1550–1800* (Cambridge: Cambridge University Press, 2008).

2 Clare Anderson, Niklas Frykman, Lex Heerma van Voss and Marcus Rediker (eds), *Mutiny and Maritime Radicalism in the Age of Revolution: A Global Survey* (Cambridge: Cambridge University Press, 2014). Lex Heerma van Voss, *Petitions in Social History* (Cambridge: Cambridge University Press, 2002).

3 A. Stanziani, *After Oriental Despotism: Eurasian Growth in a Global Perspective* (London: Bloomsbury, 2014).

4 G. Austin and K. Sugihara, *Labour-Intensive Industrialization in Global History* (Abingdon: Routledge, 2013).

5 Jan Lucassen, 'Deep Monetization, Commercialization, and Proletarization: Possible Links, India 1200–1900', in S. Bhattacharya (ed.), *Towards a New History of Work* (New Delhi: Tulika, 2014); J. Lucassen, 'Een geschiedenis van de arbeid in grote lijnen' (retirement lecture, Vrije Universiteit Amsterdam, 2012).

6 We would like to express our gratitude to Marjolein 't Hart for her stimulating and encouraging comments at the conference.

7 We are thankful for the intellectual contributions of Titas Chakraborty and Marcus Rediker, and look forward to collaborations in future missions in the study of this topic.

8 Special thanks goes to Erik Odegard for providing the maps visualizing the global dimension of this study.

9 Matthias van Rossum, *Kleurrijke tragiek: De geschiedenis van Nederlandse slavernij in Azië onder de VOC* (Hilversum: Uitgeverij Verloren, 2015).

10 Jan Lucassen and Leo Lucassen, 'The Mobility Transition in Europe Revisited, 1500–1900: Sources and Methods', IISH Research Paper 46, www.iisg.nl, p. 63.

11 M. van Rossum, 'The Rise of the Asian Sailor? Inter-Asiatic Shipping, the Dutch East India Company and Maritime Labour Markets (1500–1800)', in Bhattacharya, *Towards a New History of Work*, pp. 180–213.

12 G. Parker, *Spain and the Netherlands, 1559–1569: Ten Studies* (London: Collins, 1979), p. 102; G. Parker, *The Military Revolution: Military Innovation and the Rise of the West, 1500–1800* (Cambridge: Cambridge University Press, 1988) p. 46; J. Luh, *Ancien Régime Warfare and the Military Revolution: A Study* (Groningen: INOS, 2000), p. 13; Lucassen and Leo Lucassen, 'The Mobility Transition', p. 101.

13 Lucassen and Lucassen, 'The Mobility Transition', pp. 101–2.

14 Kaushik Roy, 'From the Mamluks to the Mansabdars: A Social History of Military Service in South Asia, c. 1500 to c. 1650', in Erik-Jan Zürcher (ed.), *Fighting for a Living: A Comparative History of Military Labour 1500–2000*

(Amsterdam: Amsterdam University Press, 2013), pp. 81–114; Dirk H.A. Kolff, 'Peasants Fighting for a Living in Early Modern North India', in Zürcher (ed.), *Fighting for a Living*, pp. 243–66.

15 David M. Robinson, 'Military Labor in China, c. 1500', in Zürcher (ed.), *Fighting for a Living*, pp. 43–80, 45, 48.

16 G.J. Knaap, *Kruidnagelen en Christenen: De Verenigde Oost-Indische Compagnie en de bevolking van Ambon 1656–1696* (Dordrecht: Foris Publications, 1987), pp. 128–35.

1

Runaways:

A Global History

Alessandro Stanziani

We usually associate runaways, fugitives and deserters with two main categories of people: maroon slaves and conscripts. In this chapter, we will take a different position, arguing that the history of runaways – from the mid-seventeenth century to the end of the nineteenth century in Europe and well into the twentieth century in other parts of the world – is a global history in the sense that it concerned all working people – slaves, serfs, indentured immigrants, bonded persons, apprentices, servants and even, up to a point, wage earners, as well as convicts, seamen and soldiers. As such, fugitive working people bypassed the conventional dichotomies between military conscription and labour markets, free and unfree labour and slaves and serfs as opposed to wage earners.

Runaways, maroons, vagrants and other fugitive people did not merely express 'resistance', as most scholars have argued.[1] They need to be seen as part of a broader picture. First and foremost, if we adopt the well-known Hirschman trilogy (voice, exit and loyalty), runaways undoubtedly expressed a form of exit where their voice was weak or non-existent, and their loyalty was therefore equally weak.[2] The question here concerns not so much the validity of the general principle as the relationships among these categories in specific historical and spatial contexts. Was exit always the opposite of voice? Were there contexts in which they played complementary roles? If so, then why?

We argue that runaways as a form of exit cannot be understood without taking into account the fact that, between the seventeenth and the early twentieth centuries, working people – slaves or serfs, day labourers or servants, conscripts or convicts – had no voice or only a very weak one in the broader sense: no political rights, very few civil rights, unequal legal rights, no social rights. They were runaways because they had no voice and thus no choice.[3]

At the same time, this tension could not have been socially and legally validated if labour had not been considered a service to the master (not the employer), the state, the village, and/or the social community.[4] Labour was a duty and, for this reason, working people were supposed to devote all their working time to their master or the head of the family, the village, the state, etc. Labour as service meant that all those who escaped from it were deemed fugitives or vagrants. Ownership of time and ownership of people were blurred categories during this period. The amount of time devoted to labour was far more crucial than its quality, and therefore elites, masters and heads of households demanded control over labour time.[5] The limitations on mobility and titles of ownership of people converged and, in extreme cases, coincided, for example in the case of slaves, serfs and certain forms of indentured immigrants. But even in other cases, the general notion of labour as service led to establishing a close normative relationship between control over time and control over people.[6]

This explains why the social order was so closely linked to the political order in issues concerning runaways and in labour issues generally during the period under study. One of the main purposes of the rules governing runaways was to maintain the market in a well-ordered, hierarchical society. There was no opposition between the market and coercion, or between public and private control of labour, as liberal interpreters of capitalism have argued since Smith; on the contrary, they were perfectly adapted to each other.[7]

To demonstrate these points, in the following pages we will briefly recall the role of fugitives in several different contexts: the Navy and the process of colonization in the seventeenth and eighteenth centuries; runaways before, during and after slavery (indentured immigrants); and finally the meaning of runaways in industrializing Europe (from the eighteenth to the early twentieth centuries).

When labour market met military markets: Fugitive seamen and colonial expansion

The long history of French seamen was that of the slow decline of the galleys and of the ever insufficient and increasingly problematic separation between military conscription and the merchant navy. In 1630, Marseille's arsenal fleet comprised approximately 6,000 galley slaves, and Colbert organized a veritable system of recruitment in prisons in order to meet demand.[8] Along with Moors and Turks, magistrates sent to the galleys thieves, salt smugglers, violent criminals, libertines, vagabonds, rebels and those who had simply been convicted of disturbing the peace, to which we must of course add smugglers and Protestants. The recourse to coercion was preferred to increasing wages not only by the Royal Navy but also by merchant and fishing communities. Sailors and seamen had limited rights, and any absenteeism was qualified as desertion and, as such, was subject to criminal law.[9] The French East India Company increased recruitment through alternative channels, i.e. more or less forcible enrolment in the ports and hinterlands. The recruitment of foreigners from Europe (Ireland, Genoa, Portugal, Naples), and then of Indians, Sinhalese and others then became more widespread. The French East India Company also used its trading post in Senegal to 'recruit' *laptots*, famous Senegalese sailors and navigators, whom it employed for four to five months to sail back up the river.[10]

As from 1644, on a large scale and in a systematic manner, England was employing the press-gang system. The Navy targeted entire districts and cared not whether the people it caught were real seamen or not; in the name of military imperative and national defence, they were seized and embarked. As from the end of the seventeenth century, some people were questioning the constitutional legitimacy of this practice, but jurisprudential decisions were all in favour of the Navy, placing individual rights behind those of the nation's military interests. Following these decisions, Royal Navy sailors were not protected by the Magna Carta. On the other hand, the 1597 Vagrancy Act included royal ships as one of the destinations for vagabonds, thus highlighting once again the close links between duress, military service and 'ordinary' work.

The 1703 Act excluded from the press-gang system anyone under the age of 18 who had already completed their apprenticeship.[11] This was a very important step as it demonstrated the link between maritime conscription, the labour market and social order. It met two demands: the first by masters, employers and guilds who said that apprenticeships were costly and beneficial not only to masters but to the nation. It would therefore be a waste to send to sea young men who had been trained in other professions. This argument was in line with the content of the 1692 Poor Law, which included apprenticeships among the conditions which excluded individuals from having to state their place of residence.

Having excluded apprentices from press-gang recruitment in both England and France, towards the middle of the eighteenth century, the question then arose of the link between these forms of recruiting and slavery. Charter companies and slave ships frequently used slaves as seamen. However, this increasingly widespread practice was causing protests from growers in the West Indies and the Americas, who were concerned about competition in the slave market from the Navy.[12]

The same problem existed with regard to the recruiting of sailors; this link was established between the recruitment of sailors and the allocation of slaves. In both cases, the American colonies protested against England, with whom they were competing for access to manpower, be it slaves or seamen, these two categories being easily confused, both in the case of African slaves employed as seamen, emancipated slaves or even sailors and embarked indentured white men.

In England, the relationship between the forcible seizure of sailors and slavery was more complicated. The famous 'Somerset case' of 1772 has often been put forward as the first real abolitionist act. The judge ruled that a slave was deemed to be emancipated as soon as he laid foot on British soil and that he could not be returned to slavery. Less familiar to historians, this same act immediately sparked a debate on sailors: if no one could be enslaved on British soil, how could the forcible recruitment of sailors be justified?[13]

Yet whilst the anti-slavery campaign led to concrete measures being taken for slaves, steps taken with regard to sailors were far more modest. Their forced recruitment in port taverns, or even on merchant vessels, continued to be practiced on a large scale. Forced recruitment was practiced with the blessing of numerous legal decisions which stressed the difference between the 'fully aware' sailor on the one hand and children and slaves on the other. Sailors' debauchery was invoked to stigmatize their behaviour and justify such abuse. In other words, in accordance with the law and with the morals of the time, children and slaves should be protected because they have no real will; on the other hand, persons who were legally free did not require protection and bore sole responsibility for their degeneration. This was the case for 'drunken sailors', prostitutes and all persons placed in workhouses.

The decriminalization of sailors' contracts was only validated in a law passed in 1880, before once again being criminalized to a partial extent in 1894. Most important, these rules did not concern colonial seamen.[14] Lascars in particular were to be found in larger numbers on English ships, to such an extent that towards the end of the century they represented 20 per cent of crews.[15] Recruiting essentially took place on site: partly in India – mainly in Bombay where the Royal Navy disembarked a large number of Indian and African slaves 'freed' from their European, Arab and African masters. This same practice was common in Zanzibar, where Africans emancipated inland by the English, along with a mass of 'vagabonds', day workers, indentured servants and slaves who had fled their masters, were to be found in ever-increasing numbers.[16] Further north, Aden was a port filled with fugitives, former slaves, etc.[17] Freed slaves were not free to go wherever they wished – the reasons given were fears of vagrancy and of them being enslaved once again. So they were dispatched to the homes of 'respectable' local elites or sent to other British enclaves in the Indian Ocean.

Strict rules against desertion were thus needed to maintain this segmented market and to perpetuate these inequalities. Indeed, what shipowners feared the most was that upon arriving in an English port, the lascars would escape and go into town to find better working conditions. In 1844 – the year in which the Poor Law was repealed and when for the very first time industrial workers won their case in Parliament in relation to the Masters and Servants

Act – a new Merchant Seamen Act was passed. The details of sailors employed on British ships were written on a 'ticket' – not just their height, weight, hair and eye colour, but also their education and maritime career. When this ticket was complete, all of the information was entered into a sailors register. The aim was to combat desertion.[18] Yet the problem of deserters persisted, also because this category was still in use in the British labour market.

Runaways in colonial production: From white indentured to black slaves to 'coloured' indentured immigrants

In the French as well as in the British colonies, the contract of indentured service was developed in the seventeenth century. It was initially intended for white settlers whose transport expenses were advanced by employers or their middlemen in exchange for a commitment to work for several years. The indentured immigrants were subject to criminal penalties and could be transferred along with their contract to other masters. The indenture contract, which historians have usually considered a form of forced labour, was not placed in this category until the middle of the nineteenth century. Until that point, ever since the seventeenth century, indenture had been viewed in the strictest sense as an expression of free contract; the individual bound by the contract was just a servant whose travel expenses were paid in advance and who committed himself for a longer period of time than a labourer but for a shorter one than a domestic servant. Like the others, however, he owed all this time to his master, who could sell the indentured servant along with any debts he still owed to someone else. Just as a master in Great Britain had the right to recover fugitives, so too in the colonies: indentured servants who fled were subject to criminal penalties. Without the Masters and Servants Acts, indenture would not have been possible. The labour contract was no fiction, but a real tool in the master's hand.

This situation was all the more important in that masters in the colonies gradually obtained broader rights than masters in Great Britain. They could exercise corporal punishment, authorize the marriage of indentured servants, etc. In Britain as in France, the indentured contract mixed the clauses of two existing contracts: the daily rural labourer and the seaman. In both cases, working people owned all their time to their master, could not move without his authorization, and were under criminal penalties (desertion, breach of contract). Nevertheless, the rate of desertion was high in both the British and the French colonies as many indentured immigrants preferred to lose eventual rights after the end of their service than to have their low wages under harsh conditions.[19] It was not by chance that the first slaves landing in the American colonies were considered either as war captives or as servants (under indentured contracts). Progressive differentiation from these other categories took place during the second half of the seventeenth century when chattel slavery was formalized.[20]

Maroons (runaway slaves) have probably been the most well studied fugitives.[21] Maroon communities that threatened the local socio-economic order existed in Brazil, Colombia, Jamaica, Mexico, Suriname, Mauritius and Reunion Islands, Indonesia, the Persian and the Arabian Gulf. Most often, the measures taken to maintain order in slave regimes were shaped by fear of maroon activity; such fears help to explain why fugitive slaves were often punished harshly.[22] In several situations, punishment was at the same time exemplary and relatively rare. Not all runaway slaves aimed at becoming free people, however, as many deserted to move to other plantations where living and working conditions were said to be better. Police inefficiency and collusion with large estate owners supported these attitudes and gave many colonists a sense of frustration.[23]

In other contexts, maroon settlement represented a serious threat to colonial societies. This was the case in Jamaica, where maroon towns were formed in the mountainous interiors and in Haiti, where maroon societies led to the abolition of slavery and the colonial yoke.[24] These different issues were related to the geographical context (small islands and mainland slave societies did not offer the same opportunities to hide), but also to the imperial and economic settings (the outcome was different in Haiti, Jamaica and Mauritius). The most important to us is that the evolution of slavery and runaways in slave societies strongly interacted with the identification of 'free labour' in the mainland and of labour in post-emancipation societies.

In England many had believed that the abolition of the slave trade would lead to the progressive abolition of slavery. This was not the case, as France, Spain and Portugal continued to import slaves, while in the West Indies planters resisted any attempt to improve the conditions of slaves. A new anti-slavery society was founded; it shifted from gradual abolition to immediate abolition of slavery. A period (usually six to seven years, which typically reproduced the timeframe of individual emancipation as well as the apprenticeship contract) was imposed during which the quasi-former slaves were given an apprenticeship status.[25] Slaves did not enjoy full legal status inasmuch as they were not yet 'civilized'.[26] Apprentices worked forty-five hours a week for their former owners in exchange for food, clothing, lodging and medical care. Absenteeism or bad performance (according to standards set by the planters themselves) led to severe penalties and increased the period and the amount of apprentices' obligations. Physical punishment, which had been suppressed under slavery during the 1820s, was now re-introduced for apprentices. Abuse was thus extremely frequent.[27] Absenteeism and vagrancy were the most common breach of rules attributed to former slaves.

The same was true with new indentured immigrants. According to one approach, the indentured contract resembled forced labour and slavery and contracts were said to express a 'legal fiction'.[28] This approach deprives the abolition of slavery of any historical significance.[29] Other scholars have opposed this view by demonstrating that the indenture contract was not considered an expression of forced labour until the second half of the nineteenth century, whereas until that date it was viewed as an expression of free will in contract.[30] Indeed, indentured labour was not just disguised slavery, but an expression of what free labour was at that time, i.e. a contract based upon unequal rights between the master and the servant, the latter being subject to criminal prosecution. Indenture contracts were governed by the provisions of the Masters and Servants Acts in the colonies.[31]

In the colonies, the inequality of the relationship increased. In Mauritius, between the official abolition of slavery in 1834 and 1910, 450,000 indentured servants arrived from India and from Madagascar. Two-thirds never returned home and, as a result, the servant Indian population grew constantly (from 35 per cent in 1846 to two-thirds of the total population in 1871).[32] These figures must be expanded to include other indentured servants from South Asia and Africa: 30,000 in 1851, and twice that number ten years later. Around 14,000 indentured and domestic servants were prosecuted every year in the 1860s; during the same period in Great Britain, proceedings were brought against 9,700 servants per year for breach of contract and almost always resulted in convictions. In contrast, masters were seldom indicted and even more rarely convicted for breach of contract, ill treatment or non-payment of wages. They could exercise corporal punishment, authorize the marriage of indentured servants, etc.[33] The law was largely enforced when immigrants were sued. Any unjustified absence was subject to criminal prosecution. In particular, the law against vagrancy took on particular importance; several restrictive laws were adopted between the abolition of slavery and the 1870s. Small landowners complained of runaway indentured immigrants; this problem also stemmed from lack of cooperation on the part of large landowners. Small plantation owners were more concerned about fugitive, insubordinate and vagrant indentured servants. On the other hand, owners of large plantations who complained of the excessive cost of slave surveillance often imposed a liberal ideology in the colonial systems; they found support for the indenture system in humanitarian and anti-slavery associations by stressing the benefits of free immigration (indenture) as opposed to slavery.[34]

Transition from slavery to 'free labour', the real rights of freed slaves, and, thus, the problem of exit and voice was equally important in post-bellum USA. The strong heritage of slavery reflects only part of the story. Former slaves were not granted 'false freedom' but freedom as it was generally understood at that time for people such as servants, apprentices and children. In the US a fundamental difference separated wage labour from indentured contracts. By 1800 wage work was different from its equivalent in England, at least for adult white native-born workers, in that penal sanctions had already been abolished; wage forfeiture was the most widespread remedy to enforce contracts. By contrast, criminal penalties were extremely important in the enforcement of indentured and seamen's contracts. With the abolition of slavery, criminal punishments were generalized to all former slaves. In agriculture, in particular in cotton fields, employers found it increasingly difficult to retain freedmen over an entire year.[35] The fixed-wage system with a year-long contract prevented a midseason reservoir of unemployed workers and contributed towards reducing the number of dismissals for neglect of work. However, it did not offer the planter enough control over seasonal variations of labour supply. Sharecropping was seen as the best solution to this problem. Under this system, supervision costs would be reduced and the supply of labour over the entire year could be ensured.

The issue was different in sugar-producing areas. In Louisiana, planters sought to counteract limited credit and financial resources with long-term contracts for gangs of workers, and later, with the collapse of the sugar price in the 1870s, with increasing pressure on labour. Workers initially reacted with increasing mobility, which gave rise to an attempt to enforce the rules on criminal punishments more strictly. Another consequence was that small planters stopped processing the sugar themselves, with 'central stations' receiving the sugar from several units. Faced with this increasing pressure, workers reacted with collective action and strikes. Repression was severe, leading to concentration and mechanization.[36]

In short, runaways were a constant problem in expanding colonial empires, not only during their initial conquest and settlement, but also after it, when the plantation system developed. Before (white indentured immigrants), during and after slavery (coloured indentured immigrants), the plantation system relied upon coercion, few rights (although increasing) and therefore high rates of desertion. In this context, desertion was sometimes a form of radical opposition to this system or simply a way of moving to other plantations, playing with the tough competition among planters. The final question we have to ask is whether these persistent anxieties about fugitives were a peculiarity of the colonial context, and as such opposed to free labour in Europe, or if they were an extension of it.

Runaways in Western Europe

From the sixteenth to the nineteenth centuries, rules on runaways were adopted not only in Russia for serfs, and in the American colonies for indentured workers, but also in Europe. In Great Britain, fugitive workers, journeymen and servants in general were subjected to severe criminal punishment under the Master and Servant Acts. Apprenticeship, advances in wages and raw materials, and also simple master–servant relations were adduced to justify such provisions. From the sixteenth to the end of the nineteenth century in Britain and Europe, free labour, even where a contract existed, was considered the property of the employer and a resource for the whole community to which the individual belonged.[37] The Poor Law related relief directly to workhouses. Any person lacking employment or permanent residence was no longer considered a 'poor' person, but became a 'vagrant', and as such was subject to criminal prosecution. Anti-vagrancy laws did not decline but became stricter in the nineteenth century, particularly after the adoption of the new Poor Law in 1834. Between this year and the mid-1870s, there were about 10,000 prosecutions for vagrancy.[38] Unlike prosecutions carried out under the Master and Servant Acts, they were conducted on the initiative of public authorities and did not respond to economic trends, but to political and social-order interests.

The workhouse system was far from marginal: it has been estimated that in periods of crisis during the eighteenth and nineteenth centuries, about 6.5 per cent of the British population was in a workhouse at any given time.[39] The Statute of Labourers (1350–51) was enacted two years after the Ordinance of Labourers had been put in place and was followed by a set of laws gathered under the umbrella of the Master and Servant Acts, which multiplied in the sixteenth century and accompanied the Statute of Artificers and Apprentices (1562).[40] During the term of service, the labour of servants was legally reserved for their masters. Even when the term of service expired, servants were not allowed to leave their masters unless they had given 'one quarter's warning' of their intention to leave.[41]

Beginning in the second half of the sixteenth century, the tradition that viewed the master's legal control as property-based became an important constituent of the new market society. Workers could be imprisoned until they were willing to return to their employers to complete their agreed-upon service. Any untimely breach of contract on the part of the servant was subject to prosecution. The word fugitive was clearly employed for apprentices and servants who left without giving notice. More generally, servants' hirings were seen as agreements to do something in the future. As such, the labour of servants was considered the legitimate property of the master. In fact, in early-modern Britain, resident servants were like wives and children: all were members of the household and all were the legal dependents of its head. This implies, on the one hand, that servants, children, and wives were entitled to be maintained by the head of the household; on the other hand, all of them were supposed to be under his authority, the family head benefiting from a higher legal status and more legal entitlements and rights than his dependants and family. In general, labour was seen as akin to domestic service, with the employer purchasing the worker's time. As the leading British legal doctrine of that time put it, by owning slaves and war captives you owned things, whereas labour services meant that you owned a certain person's time.[42] It was a lease of labour in which the borrower had the right to benefit from all the time and capacities of his labour force. As long as contracts for the hire of labour continued to be understood as conveyances of property in labour, contractarian individualism would continue to furnish support for unfree labour.

Criminal proceedings accompanied the emphasis placed on contractual free will as a foundation of the labour market. Criminal sanctions were provided because it was supposed that the worker freely agreed to engage and, thus, to face the consequences of his/her contractual failure. The measures were also applied to journeymen, daily labourers, unskilled workers, and in general, whenever short-term contracts to improve output were involved. The measures of the Master and Servant Acts grew stricter, starting in the 1720s, when penalties against servants who broke their contracts were reinforced. The first Industrial Revolution was backed by constraints on labour mobility that were tighter than ever. Between 1720 and 1792, ten acts of Parliament imposed or increased the term of imprisonment for leaving work or for misbehaviour. Almost all these acts were a new departure: the Master and Servant Acts not only attempted to provide for social and political stability but required tighter control of workers by their masters while guaranteeing 'fair' competition among masters (that is, they should not try to entice away other masters' working people). Monetary or raw material investments made by the employer were used to further justify such sanctions against wage earners who left their jobs.[43]

Competition between sectors and the intense seasonality of labour strongly buttressed these new labour laws.[44] Contrary to conventional arguments, there is no persuasive evidence that technological progress emerged as labour-saving in the eighteenth and the first half of the nineteenth century.[45] Agricultural innovations in particular tended to be labour-using rather than labour-saving: the new techniques of husbandry demanded more labour, not less.[46] Recent analyses come to the same conclusion: labour and labour intensity are identified as the main source of agricultural growth before 1850, with human and physical capital playing a secondary role.[47] Labour-intensive techniques linked to the diffusion of knowledge and attractive markets (with increasing agriculture prices) were dominant between the seventeenth and the last quarter of the nineteenth century, when this trend reversed (due to decreasing agricultural prices and increasing wages).[48] This trend was not limited to agriculture. Casting doubt on traditional views, recent analyses seem to show that the rate of capital intensification in British industry was relatively limited until the mid-nineteenth century.[49] By 1850, there were relatively few workers employed in factories; only a small proportion worked in technologically advanced industries such as cotton, iron and steel, and metalworking; the full impact of steam power in transport and production was yet to be felt.[50] The leading industries of the first Industrial Revolution were much more labour-intensive than is usually assumed, at least until the mid-nineteenth century. After that time, mechanization accelerated with the second Industrial Revolution and the emergence of new, highly capital-intensive industries.

All this helps to explain the main features of labour contracts. The labour market did not operate as an 'auction market' for several interrelated reasons: there was no unlimited supply of labour, in particular of skilled labour; the peasant-worker and unskilled workforce were the leading actors;

and the Master and Servant Acts aimed at providing a tool with which masters could discipline the labour force and fix wages outside the market mechanism.[51] Most masters and employers waged war on wage laws and exacted criminal punishment to obtain the required amount of labour. Coercion took different forms: the obligation to work under the new Poor Law and the anti-vagrancy laws; penalties for violating the factory regulations; and penalties for infringing the Master and Servant Acts.

Detailed analyses have recently been carried out on the rate of penalty enforcement in the courts of Great Britain.[52] The eighteenth century saw a sharp increase in the number of prosecutions, and within this time period there were shorter trends that appear to have significantly correlated with the rate of activity and employment. Thus the higher the rate of employment, the higher the rate of worker prosecution.

The long-term movement of labour and labour laws in Britain, therefore, hardly confirm the traditional argument that early labour freedom in the country fuelled the Industrial Revolution. On the contrary, the Industrial Revolution was accompanied by increasingly tough regulations and criminal sanctions on workers. Master and Servant Acts were a powerful tool in the hand of masters or employers in filling the increasing demand for labour in the eighteenth and nineteenth centuries. The new Master and Servant Acts were not vestiges of feudal times but a clear response to the new industrializing context. They fit the ambition of judges and British political elites to secure social and political order through laws addressing the poor, vagrancy, and labour. Masters criticized unreliable servants and workers, but they also did not hesitate to entice away other employers' labourers. Competition was particularly strong in towns but also existed between urban and rural activities. For the reasons mentioned above, economic growth from the seventeenth to the mid-nineteenth century was often labour intensive, and even when more capital was demanded, it led to greater employment of the labour force. This trend was a response to the persistent attitude of most employers (not only industrial ones, but also heads of family, especially in the countryside) and public officers, who considered labour a service. From this standpoint, working people were considered legally and practically to be close to conscripts and submitted to similar rules during their service.

Concluding remarks

Masters, heads of villages and households, and political, administrative and military elites all required working people, and their needs increased with the rise of the market economy, colonization and the military and fiscal state. Yet the extreme emphasis put on labour and its mobility also had unintended consequences. Masters and elites accused each other of engaging in 'unfair competition', i.e. keeping fugitive working people for themselves.

Rules of competition were invented not to regulate trade, but to control labour.[53] Most of the rules regarding runaways and fugitives stressed the importance of returning them to their legitimate master and/or owner. This phenomenon also revealed that it was essential for masters to have people at will and showed the intrinsic weakness of a system that drove masters to compete with each other for control of fugitives.

The final outcome of this global problem depended on the relative strength of the various groups of masters, the state and other authorities (towns, villages), and of course working people, as well as on the relationships between them. The outcomes in France and Britain were different from those in their respective colonies, and even within these areas there were considerable variations from one region to the next. In addition to tensions between individual masters and groups of masters, coercive power itself was by no means monolithic or effective. Masters sought to keep their fugitive people, but the police, the state or the militias in charge of fugitives lacked coordination and resources and, most of all, they were often acting at cross-purposes. For example, in France and Britain, the claims regarding fugitives raised by masters in the mainland conflicted with the demands of colonial and imperial expansion, which was pushing in the opposite direction, namely, for greater mobility from the home country. The same was true in competition between the cities and the countryside.

Scarcity of labour and the related law of demand and supply are said to be the origin of coerced labour and legal constraints on labour mobility. The cases of Russia, Eastern Europe and the American colonies have been used to prove this statement.[54] However, closer empirical analyses raise serious doubts about this argument and it is not by chance that historians have been showing increasing scepticism.[55] The abolition of slavery in the English colonies, despite widespread beliefs, had little to do with demographic trends; as Seymour Drescher has put it, there was no fundamental change of demographic pattern in the tropical world beyond Europe in the watershed period of 1760 to 1790.[56] Wrigley and Schofield show that the English established their overseas slave system during the very decades when their net emigration rate reached a three-century peak (1641–61); moreover, British abolitionism took off exactly when the net emigration rate sank to its tricentennial low (1771–91).[57]

In Europe and England in particular, common views stress the increasing freedom and deregulation of the labour market, followed by a growing supply of labour, urbanization and proletarianization, accompanied by an increasing use of capital. Indeed, the contrary was true, and legal constraints on labour mobility persisted until the last quarter of the nineteenth century. Thus, the critical variable was not the lack of population in itself, but the kind of social, military and economic orders that pushed to adopt and enforce rules on runaways. Our argument is that, since the mid-nineteenth century to the early twentieth century, runaways were a universal obsession because of the convergence of several forces: labour-intensive growth, highly unequal social, political, civil and economic rights and labour as a social and personal service.

In Europe itself this process did not halt with the Industrial Revolution, which required more labour, not less, but only with the second industrial revolution (capital-intensive). Together with the increasing political strength of working people (unions, socialist parties) and the first rise of the welfare state at the end of the nineteenth century, working people gained greater rights. Labour was no more considered as a service but as an agreement between working people (their unions) and employers (no more masters).

However, in Europe and the USA this outcome did not concern all working people: peasants and workers of small units in Europe, peons and former slaves in the USA were left at the edge of this new system. Even worse, the protection of some workers in the 'West' contrasted with the persisting importance of coercion and bondage outside of these areas. In the European colonies, but also in Russia and most of Asian and Latin American areas, post-slavery and post-serfdom societies maintained unequal rights, limited political and civil rights and no social rights for working people. Labour was still considered as a service to the master and the state. In these contexts, working people were still qualified as fugitives, deserters, and vagrants.

Notes

1 James Scott, *Weapons of the Weak: Everyday Forms of Peasant Resistance* (New Haven: Yale University Press, 1985); Orlando Patterson, *Slavery and Social Death: a Comparative Study* (Cambridge, MA: Harvard University Press, 1985).
2 Albert Hirschman, *Exit, Voice, and Loyalty: Responses to Decline in Firms, Organizations, and States* (Cambridge, MA: Harvard University Press, 1970).
3 Alessandro Stanziani, *Bondage: Labor and Rights in Eurasia from the Sixteenth to the Early Twentieth Centuries* (New York: Berghahn Books, 2014); Frederick Cooper, *Decolonization and African Society: the Labor Question in French and British Africa* (Cambridge: Cambridge University Press, 1996).
4 Robert Steinfeld, *The Invention of Free Labor: the Employment Relation in English and American Law and Culture, 1350–1870* (Chapel Hill: University of North Carolina Press, 1991).
5 Richard Biernacki, *The Fabrication of Labour: Germany and Britain, 1640–1914* (Berkeley: University of California Press, 1997).
6 Gary Cross, *A Quest for Time: The Reduction of Work in Britain and France, 1840–1940* (Berkeley: University of California Press, 1989); Gary Cross (ed.), *Worktime and Industrialization: An International History* (Philadelphia: Temple University Press, 1988).
7 Stanziani, *Bondage*.
8 André Zysberg, *Les Galériens: Vies et destins de 60 000 forçats sur les galères de France (1680–1748)* (Paris: Le Seuil, 1987).

9 Alessandro Stanziani, *Sailors, Slaves, and Immigrants in the Indian Ocean World, 1750–1914* (New York: Palgrave, 2014).
10 Archives Nationales Paris (AN), Col. 6, 11, 1734.
11 Nicholas A. M. Rodger, *The Command of the Ocean: A Naval History of Britain, 1649–1815* (New York: W. W. Norton and Company, 2004).
12 Emma Christopher, *Slave Ships and Their Captive Cargoes, 1730–1807* (Cambridge: Cambridge University Press, 2006).
13 Michael Fisher, 'Working Across the Seas: Indian Maritime Laborers in India, Britain, and in Between, 1600–1857', in Rana Behal and Marcel van der Linden (eds), *Coolies, Capital and Colonialism: Studies in Indian Labor History, International Review of Social History Supplements* (Cambridge: Cambridge University Press, 2006), pp. 21–46.
14 Michael H. Fisher, *Counterflows to Colonialism: Indian Travelers and Settlers in Britain 1600–1857* (Delhi: Oxford University Press, 2004).
15 Gopalan Balachandran, *Globalizing Labour: Indian Seafarers and World Shipping, c. 1870–1945* (Delhi: Oxford University Press, 2012).
16 Jonathan Glassman, 'The Bondsman's New Clothes: The Contradictory Consciousness of Slave Resistance on the Swahili Coast', *Journal of African History* 32:2 (1991), pp. 303–9.
17 Robert L. Playfair, *History of Arabia Felix or Yemen: from the Commencement of Christian Era to the Middle of the XIXth Century, Including an Account of the British Settlement of Aden* (Bombay: Education Society's Press, 1859, reprinted Farnborough: Gregg International, 1970), p. 15.
18 Alan Cobley, 'Black West Indian Seamen in the British Merchant Marine in the Mid-Nineteenth Century', *History Workshop Journal* 58 (2004), pp. 259–74.
19 David W. Galenson, *White Servitude in Colonial America: an Economic Analysis* (Cambridge: Cambridge University Press, 1981).
20 Christopher Tomlins, *Freedom Bound: Law, Labor, and Civic Identity in Colonizing British America, 1580–1865* (Cambridge: Cambridge University Press, 2010).
21 Seymour Drescher and Stanley Engerman (eds), *A Historical Guide to World Slavery* (New York and Oxford: Oxford University Press, 1998).
22 Richard Allen, 'A Serious and Alarming Daily Evil: Marronage and its Legacy in Mauritius and the Colonial Plantation World', *Slavery and Abolition* 25:2 (2004), pp. 1–17; Gwendolyn Hall, *Social Control in Slave Plantation Societies: A Comparison of St. Domingue and Cuba* (Baltimore and London: The Johns Hopkins University Press, 1971); Eugene Genovese, *Roll, Jordan, Roll: The World the Slaves Made* (New York: Vintage Books, 1976).
23 Richard Price (ed.), *Maroon Societies: Rebel Slave Communities in the Americas* (Baltimore: The Johns Hopkins University, 1996); Alvin Thompson, *Flight to Freedom: African Runaways and Maroons in the Americas* (Kingston: University of the West Indies Press, 2006).
24 Mavis Campbell, *The Maroons of Jamaica 1655–1796: a History of Resistance, Collaboration and Betrayal* (Trenton: African World Press, 1990); Barbara

Lalla, *Defining Jamaican Fiction: Marronage and the Discourse of Survival* (Tuscaloosa: University of Alabama Press, 1996).

25 Seymour Drescher, *Capitalism and Antislavery: British mobilization in Comparative Perspective* (London: Palgrave, 1987); Robin Blackburn, *The Overthrow of Colonial Slavery, 1776–1848* (London: Verso, 1988).

26 House of Commons, 'Papers in Explanation of the Condition of the Slave Population, 5 Nov. 1831', *British Parliamentary Papers*, 1830–1 (230), 16.1, pp. 59–88.

27 John R. Ward, *British West India Slavery, 1750–1834: the Process of Amelioration* (Oxford: Oxford University Press, 1988).

28 Hugh Tinker, *A New System of Slavery: the Export of Indian Labour Overseas, 1830–1920* (London: Hansib, 1974).

29 David Northrup, *Indentured Labour in the Age of Imperialism: 1834–1922* (Cambridge: Cambridge University Press, 1995); Marina Carter, *Servants, Sirdars and Settlers: Indians in Mauritius, 1834–1874* (Delhi: Oxford University Press, 1995).

30 Tom Brass and Marcel van der Linden (eds), *Free and Unfree Labour: The Debate Continues* (Bern: Peter Lang, 1997).

31 Richard Allen, *Slaves, Freedmen, and Indentured Laborers in Colonial Mauritius* (Cambridge: Cambridge University Press, 1999), p. 60.

32 Allen, *Slaves*, pp. 16–17. Also Auguste Toussaint, *Histoire de l'île Maurice* (Paris: PUF, 1974).

33 Galenson, *White Servitude*.

34 Alessandro Stanziani, 'Local Bondage in Global Economies: Servants, Wage-earners, and Indentured Migrants in Nineteenth-century France, Great Britain and the Mascarene Islands', *Modern Asian Studies* 1 (2013), pp. 1–34.

35 Ralph Shlomovitz, 'Bound or Free? Black Labor in Cotton and Sugar Cane Farming, 1865–1880', *Journal of Southern History* 50 (1984), pp. 569–96.

36 Rebecca Scott, 'Defining the Boundaries of Freedom in the World of Cane: Cuba, Brazil, and Louisiana after Emancipation', *The American Historical Review* 99:1 (1994), pp. 70–102.

37 Steinfeld, *The Invention*; Brass and van der Linden, *Free and Unfree Labour*.

38 Sureh Naidu and Noam Yuchtman, 'How Green Was My Valley? Coercive Contract Enforcement in Nineteenth-century Britain', NBUR Working Papers, 2009.

39 Derek Fraser, *The Evolution of the British Welfare State*, 4th edn (London: Palgrave Macmillan, 2009), p. 67.

40 Ann Kussmaul, *Servants in Husbandry in Early Modern England* (Cambridge: Cambridge University Press, 1981).

41 Steinfeld, *The Invention*, p. 32.

42 William Blackstone, *Commentaries on the Laws of England*, 4 vols (London: Strahan, Woodfall, 1793–95), booklet 2, p. 402.

43 Donna C. Woods, 'The Operation of the Masters and Servants Act in the Black Country, 1858–1875', *Midland History* 7 (1982), pp. 93–115;

Mark R. Freedland, *The Contract of Employment* (Oxford: Oxford University Press: 1976).

44 Douglas Hay and Nick Rogers, *English Society in the Eighteenth Century: Shuttles and Swords* (Oxford: Oxford University Press, 1997).

45 Hrothgar J. Habakkuk, *American and British Technology in the Nineteenth Century: The Search for Labour-Saving Inventions* (Cambridge: Cambridge University Press, 1962); Joel Mokyr, *The Lever of Riches: Technological Creativity and Economic Progress* (Oxford: Oxford University Press, 1990).

46 Charles Timmer, 'The Turnip, the New Husbandry, and the English Agricultural Evolution', *Quarterly Journal of Economics* LXXXIII (1969), pp. 375–95.

47 George Grantham, 'Agricultural Supply during the Industrial Revolution: French Evidence and European Implications', *Journal of Economic History* 49:1 (1989), pp. 43–72.

48 F. M. L. Thompson, 'The Second Agricultural Revolution, 1815–1880', *Economic History Review* 21 (1968), pp. 62–77.

49 Phyllis Deane and W. A. Cole, *British Economic Growth 1688–1959: Trends and Structure* (Cambridge: Cambridge University Press, 1962).

50 Simon Deakin and Frank Wilkinson, *The Law of the Labour Market: Industrialization, Employment, and Legal Evolution* (Oxford: Oxford University Press, 2005), p. 20.

51 Michael Huberman, 'Invisible Handshakes in Lancashire: Cotton Spinning in the First Half of the Nineteenth Century', *The Journal of Economic History* 46:4 (1986), pp. 987–98.

52 Paul Craven and Douglas Hay, 'The Criminalization of Free Labour: Masters and Servants in Comparative Perspective', *Slavery and Abolition* 15:2 (1994), pp. 71–101.

53 Stanziani, *Bondage*; Alessandro Stanziani, *Rules of Exchange: French Capitalism in Comparative Perspective, Eighteenth to Early Twentieth Centuries* (Cambridge: Cambridge University Press, 2012).

54 Jerome Blum, 'The Rise of Serfdom in Eastern Europe', *The American Historical Review*, 62:4 (1957), pp. 807–36; Evsey Domar, *Capitalism, Socialism and Serfdom: Essays* (Cambridge, Cambridge University Press, 1989).

55 Michael Bush (ed.), *Serfdom and Slavery: Studies in Legal Bondage* (London: Longman 1996). Martin Klein, *Breaking the Chains: Slavery, Bondage and Emancipation in Modern Africa and Asia* (Madison: The University of Wisconsin Press, 1993).

56 Seymour Drescher, *Capitalism and Antislavery: British Mobilization in Comparative Perspective* (New York: Oxford University Press, 1987), p. 11.

57 Edward A. Wrigley and Roger S. Schofield, *The Population History of England, 1541–1871: A Reconstruction* (Cambridge: Cambridge University Press, 1982), pp. 218–21.

2

Mass Exits:

Who, Why, How?

Marcel van der Linden

If my soldiers began to think, not one would remain in the ranks.
FREDERICK THE GREAT

Desertion derives from the Late Latin verb *desertare*, meaning to abandon, to leave, or to forsake. The verb denotes all manner of severing connections. In most cases, its use is intended to mean: 'The wilful abandonment of an employment or duty, in violation of legal or moral obligation; *esp.* such abandonment of the military or naval service.'[1] Desertion in this sense has existed for thousands of years. One such reference appears in the island of Rhodes, where around 900 BCE a code stipulated: 'mariners who, without sufficient reason, quit their service during the period of their engagement, shall be severely punished.'[2] Desertion is not restricted to the 'West'. In India, for example, desertions were an ongoing problem in the army of the East India Company.[3] And it has been written on the millenarian Taiping Rebellion in China (1850–64):

> The clarion call of the Taiping way of life resonated with imperial rank and file troops, many of whom were peasants themselves, and the Qings experienced, in the early years of the conflict, massive waves of desertion. Thousands upon thousands of soldiers crossed the lines at night to throw in their lot with the Son of Heaven.[4]

In this chapter I will focus mainly on mass desertion. Mass desertion can be molecular or coordinated. Molecular desertion consists of escape attempts by individuals or small groups, although such efforts may become so numerous that taken together they become a mass phenomenon. In coordinated desertion, dozens or hundreds of people try to escape together as a group. Historically, molecular mass desertion has occurred far more frequently than coordinated desertion. Historians are not always able to distinguish the two types in practice, because the reasons of the runaways are often unknown.[5]

Who?

Deserters are by definition in 'violation of legal or moral obligation'. Their flight or escape is therefore always an act of serious disobedience. *Mass desertion* assumes a high concentration of people in similar situations, detained under more or less the same conditions, with some deciding that they are fed up.

Examples from history reveal at least six such social groups that have resorted to mass desertion on occasion. Some have been covered at length in this book. Many – but not all – groups of runaways may be counted among the general working class.[6] Desertion by *soldiers and navy personnel* has been a longstanding problem for armies around the world. This practice has in some cases cost these armies large sections of their personnel and severely weakened them. During the Seven Years' War from 1756 to 1763 (the actual 'First World War'), at least 300,000 soldiers deserted the different armies.[7] Following the introduction of the *levée en masse* as an almost universal military service during the French Revolution, tens of thousands tried to evade conscription.[8] In the first year of the Great War of 1914–18, half a million men ran away from the Czarist army.[9]

Sailors on merchant fleets were similarly known for their 'mobility'. In the eighteenth century, desertion by sailors was 'one of the most chronic and severe problems faced by the merchant capitalists of the shipping industry' in the North Atlantic and elsewhere.[10]

Slaves are the third major group. The best-known example is the escape by a few dozen gladiators from their 'school', which resulted in the Spartacus Rebellion (73–71 BCE). About 70,000 slaves ended up joining. A less well-known but equally impressive case concerns the revolt in 869 of the Zanj, the East African slaves forced to work in the salt marshes in South Iraq. Just south of Basra, they founded a new, expansive city called al-Mokhtára ('the elect city'), with elaborate defence works and home to a population of 50,000 or more. Only after fourteen years were these rebels defeated.[11] The best-known case from the modern age is probably the 'Negro Republic' of Palmares (Brazil, 1605–94), where between 10,000 and 20,000 maroons lived.[12] Such large-scale *marronages* have continued to occur into the early twentieth century.

On the eve of the 1905 agricultural season the slaves of Banamba, a Maraka town in the Middle Niger valley, began to leave their masters. [. . .] Within a year of the original departures from Banamba the events had been repeated in hundreds of other locations. By 1908 the wave of departures had swept through the Middle Niger valley. Elsewhere in the Western Sudan the movement continued for years.

When the commander of Bamako asked some of the first refugees why they had fled, they replied 'that they had no animosity to their masters. They simply wanted to return [home].'[13]

Peasants fled *en masse* in some cases as well. In the seventeenth and eighteenth centuries, Russian serfs regularly 'voted with their feet'. Peter Kolchin illustrates this by mentioning the thousands of subjects who in the 1730s abandoned their lord, the wealthy nobleman Prince A.M. Cherkasskii:

> entire villages typically migrated *en masse*, leaving and settling together in new surroundings. [. . .] The decision to flee was thus a communal not an individual one, and flight resulted in the reconstitution rather than the destruction of familial and communal ties. [. . .] 86.8 percent of the fugitives went in groups to previously selected villages, where advance parties had already prepared for their arrival, sometimes even buying land from nearby pomeshchiki [noble landowners]. Most often, however, they settled on previously unused land, where they established new communities in which they passed as state peasants. Village leaders [. . .] usually organized the flight and continued to fulfill their traditional functions in the newly established communities.[14]

Similar exits occurred around the same time in East and North Germany, especially in Holstein, Mecklenburg and New Western Pomerania. Thanks to the absence of a strong central authority, the large landowners were able to establish such despotic control that they could decide to sell their serfs like cattle. Motivated in part by this practice, around the mid-eighteenth century, thousands of peasants moved away without authorization to the Russian governorate of Astrakhan or to Prussia under Frederick II, who, after the end of the Seven Years' War, hoped to draw settlers to Prussian Pomerania.[15] Somewhat later, massive numbers of poor peasants fled *inter alia* in South and Southeast Asia.[16]

Indentured labourers are the fifth group. Everywhere in the world, coolies and other contract workers have absconded over the centuries. In the early decades of the twentieth century in Assam (East India), however, such forms of desertion took on mass proportions. One particularly noteworthy example has become known as the Chargola Exodus. In May 1921 indentured labourers on the tea plantations in the Chargola Valley staged a strike for higher wages, but the managers rejected their demands. As a result, increasing numbers of men and women left the plantation permanently – ultimately, about 200,000 people departed:

> [The coolies] resolved to go back to their home districts, chanting victory cries to Mahatma Gandhi and claiming to have served under his orders. Having started from one or two gardens, by the middle of June, the entire Chargola valley looked deserted, with two gardens reported to have 'lost' virtually their entire labour force, and on an average, most gardens had suffered losses of around thirty to sixty percent. The coolies of Chargola Valley marched right through Karimganj, the sub-divisional headquarters, continuing their onward journey either by train or on foot, and also by steamer they made their way back to their home districts.[17]

Convicts and inmates of concentration camps are the sixth and final group. When inmates were not yet contained in separate, closely guarded buildings but had to perform forced labour outdoors or in mines, desertions were commonplace. Even the subsequent measures of forming chain gangs and imposing mass incarceration did not put an end to the escapes. Although the greatest resistance came from *inside* prisons, and riots were common, inmates sometimes succeeded – possibly helped by outsiders – in escaping. In a more recent jail break in 2011, about 700 Egyptian prisoners reclaimed their freedom.[18] In some instances groups even escaped from Nazi concentration camps, for example the 300 Jewish inmates of the extermination camp at Sobibor, who did so successfully in 1943.[19]

All these groups were subject to a power beyond their control and were forced to live, and often work, under what were often highly authoritarian conditions.

Why?

Generally, desertions depend both on the subjective willingness of the potential deserters and on the material opportunity. Subjective willingness to run away involves a combination of two criteria: issues and triggers. Issues are longstanding sources of discontent among the employees. Triggers are specific incidents that crystallize into feelings of discontent.

Discontent may result from many causes. In most cases, historians can ascertain them only when deserters are caught, and a written record is available of their interrogation. Three types of issues surface regularly in such sources.[20] The first concern is the social and labour relations: for example bad food, harsh discipline, racial discrimination, or overdue pay or wages. Second is the fear or horror of the future course of events anticipated: fear of imminent punishment or an upcoming battle. Other reasons include the refusal to fight a certain group out of a sense of loyalty towards this 'adversary'. Such sentiments figured, for example, during the German

Peasant War in 1525: many mercenaries were originally peasants themselves and were moreover dependent on the peasants for handouts in what was known as the *Gartzeit* (the period between mercenary contracts).[21] Third, temptations or obligations elsewhere might come into play. Sons of farmers often disappeared at harvest time to help out on the farm back home. Mercenaries might be lured into switching sides by higher rates of pay from the adversary. During the California Gold Rush in the 1850s, so many sailors wanted to try their luck that: 'Vessels travelling to California were unable to maintain predictable schedules due to the high incidence of crew desertion.'[22]

Such considerations could give rise to desertion, if a certain event made 'the fat hit the fire'. Triggers came in many different manifestations. Consider the Sepoy Mutiny in India (1857), in which festering discontent instigated a social explosion, when a new type of rifle was introduced. The powder for these rifles came wrapped in greasy paper Minié cartridges that the soldiers had to tear open with their teeth. These cartridges were rumoured to contain cow and pig fat – and were thus offensive to Hindus and Muslims. This example reveals immediately that triggers were often embedded in a religious or ideological discourse.[23]

Desertion was not a decision to be taken lightly. If caught trying to escape, deserters faced severe punishments, ranging from flogging to execution. And what prospects did successful deserters face? Their decisions are certain to have been impacted by anxiety, indignation, doubt, and hope. In many cases discontent is likely to have been fairly widespread, since all groups mentioned here were exploited and/or severely oppressed.[24]

But discontent alone is of course insufficient to independently instigate any type of collective action: opportunities and resources matter as well. Can aspiring escapees deliberate among each other? Do they have contacts outside? Do they have inspiring leaders with a viable plan? If all these conditions have been met, then an exit is possible, even under severely repressive conditions.

Those considering desertion always allow their emotions and interests to guide their decisions.[25] Theoretically, after all, aside from desertion (*exit*), two alternatives are available. These are *voice*, which means expressing discontent by attempting to improve the organization 'from within' that organization (army unit, ship, plantation etc.); or *acquiescence*: accepting an unsatisfactory situation and leaving things as they are.[26] Examining under which conditions soldiers, peasants, slaves, and others opt for voice or exit is of course immensely important for our topic.

How voice and exit relate to one another is more complicated than might appear on the surface. First, voice and exit are not always mutually exclusive. Voice may be a first step. Only when that proves ineffective, will people resort to exit, as the second step. The reverse obviously does not happen: whoever has left the organization can no longer protest from within. And there is more. There is also the 'noisy exit', combining defection and protest.

The threat of exit may strengthen voice, although in extremely authoritarian organizations any type of voice will be punished as severely as desertion.[27]

Sometimes collective actions are at the interface of exit and voice, if exit is used as leverage in negotiations. Consider, for example, the illegal *uitgangen* that Dutch textile workers organized from the fourteenth century onwards. They followed a typical pattern. The workers would leave the city in which labour relations were unacceptable and go to another city, in order to renegotiate from there. The exit of the fullers of Leiden to the city of Gouda in 1478 has been well documented:

> Although the distance between Leiden and Gouda was no more than twenty kilometres, negotiations also then took place by letter. The first letter of the fullers contained a list of thirty-four demands. After three months of negotiations, the fullers returned to Leiden.[28]

Occasionally, voice may also serve to enable an exit.[29] The best-known example is probably the exodus of the Jews from Egypt – an event that has never been proven to have actually taken place. The Egyptians, according to reports from the Old Testament, 'made the people of Israel serve with rigor, and made their lives bitter with hard service, in mortar and brick, and in all kinds of work in the field; in all their work they made them serve with rigor'. The people of Israel 'groaned under their bondage, and cried out for help'. Moses, who had killed a cruel Egyptian before, decided to lead the Exodus and tried to convince the Pharaoh to let the Jews go. But the Pharaoh was hard-hearted, and he increased the workload by telling the taskmasters:

> You shall no longer give the people straw to make bricks, as heretofore; let them go and gather straw for themselves. But the number of bricks which they made heretofore you shall lay upon them, you shall by no means lessen it; for they are idle; therefore they cry, 'Let us go and offer sacrifice to our God.' Let heavier work be laid upon the men that they may labor at it and pay no regard to lying words.

Only after Yahweh had cast many plagues on Egypt (the Nile River turned into blood; frogs, gnats, and locusts afflicted the land; and all first-born animals and sons died) did the Pharaoh give in, and were the Jews able to leave the house of bondage.[30] In this story, the exit is prepared by negotiations and reciprocal punishments. Exit coincided with voice.

The 'costs' of voice and exit are the second important factor. Voice always has a price, if only because organizing collective protest requires time and effort at the very least. The authoritarian relationships in the present book of course entail far higher costs; anybody who resists faces severe punishments, meted out not only to him but also to those around him. Nor is exit entirely without cost.[31] In the cases discussed in the present book, this is obvious. Whoever deserts should expect persecution, torture and death.

Seeking to 'curtail costs', deserters frequently chose not to escape entirely on their own. 'Whether one fled with a relative, wife, neighbor, slave, or other soldiers, departing with a person whom the deserter trusted was a key consideration. Having a running-mate encouraged desertion because soldiers benefited from the companionship, and shared resources and advice offered by accomplices in an enterprise of considerable risk.'[32]

Loyalty is the third factor that 'holds exit at bay and activates voice'.[33] When the 'members' feel a strong sense of loyalty, they tend to be very willing to try hard to make the voice option work. Loyalty is undermined, when people are recruited through coercion. This is obviously the case with chattel slaves, but it may hold true for army units as well. Because Frederick William I of Prussia (early eighteenth century) relished tall soldiers, many of his elite troops were enlisted through coercion or were misled, leading to a high propensity to desert.[34]

The cases described in this book are unlikely to have involved any significant sense of loyalty. Loyalty of 'subalterns' towards one another is a factor. Studies about different armies have revealed that soldiers hardly ever went to battle exclusively on ideological grounds but usually for very different reasons. During the Second World War, for example, the German soldier 'fought for the reasons that men have always fought; because he felt himself a member of a well-integrated, well-led team whose structure, administration, and functioning were perceived to be, on the whole [...] equitable and just'.[35]

That the fleeing peasants often left in groups or even with entire villages similarly reflects this type of loyalty. Such loyalty appears to have two potential outcomes: as long as 'acquiescence' or even voice prevails in a group, loyalty will ensure that most people participate. The reverse holds true as well: once the tipping point has been reached, and a substantial share opts to desert, this may initiate a general departure. One very revealing practice of the maroons in Suriname was that after they had deserted, they identified themselves by their plantation of origin. Slaves who had fled the plantation run by the widow of Johan (Dyan) Bosseliers called themselves *Misidyan*. Slaves who had escaped from the L'Espinasse family were called *Pinasi-lo* (lo = clan), and the *Dikan* came from the Nessenkamp plantation of the De Camp family.[36] Maroons from different plantations might become very suspicious of one another, sometimes resulting in armed conflicts. Mass desertions were thus promoted by local, ethnic, or racial homogeneity.[37]

How?

Adopting an instrumental perspective on desertion yields three distinctive elements: preparation for the escape, the escape itself, and the subsequent course of events. Regarding the first element, some information about abortive collective escapes is available from reports or court records. Still, we know fairly little about how such exits were organized, even though the essays in this collection enrich our knowledge in this field. Escapees attempting a coordinated mass exit may be assumed to have had 'a rudimentary organization and acknowledged leaders when they planned and carried out their escape'.[38] Even under highly repressive conditions, escapes or uprisings could be organized in some cases. On Barbados, male slaves managed to keep a conspiracy so secret for three years that even their own wives were unaware of it.[39]

In some cases desertion was not difficult. In eighteenth-century Suriname, the back of nearly all plantations opened onto the jungle:

> Slaves had reasonable freedom of movement. Every plantation had tracts of land that were not used to cultivate market crops; slaves could plant their own small fields, provision grounds (*goon*) to raise edible crops. Some of these provision grounds were even in the 'forest' behind the plantations. Slaves would hunt in these jungles, and they caught fish in the swamps. The slaves also had small dugout canoes, in which they paddled through creeks and swamps. The Bakaa, their white masters, owners, and foremen never went along on these journeys, so that the slaves knew considerably more than their masters about the geographic state of this terrain. *Slaves usually had little difficulty slipping away from the plantation unnoticed.*[40]

When desertion became a serious problem for the 'incumbent rulers', however, they would resort to countermeasures. For thousands of years, escapes by convicts, slaves and others have been complicated by giving them a *stigma* – the ancient Greek term for a lasting mutilation of potential runaways.

> In fact, branding, tattooing and incising the skin are traceable about as far back as one can trace things in the ancient Near East: brands and tattoos could function as signs of captivity and enslavement, record the name of the slave's owner, or warn the unwary observer (e.g., '[This is a] runaway! Arrest!'); they were apparently placed on the hands, wrists, and (perhaps less frequently) on the face or forehead.[41]

In the South of the United States, their colour made escaped slaves easily identifiable.[42] The introduction of uniforms for soldiers since the seventeenth century and prison garb since the nineteenth century also served as a stigma that facilitated recognizing runaways. Prisoners in Czarist Russia and in the Stalinist Soviet Union could not escape their camps, because they were isolated in desolate areas.[43] And the British-Indian prisoners on the Andaman islands were told that, should they try to escape, they risked death in the hands of the hostile tribal population in the surrounding forest.[44]

All kinds of other precautions were taken as well. Troops were stationed on peninsulas, sentries were posted at possible escape routes, or passes were issued, so that any soldier or slave far away from the army camp or plantation might be asked to present identification.[45] Several of these measures made for rising tensions: 'deserters learned to leave in bands and so to force their passage by violence against the guards';[46] passes were forged, etc.

The actual escape – usually at night – was often highly ingenious. Myriad methods were used. A study about the American Civil War reports, for example:

> The tactics followed by the soldiers to effect their escape are fairly obvious: passage from the picket line or rifle-pit to the enemy's line; dropping out from the column at the fords and ferries and while on the march; taking advantage of gaps and passes while traversing rough country, or of the presence of swamps in the vicinity of the camp or station; slipping away at railroad stations or even jumping from a moving train; failure to return from hospitals or from furloughs; use of stolen or forged passes; escape under the confusion of attacks or captures by the enemy; and escape in civilian clothes through the connivance of friends and relatives.[47]

The days, months and years after the escape were an entirely different matter. Runaways faced two immediate problems: how to avoid being recaptured, and how to obtain adequate provisions.[48] They basically had three options to 'solve' these problems: blend in with the locals, find a hiding place, or try to go far away, to a place where different authorities were in control, or where no central authority existed. The first option was the easiest for runaways whose appearance did not draw attention (i.e. they would not be recognized because of their complexion or a tattoo) and had formed small groups. Sometimes the escapees found shelter with friends or relatives, and in times of labour scarcity, employers would even agree to hire escapees.[49] In some cases deserters managed to settle among friendly indigenous groups.[50] This last alternative is somewhat similar to the second option of disappearing from public view by hiding in an impenetrable area – a jungle, swamp, or a rugged mountain range. The Great Dismal Swamp in North Carolina and Virginia, where between 1630 and 1865 many thousands of disenfranchised Native Americans and maroons lived, was well known.[51]

When runaways collectively settled somewhere in a new place, their logistical problems were obviously quite extensive. There was a constant danger of punitive expeditions by their former rulers. Yet the fugitives were forced to build their settlements in inhospitable areas precisely because these were difficult for punitive expeditions to access. The more rugged the terrain, the more Spartan everyday life became. Maroons on the Caribbean island of St Thomas who in the eighteenth century retreated to inaccessible caves along the coast 'went naked and subsisted on fish, fruit, small game such as land turtles, or stolen provender'.[52] Confined in surroundings that were not suitable for self-subsistence, inhabitants of such concealed settlements were often forced to resort to plundering and looting in the 'established' outside world, which in turn of course led to punitive expeditions and persecution.

The final option was departure to a remote area, where the rulers one had escaped had no direct influence. Where runaways had a place of origin which was accessible with available means of transport, they could collectively try to return to that place after their escape. Most deserters from the West African Banamba exodus had been enslaved only recently: 'This meant that many of the slaves knew another home, and even those born to slavery knew where they had originated. The slaves of the Banamba plantations formed a relatively homogeneous group, since most of them came from Samory's conquests. Thus, the capacity for cooperation was undoubtedly greater than in plantations of diverse origins.'[53] The coolies of the Chargola valley in Assam, who downed tools during their exodus, stayed in touch with their regions of origin as well. In other cases, returning to the former place of residence is not an option, because it is too far away, or because no social or emotional ties exist anymore. In that event, a new domicile must be found. Those who escaped might try to sail to a safer area. Or they could be forced to reach another country on foot. An impressive example of this practice was the Underground Railroad, which guided escaped slaves from the South of the United States to Canada.

Of course deserters were recaptured in some cases. Often they would be severely punished. But there were exceptions. Especially when the escaped persons were indispensable because of their special skills, or because they were difficult to replace for other reasons, they could expect some mercy. With mercenaries, for example, it was 'far cheaper to extend mercy to a soldier than it was to execute the offender, locate, enlist, train, clothe, and pay a further enlistment bounty to a recruit'.[54] The situation was similar with some slaves.

Avoiding the stings

Desertion by oppressed and exploited groups appears to reflect a certain logic. Still more importantly, people – however oppressed and humiliated they may be – keep trying to 'walk with dignity'. Elias Canetti has argued that commands always leave behind a painful sting in the persons forced to carry them out. However: 'Only commands which have been carried out leave their sting lodged in the obeyer. Commands which have been evaded need not be stored; the "free" man is not the man who rids himself of commands after he has received them, but the man who knows how to evade them in the first place. [. . .] There is no man who does not turn against a command imposed on him from the outside; in this case everyone speaks of pressure and reserves the right of vengeance or rebellion.'[55]

Notes

1 *A New English Dictionary on Historical Principles; Founded Mainly on the Materials Collected by The Philological Society*. Edited by Dr James A.H. Murray, with the Assistance of Many Scholars and Men of Science, Volume III (Oxford: At the Clarendon Press, 1897) p. 241.

2 Charles R. Clee, 'Desertion and the Freedom of the Seaman', *International Labour Review* 13 (1926), p. 650.

3 See e.g. Manas Dutta, 'Disciplining the Madras Army During the Early Years of the English East India Company's Dominance in South India', *Socialniu makslu studijos/Societal Studies* 4:3 (2012), pp. 887–99; Douglas M. Peers, 'Sepoys, Soldiers and the Lash: Race, Caste and Army Discipline in India, 1820–50', *The Journal of Imperial and Commonwealth History* 23:2 (1995), pp. 211–47.

4 Joseph Cummins, *The War Chronicles: From Flintlocks to Machine Guns* (Beverly, MA: Fair Winds Press, 2009), p. 95.

5 Jerome S. Handler, 'Slave Revolts and Conspiracies in Seventeenth-Century Barbados', *Nieuwe West-Indische Gids/New West Indian Guide* 56:1–2 (1982), pp. 5–42, p. 12; Michael Kaiser, 'Ausreißer und Meuterer im Dreißigjährigen Krieg', in Ulrich Bröckling and Michael Sikora (eds), *Armeen und ihre Deserteure: Vernachlässigte Kapitel einer Militärgeschichte der Neuzeit* (Göttingen: Vandenhoeck & Ruprecht, 1998), pp. 49–71, p. 51.

6 For an explanation of the broad class concept in Global Labour History, see Marcel van der Linden, *Workers of the World: Essays toward a Global Labor History* (Leiden: Brill, 2008). According to this interpretation, mercenaries also pertain to the working class, as do convict labourers. See Alex Lichtenstein and Christian De Vito, 'Writing a Global History of Convict Labour', *International Review of Social History* 58:2 (August 2013), pp. 285–325; Erik-Jan Zürcher (ed.), *Fighting for a Living: A Comparative Study of Military Labour, 1500–2000* (Amsterdam: Amsterdam University Press, 2014).

7 Thomas Agostini, '"Deserted His Majesty's Service": Military Runaways, the British-American Press, and the Problem of Desertion during the Seven Years' War', *Journal of Social History* 40:4 (2007), pp. 957–85, p. 960.

8 See e.g. Jean-Paul Bertaud, *La Révolution Armée: Les Soldats-Citoyens et la Révolution Française* (Paris: Robert Laffond, 1979), Chapter 5; Alan Forrest, *Conscripts and Deserters: The Army and French Society during the Revolution and Empire* (Oxford: Oxford University Press, 1989).

9 Joshua A. Sanborn, *Drafting the Russian Nation: Military Conscription, Total War, and Mass Politics, 1905–1925* (DeKalb: Northern Illinois University Press, 2003), p. 33.

10 Marcus Rediker, *Between the Devil and the Deep Blue Sea: Merchant Seamen, Pirates, and the Anglo-American Maritime World, 1700–1750* (Cambridge: Cambridge University Press, 1987), p. 100; Ruth de Vliegher 'Desertie bij

Oostendse Oost-Indiëvaarders', in Jan Parmentier and Sander Spanoghe (eds), *Orbis in Orbem: Liber amicorum John Everaert* (Ghent: Academia Press, 2001), pp. 171–85.

11 Theodor Nöldeke, 'A Servile War in the East', in Nöldeke, *Sketches from Eastern History*. Trans. John Sutherland Black (London and Edinburgh: Adam and Charles Black, 1892), pp. 146–75, p. 165, p. 167.

12 Robert N. Anderson, 'The Quilimbo of Palmares: A New Overview of a Maroon State in Seventeenth-Century Brazil', *Journal of Latin American Studies* 28:3 (October 1996), pp. 545–66.

13 Richard Roberts and Martin A. Klein, 'The Banamba Slave Exodus of 1905 and the Decline of Slavery in the Western Sudan', *Journal of African History* 21 (1980), pp. 375–94, quotes at p. 375 and p. 388.

14 Peter Kolchin, *Unfree Labor: American Slavery and Russian Serfdom* (Cambridge, MA: The Belknap Press of Harvard University Press, 1987), p. 279.

15 Johannes Nichtweiss, *Das Bauernlegen in Mecklenburg: Eine Untersuchung zur Geschichte der Bauernschaft und der zweiten Leibeigenschaft in Mecklenburg bis zum Beginn des 19. Jahrhunderts* (Berlin [GDR]: Rütten und Loening, 1954), pp. 136–8.

16 Aditee Nag Chowdhury-Zilly, *The Vagrant Peasant: Agrarian Distress and Desertion in Bengal, 1770 to 1830* (Wiesbaden: Franz Steiner Verlag, 1982); Michael Adas, 'From Footdragging to Flight: The Evasive History of Peasant Avoidance Protest in South and South-East Asia', *Journal of Peasant Studies* 13:2 (1986), pp. 64–86, esp. pp. 72–8.

17 Nitin Varma, 'Chargola Exodus and Collective Action in the Colonial Tea Plantations of Assam', *Sephis* e-magazine 3:2 (2007), pp. 34–7, p. 34. http://sephisemagazine.org/past/vol3-no2-jan-2007.html [accessed 10 March 2015]. On the context, see also Nitin Varma, 'Producing Tea Coolies? Work, Life and Protest in the Colonial Tea Plantations of Assam, 1830s–1920s' (PhD Thesis, Humboldt Universität zu Berlin, 2011); Rana P. Behal, *One Hundred Years of Servitude: Political Economy of Tea Plantations in Colonial Assam* (New Delhi: Tulika, 2014).

18 Reflections on the nature of recent prison riots appear in Bert Useem and Peter A. Kimball, 'A Theory of Prison Riots', *Theory and Society* 16:1 (1987), pp. 87–122; Bert Useem and Michael D. Reisig, 'Collective Action in Prisons: Protests, Disturbances, and Riots', *Criminology* 37:4 (1999), pp. 735–59. For an eighteenth-century example of a prison rebellion, see Paul Truter, 'The Robben Island Rebellion of 1751: A Study of Convict Experience at the Cape of Good Hope', *Kronos* 31 (2005), pp. 34–49.

19 Richard Rashke, *Escape from Sobibor* (Reading: Sphere Books, 1983).

20 Elihu Rose, 'The Anatomy of Mutiny', *Armed Forces and Society* 8:4 (1982), pp. 561–74.

21 Reinhart Baumann, 'Protest und Verweigerung in der Zeit der klassischen Söldnerheere', in Ulrich Bröckling and Michael Sikora (eds), *Armeen und ihre Deserteure: Vernachlässigte Kapitel einer Militärgeschichte der Neuzeit* (Göttingen: Vandenhoeck & Ruprecht, 1998), pp. 16–48, p. 41.

22 Barry L. Dutka, 'New York Discovers Gold! in California', *California History* 63:4 (1984), pp. 313–19, p. 319.

23 Peter J.O. Taylor (ed.), *A Companion to the 'Indian Mutiny' of 1857* (Oxford: Oxford University Press, 1995); Andrew Ward, *Our Bones are Scattered: The Cawnpore Massacres and the Indian Mutiny of 1857* (London: John Murray, 1996).

24 Theda Skocpol, *States and Social Revolutions: A Comparative Analysis of France, Russia, and China* (Cambridge: Cambridge University Press, 1979), p. 115, explains, for example: 'By definition, peasants are primary agricultural cultivators who must [. . .] bear the burden of varying combinations of taxes, rents, corvée, usurious interest rates, and discriminatory prices. *Peasants always have grounds for rebellion* against landlords, state agents, and merchants who exploit them. What is at issue is not so much the objective potential for revolts on grounds of justifiable grievances. It is rather the degree to which grievances that are always at least implicitly present can be collectively perceived and acted upon' (italics mine).

25 I do not mean to suggest that such decisions result from careful calculations in all cases. In some, for example, alcohol abuse led to reckless acts. See e.g. the case of the Cape desertion of 1727 in Nigel Penn, 'Great Escapes: Deserting Soldiers during Noodt's Cape Governorship, 1727–1729', *South African Historical Journal* 59:1 (2007), pp. 171–203, pp. 176–84.

26 Albert O. Hirschmann, *Exit, Voice, and Loyalty: Responses to Decline in Firms, Organizations, and States* (Cambridge, MA: Harvard University Press, 1970). Hirschman defines voice as: 'any attempt at all to change, rather than to escape from, an objectionable state of affairs, whether through individual or collective petition to the management directly in charge, through appeal to a higher authority with the intention of forcing a change in management, or through various types of actions and protests, including those that are meant to mobilize public opinion.' (p. 30) Acquiescence is also labelled as 'apathy' or 'toleration' in the literature. See e.g. Guy Bajoit, 'Exit, voice, loyalty . . . and apathy. Les réactions individuelles au mécontentement', *Revue française de sociologie* 29 (1988), pp. 325–45; Elizabeth A. Hoffmann, 'Exit and Voice: Organizational Loyalty and Dispute Resolution Strategies', *Social Forces* 84:4 (2006), pp. 2313–30.

27 Hirschman, *Exit, Voice, and Loyalty*, p. 37, p. 82.

28 Rudolf Dekker, 'Labour Conflicts and Working-Class Culture in Early Modern Holland', *International Review of Social History* 35 (1990), pp. 377–420, pp. 387–8.

29 'Through boycott, exit is actually consummated rather than just threatened; but it is undertaken for the specific and explicit purpose of achieving a change of policy on the part of the boycotted organization and it is therefore a true hybrid of the two mechanisms.' Hirschman, *Exit, Voice, and Loyalty*, p. 86.

30 *The New Oxford Annotated Bible*. Edited by Herbert G. May and Bruce M. Metzger (New York: Oxford University Press, 1973), book 'Exodus', pp. 67–121, at pp. 68–70, p. 72, pp. 75–9, pp. 82–3.

31 Albert O. Hirschmann, '*Exit, Voice, and Loyalty*: Further Reflections and a Survey of Recent Contributions', *The Milbank Memorial Fund Quarterly* 58:3 (1980), pp. 430–53, pp. 439–40.
32 Agostini, 'Deserted His Majesty's Service', p. 969.
33 Hirschman, *Exit, Voice, and Loyalty*, p. 78.
34 Willerd R. Fann, 'Peacetime Attrition in the Army of Frederick William I, 1713–1740', *Central European History* 11:4 (1978), pp. 323–34, p. 326.
35 Martin van Creveld, *Fighting Power: German and US Army Performance, 1939–1945* (Westport, CT: Greenwood Press, 1982), pp. 163–4. Of course we must not overlook the fact that ideology came into play here as well. Not necessarily the Nazi ideology as such but the conviction that one was fighting for 'a good cause', against the 'diabolical' adversary. Omer Bartov, 'Daily Life and Motivation in War: The *Wehrmacht* in the Soviet Union', *Journal of Strategic Studies* 12 (1989), pp. 200–14.
36 E. Wong, 'Hoofdenverkiezing, stamverdeeling en stamverspreiding der boschnegers van Suriname in de 18^e en 19^e eeuw', *Bijdragen tot de Taal-, Land- en Volkenkunde* 97 (1938), pp. 295–362, pp. 311–14.
37 For an excellent study on this subject, see Peter S. Bearman, 'Desertion as Localism: Army Unit Solidarity and Group Norms in the U.S. Civil War', *Social Forces* 70:2 (December 1991), pp. 321–42.
38 Monica Schuler, 'Ethnic Slave Rebellions in the Caribbean and the Guianas', *Journal of Social History* 3 (1970), pp. 374–85, p. 380.
39 Handler, 'Slave Revolts and Conspiracies', p. 15.
40 H.U.E. Thoden van Velzen and Wim Hoogbergen, *Een zwarte vrijstaat in Suriname: De Okaanse samenleving in de 18e eeuw* (Leiden: KITLV, 2011), p. 1 (my italics).
41 Chase F. Robinson, 'Neck-Sealing in Early Islam', *Journal of the Economic and Social History of the Orient* 48:3 (2005), pp. 401–41, p. 407; C.P. Jones, 'Stigma: Tattooing and Branding in Graeco-Roman Antiquity', *The Journal of Roman Studies* 77 (1987), pp. 139–55.
42 Kolchin, *Unfree Labor*, p. 16.
43 In Stalinist labour camps there was sometimes a practice known as 'internal desertion'. There was a secret fraternity of convicted criminals (mainly pickpockets) called *vory-v-zakone*, of which the members consistently refused to work. And although such behaviour was not ordinarily punished by camp authorities and Soviet courts, 'camp authorities generally avoided direct confrontation with the *vory*'. Federico Varese, 'The Society of the Vory-v-zakone, 1930s–1950s', *Cahiers du Monde Russe* 39:4 (1998), pp. 515–38, p. 518. I owe this reference to my colleague Zhanna Popova.
44 Vishvajit Pandya, 'Sacrifice and Escape as Counter-Hegemonic Rituals: A Structural Essay on an aspect of Andamanese History', *Social Analysis* 41:2 (1997), pp. 66–98.
45 In eighteenth-century Prussia, deserted soldiers were hunted very intensively. Any civilian was entitled to ask a passing soldier to present his pass. If a soldier had run away, the garrison would shoot a cannon, informing peasants from the

surrounding villages that they should assemble units immediately to search the undergrowth and other impenetrable places. Peasants were also required to occupy bridges, dams and tracks [pathways] for a while. Michael Sikora, 'Das 18. Jahrhundert: Die Zeit der Deserteure', in Ulrich Bröckling and Michael Sikora (eds), *Armeen und ihre Deserteure: Vernachlässigte Kapitel einer Militärgeschichte der Neuzeit* (Göttingen: Vandenhoeck & Ruprecht, 1998), pp. 86–111, p. 86 and p. 97.

46 Ella Lonn, *Desertion during the Civil War* (New York: The Century Co., 1928), p. 40.
47 Lonn, *Desertion*, p. 38.
48 Roberts, 'The Banamba Slave Exodus', p. 382.
49 Agostini, 'Deserted His Majesty's Service', pp. 972–3.
50 David Barry Gaspar, 'Runaways in Seventeenth-Century Antigua', *Boletín de Estudios Latinoamericanos y del Caribe* 26 (1979), pp. 3–13, p. 4.
51 Daniel O. Sayers, P. Brendan Burke and Aaron M. Henry, 'The Political Economy of Exile in the Great Dismal Swamp', *International Journal of Historical Archaeology* 11:1 (2007), pp. 60–97.
52 N.A.T. Hall, 'Maritime Maroons: "Grand Marronage" from the Danish West Indies', *William and Mary Quarterly*, Third Series, 42:4 (1985), pp. 476–98, p. 483.
53 Roberts, 'The Banamba Slave Exodus', p. 379.
54 Agostini, 'Deserted His Majesty's Service', p. 967.
55 Canetti, *Crowds & Power*, p. 58 and p. 306 (quotation).

Europe

ILLUSTRATION 2 *Map of Northwest Europe (Erik Odegard).*

3

Between Agency and Force:

The Dynamics of Desertion in a Military Labour Market, Frankfurt am Main 1650–1800

Jeannette Kamp

In 1710 – amidst the War of the Spanish Succession – Michael Thüringer and Friedrich Schwartz were arrested as deserters in Frankfurt am Main. Their case is a telling one, as it shows the international scope of early modern European armies and the way this affected the mobility of individuals. Their story comes to light through their declarations before Frankfurt's criminal court. The court officials were particularly interested in their past military employment. Aged twenty-six, Friedrich already had quite some experience with military life. He declared that he had served in the army of Hessen-Cassel for eight years but had left it three years ago. The interrogation records do not state whether or not Friedrich had left the army legally or not. Either way, after his service he went to Brabant to his brother, who served there as a corporal in the Weisenfeld regiment.[1] According to his declaration Friedrich stayed with his brother for about a year and a half until he was captured as a prisoner of war by the French. After this he immediately took service with the French and about four or five weeks before his arrest in Frankfurt Friedrich had 'deserted from the garrison in Dinant and left, to go back to Germany'.[2]

The tale of Friedrich's co-deserter Michael, aged twenty-four, is not much different. According to his declarations, he was born in Nurnberg where he 'learned the craft of shoemaking from his father'. After the completion of his training he enlisted as a servant with the *Kreisregiment* of Reischach. The investigators questioned Friedrich as to where he was employed by the French and he answered that he was taken prisoner together with 150 men near Seltz, two hours away from Lauterbourg (Alsace). Having been imprisoned in Strasbourg for seven weeks, he first enlisted with the Bavarians – who fought on the French side during the war – for three years and then enlisted with the same French regiment as Michael.

After their desertion, Friedrich and Michael headed towards Liège, a major recruitment centre for armies of the Grand Alliance. There, Friedrich enlisted with one of the Dutch regiments and Michael with Hessen-Cassel. When neither of them received the promised *Handgeld* (a bonus paid upon recruitment) they decided to desert again and were finally arrested in Frankfurt.

The employment history of both Michael and Friedrich unveils a high degree of geographical mobility and continuous change of military employers – both willingly as well as unwillingly. Recruitment, service and desertion are recurring themes in these declarations. Although this particular desertion case is set against the background of war – when there was a constant shortage of manpower and desertion rates were high – the strategies and mobility of Friedrich and Michael are exemplary. This chapter will study desertion in the context of the highly competitive early modern military labour market. It will focus on the connection between recruitment patterns, mobility and desertion from the point of view of a single city: Frankfurt am Main. Throughout the Holy Roman Empire there were several cities that acted as nodal points in the military recruitment market and Frankfurt was one of the most important. During the seventeenth and eighteenth centuries the city was an important recruiting ground for several European powers. The Prussian and Imperial armies were the most dominant players on the market, but the Netherlands (including their overseas trading companies), France, Denmark and Venice all recruited soldiers in the city at one point or another as well. From the 1760s onwards, both the Prussians and the Imperial Army coordinated their recruitment from the city. Finally, Frankfurt employed an army – albeit rather small – of its own as well. The presence of these competing military powers created an environment in which coercion and violence with regard to recruitment and drills were no exception. At the same time, it created possibilities for deserters as well, as they were able to find employment with one of the competing recruitment powers easily. Therefore, studying desertion from the point of one city instead of one army helps to shed light on the interrelationship between desertion and recruitment.

The interrogation records of the city's criminal court provide the opportunity to study the motives and patterns of desertion through the declarations of the soldiers themselves. The records contain both deserters from Frankfurt's own army, as well as deserters from other armies that were arrested in the city. While these interrogation records form the core of this research, it also includes other legal sources from the city of Frankfurt and an extensive consultation of other literature on desertion in Germany. The first part of this chapter will investigate the context of the military labour market in the early modern period and focus on the methods of recruitment. Particular attention is paid to the way soldiers entered military employment, the competition between recruiters and the efforts to regulate this by the city council of Frankfurt. The second part will focus on desertion itself: the patterns and motives of individual deserters and the regulation and punishment by the city council of Frankfurt. By doing so, this chapter seeks to uncover the dynamics between the bound nature of military employment and the soldiers' own agency.

Historiography

The days that military history was an isolated field in academia are long gone. Historians have increasingly integrated military history in social history, political history and lately even migration and labour history.[3] One of the main accomplishments put forward by these studies is that soldiers are no longer merely viewed as a sum of people that constituted an army, but as historical actors in their own right. Soldiers engaged in contacts with civilians during campaigns, became a vital part of city life in (garrison) towns and often supplemented their pay with other forms of casual labour.[4] In other words, it is no longer possible to make a clear-cut distinction between civil and military life in the early modern period. While the problem of desertion is rarely studied for most countries, German historiography has paid particular attention to the phenomenon. Historians, Michael Sikora in particular, have studied desertion against the backdrop of changes in military labour organization.[5]

Desertion seems to have been a particular late-seventeenth- and eighteenth-century phenomenon. Firstly, (military) authorities paid increasing attention to desertion and sought to control it by issuing numerous edicts and decrees. At the same time, desertion, and what it actually entailed, was defined more precisely in legal texts.[6] Secondly, the rise of desertion was not only a manifestation of increased attention by authorities, but also a reflection of changing labour relations faced by soldiers. Historians have distinguished two important transformations that altered the repertoires of actions available to soldiers. The first transformation is related to the rise of standing armies, which led to an increasing need for manpower.[7] Recruitment officers were not always able to fulfil the (increased) demand for labour and turned to alternative methods of recruitment. Luring soldiers into service by way of deceit – or even the use of violence and force – were characteristic of this period.[8] Authorities also resorted to handing out military service as punishment, especially to vagrants or beggars. The lines between voluntary and involuntary recruitment were often vague but these methods hardly ever produced loyal soldiers and they altered the way soldiers entered military service drastically. The second transformation is related directly to the labour conditions. While the soldiers of classical mercenary armies were independent with a high degree of autonomy, their eighteenth-century counterparts were more restricted in their actions. Soldiers lost a great deal of their power to negotiate terms of contract, particularly with regard to the duration of service. While mercenaries traditionally were self-governing units in which soldiers had the right to select their own officers and administer justice, (military) authorities took control over these matters. Additionally the daily life of soldiers saw an increase in the enforcement of harsh discipline which also forced them to perform duties from which their predecessors were exempted like performing road work, digging trenches and other heavy physical labour.[9]

Historians have generally agreed that these transformations had a major impact on the motives of soldiers to desert. The motives of soldiers were often a combination of factors, both structural as well as personal. Michael Sikora has pointed out that desertion was not just a final action of despair, but that it could also be used strategically to enforce negotiations of labour relations or to protest against the breach of contract.[10] Investigating a recruitment city like Frankfurt am Main is especially interesting because it enables us to study how the presence of competing recruitment forces created an environment marked by coercive methods of recruitment as well as the possibility to negotiate one's labour opportunities.

Holding on to 'free will': The recruitment of soldiers

The recruitment of all early modern European armies (as well as those of their trading companies overseas) took place on a scale between voluntary and involuntary recruitment. In order to understand the position of soldiers and their labour relations within the army (as well as society) it is important to take notice of the practices that were involved with transforming civilians into soldiers. With the rise of standing armies, authorities, and, by extension, army commanders and their recruitment officers, were in constant need of sufficient supply of manpower – a problem which was especially pressing during times of war.[11] Finding enough manpower made recruiters inventive and throughout the entire period recruitment by force and deception was a commonly applied method whenever (legal) methods of voluntary recruitment did not provide enough potential recruits.[12]

Involuntary recruitment could range from being pressed into the army by force and physical violence, being lured into the army with deception or being convicted to serve by a criminal court. It is impossible to assess to what extent armies depended on forced recruits. Historians generally assume that the dominant way of recruiting remained voluntary enlistment.[13] However, the line between voluntary and involuntary recruitment is often vague and the examples of people being lured into the army under false pretences are numerous. Soldiers could, for example, be promised more *Handgeld* than they would actually receive or be hired under the presumption of obtaining a high rank, only to find themselves ending up as common foot soldiers.[14]

It is important to remember that recruitment by force and deception occurred especially in times of shortage of manpower and that dynamics were different in times of peace. Recruiters did not just take on anyone randomly and there could be a labour shortage on the military market from the perspective of potential soldiers as well. For many mobile poor, going into service was often a means of securing survival for at least a certain period of time. In times of war, when demand for manpower was high, there was an abundance of military labour available to them. In times of peace, however, recruiters were more selective and not willing to engage vagrants or beggars.

Recruitment officers depended heavily on civilians who acted as middlemen and delivered young men in exchange for financial rewards. A common tactic of these middlemen was to pretend to be willing to enlist themselves. In 1787 the *Tuchmachergesell* (cloth maker journeyman) Christoph Andrea was convicted to work in the trenches for a quarter of a year because he had 'sold' four of his fellow journeymen to the Dutch recruitment officer.[15] According to the statement of one witness the journeymen were persuaded by Andrea to enlist with the Dutch because 'this *Seelenverkäufer* assured them, that if they would accept the bounty from the recruiter and follow him, they would desert together the next day and he would bring them back'.[16] After arriving at the recruitment officer the journeymen soon discovered Andrea's true plan. Andrea handed the journeymen over to the officer with the words: 'I hereby bring you four recruits'.[17] The four journeymen, however, protested and said 'that they were no recruits yet, because they were not yet enlisted, therefore still possessed their free will'.[18] After the journeymen chased Andrea back to Frankfurt, they were offered enlistment by another Dutch recruitment officer, which they accepted 'without protest and under free will'.[19]

This case not only exemplifies how civilians were an important aspect of (forced) recruitment, but also highlights the transition from being a free person to becoming a recruit bound to his contract.[20] A crucial step in the military recruitment was the acceptance of the *Handgeld*. This was considered as the moment a soldier was officially contracted and bound to the army, thus even before taking the oath and hearing the *Kriegsartikel* (military rules and contract). In the case of voluntary recruitment this was an important moment of bargaining. Although many conditions (such as the length of service and the pay) were set, the sum of the bounty could be negotiated. During his trial in 1785, Georg Philipp Breidt, a Danish NCO, recalled how he had negotiated his terms of contract with the Danish recruitment officer in Worms. Breidt had already served under the Danish crown before and this gave him a good position to negotiate favourable conditions. He declared that he had only been willing to enlist if he would serve in the regiment of the crown prince, that he 'would be treated free and without coercion and that he would be granted his freedom until he accepted the bounty of 105 guilders'.[21] Thus, before the moment Breidt would receive his *Handgeld* the recruitment was not supposed to be finalized. In the end, things turned out differently: Breidt was suspected of having shot the officer accompanying the soldiers to the regiment, robbing the recruitment transport and finally desertion. According to Breidt's own account things were very different and he claimed that the officer did not uphold any agreements with regard to resting days along the way and conditions of travelling under bad weather. While the interrogation records do not reveal how the case ended, it shows how the period before accepting the bounty was a moment of negotiation and, more importantly, a period in which one still possessed one's own freedom – at least in the view of the recruits.

The payment of bounty was not only a moment of transition during voluntary recruitment; the practice was very similar if soldiers were recruited with deception. A great deal of deceptive recruitment took place publicly in inns and taverns. Under the influence of alcohol, young men were particularly vulnerable to the ways of the recruiters. They would offer them free meals or drinks, or even secretly slip money into their pockets. Recruiters then used this as a proof that the men had accepted the bounty and therefore enlisted 'voluntarily'. The presence of witnesses (who were often accomplices) enforced this argument.[22]

There was thus a clear moment that soldiers were considered to be bound to the military. Interestingly enough, this is not the moment a soldier swore the oath, even though desertion is often considered an act of perjury by authorities because they had broken the oath. After acceptance of (the promise of) the bounty, leaving the military legally was extremely difficult.

Regulating the recruitment market

Recruitment cities like Frankfurt attracted a great number of competing military recruiters. The story of the Hanoverian colonel Scheither, who travelled through several recruitment cities along the Rhine in 1775 illustrates this very well. Scheither was contracted to provide 2,000 German recruits for the British regiments in their war against America. However, he was unable to fulfil his obligations as he faced heavy competition from the Prussian, Austrian, and the Dutch East India Company recruitment officers. Scheither, being responsible for the financial side of recruitment as well, was not able to match any of the bounties offered by these powers if he wanted to make a profit.[23] Such competition and the presence of illegal recruiters fuelled methods of coercion and deception. The city council of Frankfurt tried to regulate recruitment practices in the city and issued many decrees in order to do so throughout the seventeenth and eighteenth centuries. It was the city council who decided which recruiters were allowed in the city and which were not.

States that received permission to recruit in the city were subjected to rules. It was common for recruiters to make their presence known to the public and potential volunteers by parading through the streets while beating the drum and establishing a post at an inn, hanging out a uniform to indicate which army was recruiting. The city council – knowing that these recruiters were competition for their own army as well – forbade all forms of public display by foreign recruiters. More importantly, they strictly stipulated who was allowed to be recruited and who was not. According to the *Werbungsordnung* from 1735, all servants and journeymen in service in Frankfurt were off limits, in addition to any citizen and their sons or any other individuals under the legal protection of Frankfurt, soldiers of the Frankfurt army and known deserters from the Imperial army and other allies.[24]

The city council, however, lacked the necessary means of enforcing these rules and was repeatedly confronted with complaints of forced recruitment in the city. Between 1640 and 1805, no less than twenty-one decrees were (re-)issued by the city council regulating or prohibiting recruitment by foreign powers.[25] Illegal recruitment (i.e. recruitment without the permission of the city council) often went hand in hand with force and coercion. Several taverns, such as Im Tannenbaum, Zum Storch and Zum Bock, were widely known as centres of recruitment in the city, with all the problems that went along with it. Although it was impossible for recruiters to find new men without the assistance and help of middlemen (and women), citizens also turned against them and 'entered the taverns rioting, forcefully removing and freeing new recruits'.[26] Frankfurt's authorities prohibited its citizens from taking matters into their own hands and ordered them to report any violations of the recruitment ordinances to the authorities. The city council often had to mediate between their own interests with regard to their army and public order and the interests of their citizens, as well as maintaining good diplomatic and political relationships with the most dominant powers in the Holy Roman Empire. These interests did not necessarily match. As a dominant military and political power, Prussia often transgressed Frankfurt's regulations, taking people violently and against their will. This put Frankfurt in a difficult position: they had to keep a diplomatic relationship with the powerful Prussians, while at the same time protecting their own people.

So, on the one hand, regulating recruitment practices was necessary to maintain public order and diplomatic relationships with other powers in the *Reich*. More importantly, however, regulating the recruitment market also meant trying to keep in check the competition and making sure that the city would be able to find enough recruits for its own army. As the example of Colonel Scheither has already shown, in the world of the highly competitive military labour market the amount of *Handgeld* that employers were able to offer played an important role. Unfortunately for Frankfurt, it was not able to offer a bounty that could compete with the other powers. The recruitment officers of Austria and Prussia were known (although it was exceptional) to offer sums up to 100 guilders for men who would fit their strict requirements with regard to height. Ralf Pröve estimated that the average sum in Göttingen was about eight *Talern* – the equivalent of the net wage for six months.[27] In Frankfurt the Dutch offered around ten guilders and the Danes six to eight guilders. Frankfurt itself was not able to offer its recruits more than one guilder and thirty *Kreuzer*.[28] Thus, the city council had to take other measures to secure enough manpower for themselves.

In order to prevent the best potential recruits being lost to other powers, the city guards were ordered to bring every person that entered the city gates willing to recruit to the *Hauptwache* first. There, his personal details would be registered and then he was to be taken to the city's recruitment officers. If the recruit fitted the city's requirements, he would have to enlist with the Frankfurter regiments. Only those found unfit (or if no new recruits were needed) were allowed to be handed over to one of the other recruitment officers in town.[29] This regulation of course only applied to those coming into town with the explicit wish to enter military service, and in order for the regulation to work the city guards had to question every person's motive upon entering the city – something which did not necessarily happen all the time.

Frankfurt's army not only faced competition from other powers by the fact that they were more lucrative for men to enlist due to the higher amount of *Handgeld*. It was not uncommon for foreign recruiters to seduce Frankfurter soldiers to desert and enlist with their own regiments. In 1791 the *Kriegszeugamt* complained that the Prussians 'have seduced many of our best people by their non-commissioned officers who were wandering around the city daily and it happened repeatedly that they enticed the men to desert while they were on duty. They approach the grenadiers publicly, on the street, and ask them if they would want to enlist with them [...] The deserters are disguised and smuggled out of the city.'[30] Seducing soldiers to desert from Frankfurt's army to another was not limited to foreign recruitment officers only: civilian middlemen and even Frankfurt's own soldiers were willing to hand over their comrades to foreign armies in return for money.[31] This again shows how recruitment, desertion and re-enlistment were often intertwined. One army's deserter was another one's recruit.

Quantifying desertion

Military authorities considered the loss of manpower through desertion as one of the biggest challenges of military organization. Because of their emphasis on desertion, both in the actual military regulations as well as in printed military commentaries and newspapers, the eighteenth century has become known as the 'age of deserters' (*Zeit der Deserteure*). Assessing how big the problem actually was numerically has proven to be a difficult task as evidence is scattered and often unreliable. There is therefore little consensus on the scope of the 'problem' and whether or not it should be perceived as a problem at all. Michael Sikora came to the conclusion that an annual desertion rate of two to three per cent represented the upper limit during peace time.[32] Peter Wilson has estimated the levels of peacetime attrition a little higher than Sikora. He concluded that there was an annual loss through desertion of 6 per cent in Prussia and 10 per cent in other German armies.[33] Both authors agree, however, that the 'popular belief that *ancien regime* soldiers deserted in droves' is unfounded and that desertion levels were 'rather low'.[34] However, it is important to distinguish between annual desertion rates and the average desertion rates. Sikora acknowledges that the annual desertion rates do not provide an accurate indication of the total percentage of soldiers lost through desertion, because one cannot account for the average duration of service. Since the majority of soldiers were in service for longer than a year, the number of deserters grows in proportion to the number of soldiers that remained in service. The total calculated loss through desertion, therefore, paints a very different picture. Prussia lost between 20 and 30 per cent of its troops through desertion, while the numbers were even bigger for Kursachsen: between 40 and 50 per cent.[35] These numbers, of course, multiplied in times of war. In any case, the proportion of manpower lost to armies by desertion generally exceeded the proportion lost by death.[36]

Unfortunately, there are no annual or average desertion rates known for Frankfurt for the early modern period besides some numbers for the Seven Years' War provided by Isidor Kracauer. During the war, Frankfurt's troops in the Upper Rhenish Circle (*Oberrheinischer Kreis*) endured considerable losses. During the marching off in June 1757 the regiments had lost between 8.5 and 39 per cent of their manpower through desertion.[37] Refilling their ranks proved to be extremely difficult: out of the 159 soldiers that were recruited between February 1760 and May 1761 almost two-thirds deserted.[38] This was not only a result of a fear of war and deteriorating conditions with regard to pay and provisioning, but also of an increase in alternative opportunities for enlistment.

In Frankfurt, the city council itself, rather than the *Kriegszeugamt* (the military office), possessed the authority to punish deserters.[39] This means that the desertion trials are found in the criminal records of the city.[40] The same records also contain cases against deserters from other military powers that were caught and tried in Frankfurt, as well as correspondence with other states about wanted deserters or correspondence about the extradition of soldiers. The records contain a total of 154 cases dealing with desertion spanning the years from 1667 to 1805.[41] The majority of these cases, 68 per cent, are related to deserters from other armies. Only 18 per cent of the cases are related to deserters from the Frankfurt army; the rest is unknown.[42]

The overrepresentation of foreign recruiters can partly be explained by the fact that one-third of the cases merely contain correspondence with other powers. In the eighteenth century, Frankfurt had entered bilateral agreements with Hessen-Kassel and Hessen-Darmstadt to extradite and exchange each other's deserters. A great deal of the correspondence is between Frankfurt and one of these two states. Although Frankfurt was not bound by bilateral agreements to extradite deserters to other states, they would still do so. More importantly the overrepresentation of foreign deserters in Frankfurt's court cases reflects the city's importance as a recruitment centre: there were soldiers who had deserted immediately after recruitment but were caught in the city, as well as deserters from elsewhere looking for re-employment in Frankfurt. Friedrich Schwartz, one of the two deserters who is mentioned in the introduction, was questioned at the city's gates for his reasons for entering the city. He stated that 'because they [i.e. Friedrich Schwartz and Michael Thüringer] were out of money, they wished to enlist and *kapitulieren* (to enter a military contract)'.[43] The criminal court records regarding desertion, as well as those investigating illegal recruitment, offer a good perspective on the conditions that led to desertion as well as the tactics employed by soldiers after their desertion.

Motives for desertion

It is clear that the nature of military service in the early modern period, and especially its recruitment practices, has considerably influenced the patterns and motives for desertion. Michael Sikora has stated that 'the motives for desertion must be regarded as diverse, but certainly enforced enlistment, violent modes of training and disciplining, and controversies over the conditions of service played a major role during peacetime'.[44] These motives come to light in the many court cases of the criminal court in Frankfurt am Main as well.[45] In general, historians have distinguished three types of motives for desertion. Firstly, desertion as a result of recruitment practices; secondly, desertion as a reaction against conditions of military service (such as drills, maltreatment, etc.); thirdly, desertion due to private and personal circumstances (debts, family circumstances, escape from punishment).[46]

One of the most frequently recurring motives voiced by deserters in their criminal records was the escape from forced or deceptive recruitment.[47] In 1734 Johann Ulrich Schwalbach from Kronenburg was imprisoned at the request of General von Iselbach from Churpfalz. During his interrogation Johann Ulrich admitted to his desertion but defended himself by stating: 'as a pressed person (*ein gezwungener Mensch*) he had repeatedly requested his discharge from the captain, but it was never granted to him'.[48] At the time of his recruitment Johann Ulrich was misled with the promise of a high rank and a large sum of bounty. After he found out that he would receive neither of these things it was too late: he had already taken the oath and thus was bound to the contract. Before deserting, Johann Ulrich tried to receive his discharge legally by mobilizing support from his mother and the *Regierungsrath* von Löwenthal. The latter had even issued a decree that required his discharge: with no result. Even after finding two new recruits for his replacement, the captain refused to let Johann Ulrich go. This case shows just how difficult it could be to get a discharge legally.

The relation between involuntary recruitment and desertion is also reflected in the prosecution patterns of the criminal court in Frankfurt. Periods with a high number of cases against illegal recruitment coincided with periods of a large number of desertion cases. Between the years 1730 and 1735 the prosecutions reached a peak: there were twenty-eight cases of (help with) illegal recruitment and twenty-four cases against desertion. This peak was probably a result of the intensified control of the city's authorities with regard to recruitment as well as desertion. In this period alone six decrees were issued against abuses by recruiters and to reinforce control over deserters.[49]

While the competitive nature of the military labour market enforced methods of coerced recruitment, it also created possibilities for soldiers. The pay of a good sum of *Handgeld* was one of the most important instruments used by officers to attract potential recruits. In order to be able to compete, recruitment officers were willing to offer as much bounty as they were able to afford. While it was not uncommon for soldiers, like Johann Ulrich Schwalbach, to find out that officers had deceived them and paid less, others used the practice of up-front cash payments to their advantage. Johann Bartholomäus, from Seefeld near Munich, stated that he had deserted the Frankfurt army because his comrades had told him that he could receive a good bounty in 'Heidelberg, Strasburg, Nurnberg or other recruitment cities in the Empire'.[50] The interrogation records reveal that soldiers were well aware of which powers recruited where and who offered the best bounty.[51] Such information was often distributed by the soldiers among each other. Recruiters themselves also publicly advertised where and when they would recruit through pamphlets, by the beating of the drum or through other forms of advertising. This means that information on where to find the highest bounty was always at hand – and could be crucial for the survival strategies of deserters. Even if one was not a *Handgeldjäger* (making a living by collecting the bounty and deserting immediately after), knowing where to find easy employment if nothing else was available was vital knowledge. Soldiers who managed to desert were faced with the fact that without the necessary documents to prove their good conduct and legal discharge, military labour often remained the only available option to earn a regular income.

The introduction of the standing armies not only significantly changed the way soldiers were recruited and entered military life, but also the way they experienced their service. In the sixteenth and seventeenth centuries, military organization and labour were characterized by a process of standardization and increased disciplining.⁵² Overall, the changes were characterized by a deterioration of the position of soldiers and their ability to negotiate a great deal of their labour conditions. The length of service and pay were now standardized; the duties of soldiers were expanded with mandatory physical labour such as working on the trenches; soldiers and companies had lost a great deal of their self-rule, especially with regard to administration of justice.⁵³

As the room to negotiate had decreased, conflicts with regard to the period of leave and service or consent of marriage increasingly became motives for desertion, next to 'standard' reasons like lack of pay or maltreatment by officers.⁵⁴ Although physical force was accepted as part of the job to some extent, excessive violence was certainly not. In 1702, Kaspar Götz cited as one of the reasons for his desertion that he was beaten repeatedly because he did not hear properly.⁵⁵ According to the statements of Hans Jakob Hauss in 1685, approximately one third of his regiment had deserted because their officer major Martini not only mistreated them physically but also did not provide them with sufficient lodging, food or pay.⁵⁶

The city council of Frankfurt took such conditions seriously, but only when it came to soldiers of their own. They specifically asked whether or not a soldier hadn't received what was promised to him and if there was any case of maltreatment from the officer that could be cited as a reason for his desertion. While such circumstances could be considered as mitigating factors, it seems that the city council was mainly concerned with controlling any misconduct by its officers that might have enhanced desertion.

Desertion was not the only option available to protest against maltreatment in the army. In 1746 the musketeers of the Frankfurt Adelsberg company handed over an official complaint to the city council about their captain – who was then disciplined by the city council. In another instance, two years later, fifteen soldiers from the company of lieutenant Bienenthal also issued a complaint and stated that they were treated 'extraordinarily hard and barbarous'.⁵⁷ Soldiers in the Frankfurt army had an advantage compared to others. The distance between them and the government was small, both literally as well as figuratively. On average half of the soldiers from the Frankfurt army were born in the city itself. They knew the city well, had access to its institutions, and the presence of their family could generate support if there were any conflicts. There are only few soldiers from Frankfurt (that served in the Frankfurt army) that appear in the desertion cases. However, soldiers that were from outside of the city or Frankfurt-born soldiers in the armies of other powers usually lacked such support and were more susceptible to desertion.

The motives to desert were diverse and it was often multiple factors that led a soldier to run away. Although the men had individual reasons for their desertion, it was not necessarily an individual act. In more than two-thirds of the cases the soldiers had either deserted together with comrades or were later accompanied by fellow deserters on the road.⁵⁸ Travelling together had certain advantages over escaping the army alone. It provided protection on the road and together one had more information available on, for example, where to find (false) passports and which cities were less strict in controlling their entrance gates than others.[59]

In the court cases of Frankfurt it appears that more often than not, desertion was not necessarily the end point of one's military career. Soldiers 'deserted', for example, because they were deceived by other army recruiters to join their ranks. As said before, they strategically chose recruitment cities as places to go to in order to be sure that they would find employment. Henrich Hermann stated that he was planning to go to 'Heidelberg, if he would not manage to find work he wanted to re-enter the army'.[60] The majority of the deserting soldiers in the criminal court cases appeared to have led a mobile lifestyle even before their employment in the army. There are very few men who seemed to have been incorporated in solid community networks through family or marriage – or at least it did not seem to affect their desertion patterns. For many of the men that appear in the court cases, desertion was just as much part of their military service as recruitment.

Mechanisms of control

The way that (military) authorities dealt with desertion varied between executing hard physical punishment, with the death penalty at one end, and pardon and re-enlistment of the deserting soldier on the other end.[61] For the most part, this discretion was the result of the problems of the competitive military labour market and the struggle to find enough (adequate) manpower. Additionally, recruitment cities like Frankfurt am Main were faced with dealing with deserters that did not belong to their jurisdiction: neither as a civil subject nor a military one. It mattered a great deal if the deserter to be tried was part of one of the city's regiments and if he was a burgher or not.

The daily discipline of soldiers enlisted in Frankfurt army was handled by the city's *Kriegszeugamt*. They handled all minor violations of the military regulations and were responsible for maintaining public order. More serious crimes, including desertion, were dealt with and punished by the city council.[62] This was certainly not the normal practice in other territories in the Holy Roman Empire. Usually desertion was judged by a court martial of the respective regiment. Although they often had to receive confirmation by a higher (civil) authority, the decision-making was in their own hands.[63]

According to the letter of the law, as stipulated in the *Kriegsordnung* from 1784, any 'soldier that walks away, deliberately and perjuriously, either on march, on the field or in garrison, whether it is to the enemy or not [. . .] will be sent to the gallows after deliberation'.[64] The city council explicitly reserved the right to adapt and mitigate punishment – something they did more often than not, as in reality the death penalty was hardly ever executed. The city's criminal records only mention one death penalty actually executed for desertion in the eighteenth century. In 1707, Gottfried Pflanz was put to death because he had deserted repeatedly. And even in this case the judges did not follow the letter of the law meticulously: instead of being hanged at the gallows Gottfried was allowed to choose the method of execution.[65] Even though the death penalty was almost never executed, it was often used as a deterrent. In 1705, the soldiers Johann Eberhard Mumm and Johann Jacob Göbel deserted while they were supposed to be on guard. This of course made matters worse: running away while on duty was considered an even bigger transgression because it meant a direct threat to the safety of the troops and the city. In their judgement the city council stated that 'although they deserved death according to military law, one, considering their youth [. . .], wanted to spare them'.[66] Instead of the gallows, Mumm and Göbel were now condemned to run the gauntlet four times a day, four days in a row.[67]

Running the gauntlet was the most common punishment for deserters executed by the city council of Frankfurt. This type of punishment was also favoured by other (military) authorities because it enabled them to adapt the sentence. Depending on possible mitigating factors such as youth, drunkenness, absence of recidivism and previous conduct, one could choose the number of times a soldier had to run through the gauntlet.[68] The sentences were often accompanied by additional stipulations such as banishment and dishonourable discharge. Many of these punishments were not only aimed at physical harm, but also at the loss of honour. This had far-reaching consequences for the person in question since it often resulted in social exclusion.[69] Such naming and shaming was not only confined to those deserters that ended up getting caught. The names of those that managed to escape successfully were pinned on the doors of the court for all to see.[70] Such practices were common throughout the Empire. In Augsburg, authorities held a public degradation ritual in order to induce deserters to turn themselves in. If a soldier turned himself in, and authorities were willing, his honour would be restored by another public ceremony in which his name would be removed from the gallows.[71]

The punishments as described above were directed to all deserters of the army in Frankfurt, regardless of their citizen status. Like any other early modern army, Frankfurt employed both citizens and foreigners alike. In the eighteenth century the number of soldiers born in Frankfurt or one of its villages varied between 43 per cent in 1753 and 54 per cent in 1778. The majority of the non-Frankfurt soldiers came from the neighbouring territories like Darmstadt and Hessen-Cassel or those close by like Nassau.[72] While the place of birth does not directly relate to a soldier's citizen status – soldiers born outside of Frankfurt could have acquired citizenship and become burghers or gained protection as *Beisasse* – it is safe to assume that the majority of the soldiers born outside of Frankfurt were not citizens.

According to Frankfurt's regulations, citizens charged with desertion faced additional punishment. Not only were they punished physically, but also with the loss of their citizenship and the confiscation of any of their property and capital.[73] Thus, they faced a greater risk when deserting. While soldiers from outside of the city might have found support networks and family in their place of birth, and therefore something to run to, deserting for soldiers with burgher status meant quite the opposite. Not only did they have to run away from the city and all their support networks, they additionally lost their entire means of existence. At the same time, as has been mentioned above, their family could file petitions to the city council to request a reduction of sentence and restoration of honour.

The judges and military authorities had a great deal of freedom to adapt punishments to individual circumstances. This discretion was also important to deal with changing demands in the labour market. Authorities had to act pragmatically when it came to the punishment of desertion. The death penalty was hardly ever executed because the soldiers were too valuable: every executed soldier had to be replaced. Recruiting and training a new soldier meant making an investment that was better avoided by punishing the soldier otherwise if possible. It was therefore not exceptional that soldiers, who were caught and punished, re-entered the army.[74] In times of extreme desertion Frankfurt's authorities resorted to issuing so-called *Generalpardons*. Such a general pardon promised to grant every deserter that returned to the garrison within three months complete impunity and re-enlistment.[75]

The effectiveness of such measures has been disputed by contemporaries and historians alike. Authorities often extended the period of the pardons because the number of returned soldiers proved to be insufficient.[76] Military commentators complained that the pardons increased the problem of desertion. Soldiers could anticipate that at some point or another a pardon would be issued, providing them with the possibility to return after desertion if necessary.[77] The discretion of (military) authorities towards the punishment of desertion gave soldiers the possibility to manoeuvre and negotiate terms of contract and improve their labour conditions – especially in times of labour shortage.[78]

At the same time, the executed punishments were extreme and feared by soldiers. Running the gauntlet was a brutal form of physical (and psychological) punishment: the convicted soldier had to run between two rows of his own comrades who had to strike him repeatedly. Depending on the severity of the transgression, the number of soldiers one had to pass and the times one had to run were set. It was almost impossible to escape serious injury if one was condemned to run the gauntlet. In his famous journal Ulrich Bräker, the Swiss soldier who had been pressed into the Prussian army, wrote: 'But no! I won't desert. Rather die than run the gauntlet.'[79] It is not without reason that the fear of punishment was an often cited excuse for desertion. Soldiers that for some reason or another had failed to return to the army on time after their leave chose not to return at all than face the possibility of punishment.[80]

But even if one managed not to get caught, desertion almost never offered a prospect of a secure life. Deserters had to face the loss of honour and the destruction of their social existence. The number of former soldiers and deserters among vagrants was extensive. Of the male vagrants arrested on the main roads in southwest Germany, a quarter had been in service at one point in their lives.[81] Resorting to petty theft or more organized robberies was often a necessary part of the broader economy of makeshifts.[82]

Besides controlling desertion from their own ranks, however, Frankfurt authorities also faced the problem of dealing with deserters from other powers. Due to the presence of foreign recruitment officers, Frankfurt was a favourable location for deserters who were looking for re-employment. At the same time, there were many new recruits that tried to escape after being pressed or lured into the service of these foreign powers.

A problem faced by all early modern authorities was that once a deserter managed to make it past the borders of their jurisdiction, they were basically powerless to prosecute him. In order to prevent this, Frankfurt, like many others, entered into contractual agreements with other territories to extradite each other's deserters. In the eighteenth century Frankfurt had entered a deserter exchange cartel with their neighbouring territories, Hessen-Cassel and Hessen-Darmstadt. While the parties agreed not to employ any of their partners' deserters, there were certain limitations on which soldiers could be extradited. If a soldier had taken service with any other military power recruiting in the respective territory, for example Prussia, it was no longer possible to hand him over. However, if the soldier was recruited by this foreign military power under false pretences or with force, he would be taken into custody, and his former (military) authority would be notified. They, in turn, had to take it up with those that had pressed him into service themselves and claim him back.[83] Such cartels were often part of complicated diplomatic relationships and partners often failed to uphold the mutual agreements – especially if there was an unequal power relation between the two states.[84] Re-enlistment with another army unit could therefore also act as a means for deserters to escape punishment by their former army officials.

By controlling the city gates Frankfurt tried to prevent deserters from entering the city in the first place. These controls, however, were not always effective and deserters still managed to come into the city looking for any kind of employment. If they were exposed as deserters and caught by the city's authorities, the general response was to banish them from the city. In some instances they were even handed over to the Imperial recruiters outside of the city gate.[85]

The city magistrates not only tried to control desertion by the demonstration of their direct power (i.e. criminal punishments, military control, bilateral agreements, etc.) but also through more indirect ways. Preventing desertion was, for example, an important issue in ordinances that prohibited the provision of loans to soldiers.[86] Citizens were instructed not only to withhold any form of help to deserters, but also to actively engage in their detection. They were instructed to stop individuals suspected of desertion and demand that they show identification. If the person failed to prove he was not a deserter by showing a valid passport, he was to be captured and taken to the authorities.[87] The court cases do not show if civilians were in fact actually active in controlling desertion; they do, however, often provide insight into the way that they were providing 'help' along the way. Selling or exchanging uniforms, acquiring false passports, food, lodging, etc. all demanded the help of civilians, whether they did this out of social or emotional considerations or to earn some money.

Conclusion

The analysis of the desertion records in Frankfurt am Main has shown just how much the motives and patterns of desertion were interwoven with the conditions of the military labour market. Military authorities in the early modern period were often faced with shortages in manpower and heavy competition among recruiters. Such conditions gave raise to recruitment by force and deception. Many soldiers found themselves bound to the army involuntarily or under different conditions than they had anticipated. It may come as no surprise that desertion as a result of forced recruitment appears regularly in the interrogation records of the city's criminal court. The records show how the payment of *Handgeld* was perceived as a moment of transition by soldiers and recruiters alike. Before one accepted the payment, one still possessed one's 'free will'.

Regulating recruitment practices by foreign powers was one of the key efforts of recruitment cities like Frankfurt am Main because they were unwanted competition for the recruitment of their own army and a threat to public order. The knowledge of readily available military work also attracted many deserters to the city. They were either looking to simply collect the bonus paid upon recruitment and desert again, or had failed to make a living elsewhere. Re-enlistment with rival powers could also provide protection from prosecution. Due to the advertisement of recruitment officers and information provided by their comrades, soldiers seemed to be very much aware of which powers were recruiting where and how much bonus could be collected.

The pressure of the market meant that authorities were often pragmatic when it came to handing out punishments. Although military regulations and laws prescribed the death penalty for desertion, this was hardly ever executed. More often, authorities condemned deserters to running the gauntlet. One must not forget that this was hardly a 'humane' punishment and that the threat of this punishment was taken very seriously by soldiers. Depending on market conditions, however, soldiers could also use desertion as a way of renegotiating their labour conditions and be re-enlisted after only little or no punishment at all.

ILLUSTRATION 3 *Two soldiers near a river*, Romeyn de Hooghe, 1655–67. Collection Rijksmuseum Amsterdam, RP-P-1933-294.

Desertion was thus part of military life as much as anything else. It was not necessarily the end point of a military career but could be a strategic step as well. The tales of the deserters in Frankfurt's criminal records show just how mobile early modern soldiers were. They travelled across great distances to be enlisted, as part of a company or as runaways.

Notes

1 Institut für Stadtgeschichte (IfSG), Historisches Archiv (vor 1866), Criminalia, 2595 (1710).
2 Translated from the German original: 'Seye er zu Dinant aus der Garnison desertiret u. weggangen, umb wieder nach Teutschland zu gehen.' IfSG, Criminalia, 2595 (1710).
3 Jan Glete, *War and State in Early Modern Europe: Spain, the Dutch Republic and Sweden as Fiscal-Military States, 1500–1660* (London: Routledge, 2002); Frank Tallett, *War and Society in Early-Modern Europe: 1495–1715* (London: Routledge, 1992); Ralf Pröve and Bernhard R. Kroener (eds), *Lebenswelten: militärische Milieus in der Neuzeit; Gesammelte Abhandlungen* (Berlin and Münster: LIT, 2010); Erik-Jan Zürcher (ed.), *Fighting for a Living: A Comparative History of Military Labour 1500–2000* (Amsterdam: Amsterdam

University Press, 2013); Jan Lucassen and Leo Lucassen, 'The Mobility Transition Revisited, 1500–1900: What the Case of Europe Can Offer to Global History', *The Journal of Global History* 4:4 (2009), pp. 347–77; Matthias Asche (ed.), *Krieg, Militär und Migration in der Frühen Neuzeit* (Münster: LIT, 2007).

4 Ralf Pröve, *Stehendes Heer und städtische Gesellschaft im 18. Jahrhundert: Göttingen und seine Militärbevölkerung, 1713–1756* (Munich: R. Oldenbourg, 1995); Griet Vermeesch, *Oorlog, steden en staatsvorming: de grenssteden Gorinchem en Doesburg tijdens de geboorte-eeuw van de Republiek (1570–1680)* (Amsterdam: Amsterdam University Press, 2006).

5 Michael Sikora, *Disziplin und Desertion: Strukturprobleme militärischer Organisation im 18. Jahrhundert* (Berlin: Duncker und Humbolt, 1996); Ulrich Bröckling and Michael Sikora (eds), *Armeen und ihre Deserteure: Vernachlässigte Kapitel einer Militärgeschichte der Neuzeit* (Göttingen: Vandenhoeck und Ruprecht, 1998); Martin Winter, '"Der Untertan auf Posten". Deserteursverfolgung an der brandenburgisch-mecklenburgischen Grenze im 18. Jahrhundert', *Militär und Gesellschaft in der Frühen Neuzeit* 10 (2006), pp. 139–80.

6 Michael Sikora, 'Change and Continuity in Mercenary Armies: Central Europe, 1650–1750', in Erik-Jan Zürcher (ed.), *Fighting for a Living: A Comparative History of Military Labour 1500–2000* (Amsterdam: Amsterdam University Press, 2013), pp. 225–6; Peter Burschel, *Söldner im Nordwestdeutschland des 16. und 17. Jahrhunderts: Sozialgeschichtlichen Studien* (Göttingen: Vandenhoeck & Ruprecht, 1994), pp. 217–25.

7 For discussion on the nature of the military revolution see: Geoffrey Parker, *The Military Revolution: Military Innovation and the Rise of the West, 1500–1800*, 2nd edn (Cambridge: Cambridge University Press, 1996); Janice E. Thomson, *Mercenaries, Pirates and Sovereigns: State-building and Extraterritorial Violence in Early Modern Europe* (Princeton: Princeton University Press, 1994); John Childs, *Armies and Warfare in Europe 1648–1789* (Manchester: Manchester University Press, 1982); John A. Lynn, 'The Evolution of Army Style in the Modern West, 800–2000', *International History Review* 18:3 (1996), pp. 505–45.

8 Ralf Pröve, 'Zum Verhältnis von Militär und Gesellschaft im Spiegel gewaltsamer Rekrutierungen (1648–1789)', *Zeitschrift für historische Forschung* 22 (1995), pp. 191–223; Sikora, *Disziplin und Desertion*, pp. 216–35; Peter Burschel, 'Die Erfindung der Desertion. Strukturprobleme der deutschen Söldnerheeren des 17. Jahrhunderts', in Ulrich Bröckling and Michael Sikora (eds), *Armeen und ihre Deserteure: Vernachlässigte Kapitel einer Militärgeschichte der Neuzeit* (Göttingen: Vandenhoeck und Ruprecht, 1998), pp. 73–6.

9 Burschel, 'Die Erfindung der Desertion', pp. 77–8; Frank Tallett, 'Soldiers in Western Europe, c. 1500–1790', in Erik-Jan Zürcher (ed.), *Fighting for a Living: A Comparative History of Military Labour 1500–2000* (Amsterdam: Amsterdam University Press, 2013), p. 155.

10 Michael Sikora, 'Verzweiflung oder Leichtsinn? Der Militärstand und die Desertion im 18. Jahrhundert', in Bernhard R. Kroener and Ralf Pröve (eds),

Krieg und Frieden. Militär und Gesellschaft in der Frühen Neuzeit (Paderborn: Schöningh, 1996), pp. 237–64.

11 Burschel, 'Die Erfindung der Desertion', pp. 73–6; Tallett, 'Soldiers in Western Europe', pp. 136–42; Michael Sikora, 'Das 18. Jahrhundert: Die Zeit der Deserteure', in Ulrich Bröckling and Michael Sikora (eds), *Armeen und ihre Deserteure: Vernachlässigte Kapitel einer Militärgeschichte der Neuzeit* (Göttingen: Vandenhoeck und Ruprecht, 1998), pp. 92–6.

12 For practices of forced recruitment in Kurhannover, see Pröve, 'Zum Verhältnis von Militär und Gesellschaft', pp. 191–223.

13 Sikora, *Disziplin und Desertion*, p. 206.

14 See for examples of this in relation to desertion further on in this chapter.

15 The early modern authorities considered the delivery of young men by middlemen in exchange for money as a '*Verkauf*' (i.e. a sale or a trade). The term soldier trade is widely used by historians and it primarily refers to the practices of rulers hiring out their soldiers to other states. See Peter H. Wilson, 'The German "Soldier Trade" of the Seventeenth and Eighteenth Centuries: A Reassessment', *The International History Review* 18:4 (1996), pp. 757–92. These perceptions conceal the practices of individual civilians who made a living or supplemented their income by collecting fees for delivering young men, voluntarily or not, to recruitment officers. See, for example, Marianne Sophia Wokeck, *Trade in Strangers: The Beginnings of Mass Migration to North America* (University Park, PA: Pennsylvania State University Press, 1999), pp. 59–112.

16 Translated from the German original: '[sie hätten] versprochen holländische Dienste anzunehmen weil sie dieser Seelenverkäufer versichert habe, dass, wenn sie nur von denen Werbern das Handgeld annehmen, und mit ihme fortgehen würden, er so dann mit ihnen des andern Tags wieder dessertieren und sie wieder anhier bringen wollte'. IfSG, Criminalia, 9709 (1787).

17 The original reads: 'hier bringe er ihnen 4 recruten'. IfSG, Criminalia, 9709 (1787).

18 Original: 'das sie noch keine Recruten seien, weil sie noch nicht angeworben worden, mihtin noch ihren freien Willen hätten'. IfSG, Criminalia, 9709 (1787).

19 Original: 'welche sie [. . .] dann annoch ohne wiederreden und aus freien Willen angenommen hätten'. IfSG, Criminalia, 9709 (1787).

20 Pröve, 'Zum Verhältnis von Militär und Gesellschaft', pp. 202–3.

21 IfSG, Criminalia, 9542 (1785). Original: 'dass er unterwegs frei und ungezwungen behandelt und ihm die Freiheit solange gelassen würde bis er das auf 105fl. reichsgulden sich ausbedungene handgeld unterwegs oder an Ort und Stelle annehmen und sich auszahlen lassen würde'.

22 Pröve, 'Zum Verhältnis von Militär und Gesellschaft', p. 212; IfSG, Criminalia, 4259 (1734–35).

23 This example is described in Rodney Atwood, *The Hessians: Mercenaries from Hessen-Kassel in the American Revolution* (Cambridge and New York: Cambridge University Press, 1980), p. 10.

24 Werbungsordnungen, 25 January 1735, in J.C. Beyerbach, *Sammlung der Verordnungen der Reichsstadt Frankfurt: Sechster Theil: Fürsorge bey der*

häußlichen Niederlassung und bey dem Aufenthalte im Frankfurter Staat (Frankfurt am Main, 1799), pp. 1312–14.

25 Karl Härter and Inke Worgitzki (eds), *Repertorium der Policeyordnungen der Frühen Neuzeit. Bd. 5: Reichsstädte I: Frankfurt am Main* (Frankfurt am Main: Klostermann, 2004).

26 Original: '[. . .] tumultarisch einzudringen, und wohl gar den oder die Neuangeworbenen mit Gewalt herauszunehmen und zu befreyen'. The quote is taken from an edict from the city council dated on 24 June 1766, in Beyerbach, *Sammlung der Verordnungen*, pp. 1318–19.

27 Pröve, 'Zum Verhältnis von Militär und Gesellschaft', p. 202.

28 Isidor Kracauer, 'Das Militärwesen der Reichsstadt Frankfurt a. M. im XVIII. Jahrhundert', *Archiv für Frankfurts Geschichte und Kunst* 3:12 (1920), p. 33.

29 Ibid., pp. 20–3.

30 Quote taken from: Kracauer, 'Das Militärwesen der Reichsstadt Frankfurt', p. 4. The original quote reads: '[. . .] haben uns viele der besten Leute durch ihre in hiesiger Stadt täglich herumschwärmenden Unteroffiziere verführt und die Leute sind öfters auf dem Posten zur Desertion verleitet worden. Auf offener Strasse sprechen sie die Grenadiers an, ob sie nicht Dienst bei ihnen nehmen wollten [. . .] Unter Verkleidung schaffe man die Deserteure aus der Stadt.'

31 IfSG, Criminalia, 7502 (1758); 4133 (1733); 4227 (1734); 5121 (1740).

32 Sikora, *Disziplin und Desertion*, p. 74.

33 Peter H. Wilson, 'The Politics of Military Recruitment in Eighteenth-Century Germany', *English Historical Review* 117:472 (2002), p. 539.

34 Ibid.

35 Sikora, *Disziplin und Desertion*, pp. 75–7.

36 Ibid.

37 Kracauer, 'Das Militärwesen der Reichsstadt Frankfurt', pp. 87–8.

38 Ibid., p. 87.

39 Johann Anton Moritz, *Versuch einer Einleitung in die Staatsverfassung derer Oberrheinischen Reichsstädt: Zweyter Theil, Reichsstadt Frankfurt* (Frankfurt am Main, 1786), pp. 432–3; Kracauer, 'Das Militärwesen der Reichsstadt Frankfurt', p. 67.

40 For more information on the background of the criminal system and sources in Frankfurt see: Joachim Eibach, *Frankfurter Verhöre: Städtische Lebenswelten und Kriminalität im 18. Jahrhundert* (Paderborn: Schöningh, 2003), pp. 29–35.

41 IfSG, Criminalia. An online repository of the criminal cases is available through: http://www.ifaust.de/isg/zeig.FAU?sid=813301E210&dm=1&ind=2&ipos=Criminalia:+Akten [accessed 9 March 2015].

42 Ibid.

43 IfSG, Criminalia, 2595 (1710). Original: 'Sie hätten nach seinen nahmen nicht gefraget, hätten auch keinen pass gezeichet sondern hätten gesaget wie sie kein geld, so wollten sie diensten allhier nehmen u. capituliren.

44 Sikora, 'Change and Continuity in Mercenary Armies', p. 226.

45 Between 1667 and 1806 there were 154 cases of desertion dealt with by the criminal court (these are not always investigation records but also include correspondence with other states regarding deserters and requests for extradition, etc.) as well as 124 cases of forced recruitment or help with forced recruitment.
46 Pröve, *Stehendes Heer*, pp. 49–56; Burschel, *Söldner im Nordwestdeutschland*, pp. 217–25; Sikora, 'Zeit der Deserteure', pp. 19–21.
47 See for example: IfSG, Criminalia, 3610 (1727).
48 IfSG, Criminalia, 4231 (1734). Original: 'er habe als ein gezwongener Mensch zum öffteren beij seinem Hauptmann umb den Abschied angehalten, selbigen aber niemahlen erhalten können'.
49 Härter and Worgitzki, *Repertorium der Policeyordnungen*. See nos. 3073 (1730); 3051 (1731); 3091 (1734); 3094 (1734); 3101 (1734); 3115 (1735).
50 IfSG, Criminalia, 1409 (1673).
51 IfSG, Criminalia, 10392 (1795); 5121 (1740); 2615 (1710); 2595 (1710); 1656 (1685).
52 Tallett, *War and Society*.
53 Burschel, 'Die Erfindung der Desertion', pp. 76–9.
54 Disagreements about absence or leave: IfSG, Criminalia, 2625 (1710); 10392 (1795). Denial of consent to marry: 8390 (1768); 4227 (1734). Lack of pay 2615 (1710); 2595 (1710). Maltreatment by officers: 1656 (1685); 7649 (1760); 1334 (1668); 2328 (1702); 2337 (1702).
55 IfSG, Criminalia, 2337 (1702).
56 IfSG, Criminalia, 1656 (1685).
57 Kracauer, 'Das Militärwesen der Reichsstadt Frankfurt', p. 67.
58 See for example: IfSG, Criminalia, 2595 (1710); 9542 (1785); 10392 (1795); 1656 (1685).
59 IfSG, Criminalia, 2615 (1710).
60 IfSG, Criminalia, 1656 (1685).
61 See for modes of punishment: Sikora, *Disziplin und Desertion*, Chapter 4.
62 Moritz, *Versuch einer Einleitung*, pp. 432–3.
63 Kracauer, 'Das Militärwesen der Reichsstadt Frankfurt', p. 67.
64 Erneuerter Articuls Brief und Kriegs-Ordnung, 10 February 1784, in J.C. Beyerbach, *Sammlung der Verordnungen der Reichsstadt Frankfurt: Neunter Theil: Allgemeine Sicherheits-Anstalten und Vollziehungsgesetze* (Frankfurt am Main, 1799), pp. 1696–711. The original quote reads: 'Welcher Soldat vorsetzlich und meineidiger Weise, es seye auf dem Marche, im Feld oder Garnison, es sey zum Feind oder sonsten, davonlauft [. . .] nach Befindung, mit dem Strang vom Leben zum Tode gebracht', p. 1705.
65 IfSG, Criminalia, 2491 (1707).
66 IfSG, Criminalia, 2434 (1705). Original: 'das sie dem gehaltenen kriegsrecht gemäss den todt zwar verdient, mann ihnen aber in ansehung ihrer jungen jahren [. . .] das leben schencken wollte'.

67 Ibid.
68 Sikora, 'Zeit der Deserteure', p. 105.
69 For the role of honour in early modern punishments, see Gerd Schwerhoff, 'Verordnete Schande? Spätmittelalterliche und frühneuzeitliche Ehrenstrafen zwischen Rechtsakt und sozialer Sanktion', in Andreas Blauert and Gerd Schwerhoff (eds), *Mit den Waffen der Justiz: Zur Kriminalitätsgeschichte des Spätmittelalters und der frühen Neuzeit* (Frankfurt am Main: Fischer Taschenbuch Verlag, 1993), pp. 158–88; Peter Schuster, 'Ehre und Recht. Überlegungen zu einer Begriffs- und Sozialgeschichte zweier Grundbegriffe der mittelalterlichen Gesellschaft', in Sibylle Backmann et al. (eds), *Ehrkonzepte in der frühen Neuzeit: Identitäten und Abgrenzungen* (Berlin: Akademie Verlag, 1998), pp. 40–66.
70 Beyerbach, *Sammlung der Verordnungen IX*, p. 1705.
71 Kathy Stuart, *Defiled Trades and Social Outcasts: Honor and Ritual Pollution in Early Modern Germany* (Cambridge: Cambridge University Press, 1999), pp. 142–3.
72 Kracauer, 'Das Militärwesen der Reichsstadt Frankfurt', pp. 27–9.
73 'Mandat gegen die Desertion der Soldaten', 12 April 1791, in Beyerbach, *Sammlung der Verordnungen IX*, pp. 1712–13.
74 Jörg Muth, *Flucht aus dem militärischen Alltag. Ursachen und individuelle Ausprägung der Desertion in der Armee Friedrichs des Großen* (Freiburg im Breisgau: Rombach Verlag, 2003), p. 109; Pröve, *Stehendes Heer*, p. 56; Sikora, *Disziplin und Desertion*, p. 138.
75 Kracauer, 'Das Militärwesen der Reichsstadt Frankfurt', p. 89; Härter and Worgitzki (eds), *Repertorium der Policeyordnungen*, no. 3094: 'Pardon wegen Desertirens der hiesigen Soldaten betreffend', 2 February 1734. For *Generalpardons* in other territories, see Sikora, *Disziplin und Desertion*, pp. 138–40.
76 Ibid., p. 140.
77 Ibid.; Burschel, 'Die Erfindung der Desertion', p. 81.
78 Sikora, 'Zeit der Deserteure', p. 105.
79 Ulrich Bräker, *The Life Story and Real Adventures of the Poor Man from Toggenburg*. Trans. Derek Bowman (Edinburgh, 1970), p. 129.
80 IfSG, Criminalia, 3674 (1728); 10392 (1795).
81 Carsten Küther, *Menschen auf der Strasse: Vagierende Unterschichten in Bayern, Franken und Schwaben in der zweiten Hälfte des 18. Jahrhunderts* (Göttingen: Vandenhoeck & Ruprecht, 1983), p. 36 and Chapter 7. See for similar numbers in England: Sebastian Schmidt, 'Armut und Armenfürsorge im frühneuzeitlichen England: Das Beispiel der Grafschaft Essex', in Gerhard Ammerer et al. (eds), *Armut auf dem Lande. Mitteleuropa vom Spätmittelalter bis zur Mitte des 19. Jahrhunderts* (Vienna: Böhlau Verlag Wien, 2010), p. 134.
82 Uwe Danker, *Räuberbanden im alten Reich um 1700: ein Beitrag zur Geschichte von Herrschaft und Kriminalität in der Frühen Neuzeit* (Frankfurt am Main: Suhrkamp, 1988), p. 239 and p. 720; Florike Egmond, *Underworlds. Organized Crime in the Netherlands, 1650–1800* (Cambridge: Polity Press, 1993), pp. 48–50.

83 See, for example, the treaty with Hessen-Kassel from 1786; Beyerbach, *Sammlung der Verordnungen IX*, p. 1716.
84 Wilson, 'The Politics of Military Recruitment', pp. 566–7.
85 Kracauer, 'Das Militärwesen der Reichsstadt Frankfurt', p. 25 (note 2) and p. 89.
86 Beyerbach, *Sammlung der Verordnungen II*, pp. 202–4.
87 Mandat gegen die Desertion der Soldaten, 12 April 1791: Beyerbach, *Sammlung der Verordnungen IX*, pp. 1712–13. Winter, 'Der Untertan auf Posten'; Jan Willem Huntebrinker, *'Fromme Knechte' und 'Garteteufel': Söldner als soziale Gruppe im 16. und 17. Jahrhundert* (Konstanz: UVK, 2010).

4

'The Privilege of Using Their Legs':

Leaving the Dutch Army in the Eighteenth Century

Pepijn Brandon

Introduction[1]

The most famous desertion in world literature was an altogether prosaic affair. On a beautiful spring day, bored from endless military exercise, Voltaire's Candide took a walk, believing that 'men and animals have the privilege of using their legs the way they themselves choose'.[2] When caught, the commander of his regiment thought otherwise and liberally gave him a choice between death in front of the firing squad and running the gauntlet. Much wiser because of the punishment meted out for his first crime of walking, Candide's second desertion was less light-hearted. 'Shaking like a philosopher', Candide took the philosopher's way out, pondering the causes and effects of warfare.[3]

Candide's second flight from the army comes closest to the popular image of the deserter as a conscientious war objector. But there is ample reason to believe that the first, more prosaic act of walking to escape from the daily routine of military labour as much captures the historic experience of desertions.[4] Focusing on the Dutch army in the eighteenth century, this chapter examines the tension that existed between a judicial framework that, without exception, treated desertion as a form of treason and a threat to the integrity of the army, and an everyday reality in which desertion was extremely common. Its core argument is that in fact desertion was so endemic and the prospect for soldiers getting away so good, that military authorities felt forced to alternate between extreme exemplary violence and more pragmatic approaches that acknowledged the mobility of soldiers to some extent. In order to sketch this dynamic, the chapter will start by locating the binding contracts that inhibited soldiers' freedom within the wider context of labour contracting in the Dutch Republic and its empire. It will then continue to trace important legal shifts in the treatment of desertion that took place in the eighteenth century, focusing on a number of concrete cases that became the subject of judicial debates. These cases show how jurisprudence shifted to take into account some of the realities of soldiers' lives, allowing for mitigating circumstances that made some forms of desertion more pardonable than others. Finally, it will take a closer look at desertion practices following a specific group of soldiers, recruited to the States' Army in the Dutch-speaking areas of the Prince Bishopric of Liège, during the second half of the eighteenth century. This will shed some light on the question how soldiers, just like other workers who were defined as servants in bonded labour contracts, still found ways to exercise 'the privilege of using their legs'. They did so even where the law did not acknowledge this freedom and promised to counteract disobedience with brutal violence, making desertion practices an important element of reclaiming agency for ordinary soldiers to whom this agency was otherwise violently denied.

Freedom, contract and service in the Dutch world

The extent to which soldiers were restricted in their mobility was defined by the nature of their labour relation. Soldiers form a counterpoint to ordinary wage labourers within the Dutch Republic in that they were subject to law-sanctioned violence in all aspects of their working careers. In this, they were connected to their colleagues across the firing line, as well as to special categories of labourers such as sailors who fell under disciplinary regulations that also allowed extreme forms of physical violence on the part of their superiors.[5] And, as with sailors, one crucial field in which this violence was employed was in enforcing the binding nature of their long-term labour contracts. In an overview of worldwide patterns of military employment, Erik-Jan Zürcher has rightly noted that:

> very few soldiers in history have been legally completely free actors in the sense that they could terminate or change their employment without

being subject to prosecution under criminal law. In almost every country, joining the army altered people's legal status.⁶

But what exactly did this change in legal status entail? Historians have long stressed the exceptionally 'free' character of the labour market of the Dutch Republic, in effect making soldiers the ultimate outsiders to the story of the development of labour relations in the Dutch Republic.⁷ Here, the most poignant comparison is with England, where from at least the fourteenth century onwards laws were introduced that put severe restrictions on the freedom of workers to leave their employers. Breaches of labour contracts remained subject to criminal prosecution until the nineteenth century. Corporal punishment and long periods of forced labour were part of the standard repertoire of employers and the state in restricting labourers' mobility.⁸

In the Dutch Republic, especially its core province Holland, central labour laws were notably absent and local labour laws usually sanctioned a breach of contract by leaving before having served the required period with no more than a fine.⁹ An important part of the explanation of this relative reluctance to bind labour by force of law was the overwhelming significance of migrant labour for the main urban centres and the manning of the merchant fleet, creating an exceptionally wide labour pool for employers to draw on.¹⁰ An abundant supply of labour with a wide range of skill levels made it possible for employers to rely on economic force, or forms of 'recruitment by poverty', to provide a stable workforce of often casual labourers. An additional factor is that from early on the competition for labour power between strong and autonomous towns formed an impediment to the introduction of central labour regulation.¹¹ Within the borders of the Dutch Republic, even very large and powerful institutions such as the Amsterdam naval shipyards recruited the majority of their workforce as short-term labourers without binding, long-term contracts. In comparison to their English counterparts, managers of these institutions had few legal means to force their workers to stay. Instead, they relied on a more subtle combination of preferential treatment on the labour market guaranteed by urban regulations and economic rewards and punishments to buy workers' attachment to their jobs.¹²

While stressing the relative freedom – although one which was often precarious – of wage workers in the core of the Republic, the literature also acknowledges that there were severe limitations to this freedom outside the core region.¹³ These limits were clearest in the large-scale use of slave labour and otherwise forced labour in the East and West Indies. But they were by no means confined to this aspect of Dutch commercial-colonial expansion. It seems to be a strangely under-theorized paradox of Dutch history that the country with the most lenient labour laws of early modern Europe at the same time pioneered subjecting soldiers to the strictest forms of military discipline, in using the workhouse for castigating the 'undeserving poor', and in introducing racialized immigration controls to bar enslaved Africans access to the Dutch Republic.[14] Combined with the severe *de jure* as well as *de facto* restrictions on the freedom to leave their jobs of such diverse and large groups as sailors, children working as apprentices, housemaids, and contract labourers overseas, we are forced to rethink the boundaries between free and forced labour within the Dutch world as much as it has been done for other regions.[15] While the chances of engaging in legally 'free labour' seem to have been greater in the Dutch Republic than elsewhere, it was still well possible within one working life to move between situations where restrictions on mobility and direct physical control over one's own labour power were relatively absent to ones where they were ominously present.

What unites soldiers with all these other groups of workers whose contracts put severe, and sometimes lethal, boundaries to their mobility is that their labour was defined as 'service'. Service contracts created long-term obligations to work for a single employer in a patriarchal setting in which the master's control extended even beyond the workers' labour-time. As Alessandro Stanziani has powerfully argued for the case of France and its colonies, service contracts should not be seen as the polar opposite of wage labour contracts, but rather as one of the legal strands from which the modern labour contract developed. Furthermore, the expansion of wage labour did not simply lead to the gradual replacement of service practices, but instead led to a refinement of service contracts that again influenced the development of legal practices for wage labour.[16] Very similar processes can be discerned in the Dutch Empire, although for now their interconnections remain understudied. It is noticeable, for example, that while labour law remained in its underdeveloped state within the Dutch Republic, elaborate government regulations were introduced for white servants in Suriname. Contrary to the image of labour immigration in the Dutch Atlantic as largely 'free' migration, long-term contracts with high penalties on leaving the job before the end of the contract, commonly categorized as indentured labour in the historiography of other European Atlantic empires, were the norm.[17] As in the case of soldiers, governors cited political considerations – the supposed threat that a mobile labour force created to the control of slaves – as a reason to introduce severe legal restrictions on the movement of white plantation personnel.[18] For example, 1784 regulations for 'white servants' explained that a lack of white personnel on the plantation, whether temporary through absenteeism or permanently if white servants did not hold to their contracts and left their jobs, would endanger 'the planter or owner in particular and this colony in general', even threatening that this could 'lead to complete downfall'.[19]

Seeing the development of soldiers' contracts and the means of their enforcement as part of a wider development of service practices that bridged core and periphery and forms an integral part of the history of Dutch early modern commercial expansion, helps to put desertion and its treatment by authorities back into the main story of Dutch labour relations and the resistance it engendered.

'Punished with his life'

The legal framework that defined and restricted the possibilities for soldiers to leave the States' Army obtained its durable form in the course of the Dutch struggle of independence against Habsburg Spain. Given the essentially military character of this struggle, the evolution of military regulations, inscribed in the so-called Military Articles, should be considered one of the foundation stones of the new state. Recent scholarship describes this development as a forceful break from older attitudes to soldiering as a craft characteristic of the traditional German *Landsknecht* organization, to a situation in which soldiering became a highly regulated form of wage labour.[20] It has been well documented that this proletarianization denoted a substantial loss of freedom to the individual soldier. This had an impact on the legal routes available to soldiers to leave service. During the first half of the sixteenth century, the terms of contract for German soldiers in the Low Countries often specified a clear end date to their obligations, with a very short minimum of three months service. After this term, soldiers were legally free to leave, or to renegotiate the conditions of their further employment. After 1550, a clause became customary that stipulated the continued availability of soldiers after the end of their contract, and the Articles introduced first under Charles V and then under William of Orange did not make mention of any limits to the length of service. Erik Swart suggests that at this point, soldiers were contracted for life and could only leave their regiments by request, at the discretion of their officers.[21]

These limits on the possibilities for soldiers to leave employment in lawful fashion were strongly affirmed in the famous Military Articles of *stadtholder* Maurits of Nassau of August 1590. These articles added the monotonous promise of death for escaping the army in any form. Fourteen out of eighty-two clauses dealt with desertion or absenteeism in various contexts. Article 16 stated that whoever wanted to leave his unit to join another, or to leave the army altogether, had to be in possession of a passport provided by the captain or be punishable by death.[22] The next article prohibited captains from trying to recruit soldiers from another regiment who did not possess such a passport, also stipulating death for offenders.[23] Article 21 defined the distance beyond which a soldier without permit would be considered a deserter as the length of one cannon-shot.[24] Any soldier found beyond this point without a permit would be 'punished with his life'. And so the articles went on in regular repetition. The most important variations on this theme were the clauses against desertion in an immediate situation of battle. For this crime of treason mere execution was not deemed severe enough, so death by hanging – considered more dishonouring than other forms of execution – was prescribed.[25]

Much has been written about the historical significance of Maurits' army regulations. They have been interpreted as a crucial moment in a military revolution in which states achieved greater control over their armed forces, a disciplinary revolution in which even the tiniest minutiae of the soldiers' daily routine were subjected to a rigid Calvinist work ethic, and as an aspect of the development of state terror directed towards the working classes accompanying the 'primitive accumulation' stage in the history of capitalism.[26] Severe punishment for deserters logically formed one of the cornerstones of making these rules effective. It helped delineate the soldiers' field of work as a separate sphere of life, creating both temporal (unbreakable labour contracts for life or for very long periods) and spatial (the one cannon-shot limit) boundaries to the soldiers' mobility. The harshness imposed in this form of labour contract reflected the deadly nature of the soldiers' profession itself, but also the fact that in this crucial area of the states' security, physical force took precedence over economic force in regulating the terms of employment.

However, it should also be noted that the negation of soldiers' freedom even under these stringent military laws was never absolute. It is hard to see how it could have been, given the realities of sharp competition between armies for soldiers that characterized early modern military labour markets. At least partial mobility for soldiers – of course outside the direct confines of battles – was in the direct interest of states, who for cost-cutting reasons kept to the practice of rapidly increasing the number of soldiers under their pay under the immediate threat of war, and dismissing troops *en masse* once war was over. Especially in wartime, soldiers were often able to negotiate shorter terms of service.[27] Captains had their own strong incentives to be permissive towards short-term absenteeism, as long as they could avoid having to report this as desertion. Apart from the obvious boost in morale that could stem from a brief bout of drinking or other transgressions, there might have been financial reasons as well. Since the captains themselves were responsible for the upkeep of their soldiers for which they received a lump sum, temporarily holding on to fewer soldiers than formally stood on the payroll became an important (though illegal) source of profit. Only when marked as dead or a deserter were soldiers struck from the payroll. Despite improvements in mustering practices, incompleteness of army companies remained the norm.[28] Finally, the agency of the soldiers themselves must be accounted for as an important factor in moulding legal practices on desertion. Especially in times of peace, running remained one of the important forms of protest against maltreatment, lack of pay or other forms of mismanagement by the officers. In the peace year 1663, one author commenting on the application of military regulations on desertion characteristically, though certainly with exaggeration, complained:

> This crime, even though it is one of the heaviest military offences, nowadays is punished very lightly, and the Soldiers, without shame, walk from one Company to the other, yes they even run from their service

completely, without anyone caring for it. Whether this strengthens or destroys military discipline, I leave for the consideration of those that should and can remedy this.[29]

One of the important legal windows for temporarily exiting the army offered to soldiers, and at the same time one of the clearest connections between the legal position of soldiers and that of other labourers falling under servants' contracts, was the possibility to obtain official permits or passports to move about.[30] Even when they remained tied to their units, soldiers enjoyed a certain liberty to come and go, provided they obtained the required permits from their officers. Such permits had to be acquired for every journey outside the 'one cannon-shot boundary', ranging from temporary returns to the family home to take care of family business or to get married, to shorter periods of work outside the unit, to ending one's legal term of military employment. Over time, an elaborate set of regulations developed on how, and at what costs to the soldier, these passports could be obtained. Ultimately, the granting of permits remained at the discretion of the military authorities.[31] This affirmed the patriarchal hierarchy and dependency that characterized the soldiers' position *vis-à-vis* his captain, but also opened up a legal framework for negotiation, as well as a possible escape route from bonded labour.[32] This of course was known by soldiers as well as officers, but the very routine of army life depended on a certain level of mobility of soldiers beyond the stringent limits prescribed by the Military Articles. Thus, for example, at the same time that harsh restrictions against absenteeism and desertion were introduced in the second half of the sixteenth century, there also took place an expansion of the employment of soldiers in physical labour outside the immediate context of their regiments, such as in digging trenches, building earthworks and doing repair work on fortresses. All of these took soldiers beyond the immediate range of their units.[33]

Binding soldiers to the army thus in practice depended on a rather complex negotiation between the basic need to grant a certain amount of mobility, and the fear of the authorities that this mobility would induce soldiers to claim 'the privilege of using one's legs'. However, until very late, military law remained completely inflexible in this respect. The first general revision of the Military Articles, introduced in 1705, continued to prescribe the death penalty for all instances of running away, without exceptions. Only in 1748 did the States General agree to an amendment replacing the death penalty with lifelong forced labour as the preferred sanction for desertion in peacetime. Substantial legal discussions preceded this shift. Nevertheless, the practice of persecution was considerably more flexible than the theory prescribed, at least in part because soldiers enforced tolerance towards a certain amount of mobility by walking away from their units on a massive scale. Over time, this reality also started to influence legal texts.

Boomhouer's *Miles Desertor* and eighteenth-century legal debates

In 1731, the military procurator of the city of Namur published a handbook on how to deal with desertion, *Miles Desertor, ofte verhandeling van de desertie*.[34] The book consisted of a summary of the clauses in the military articles that dealt with desertion accompanied by legal commentary, as well as a rendition of cases in which law had been applied with different effects. In general, Boomhouer's text can be read as an argument for applying the military articles on desertion with a certain amount of sensibility to the circumstances under which soldiers ran away, that reflected shifting opinions among legal specialists during the eighteenth century and culminated in the 1748 resolution of the States General.[35] However, the book opened with a revealing case in which this sensibility had definitely not been applied. In August 1723, three soldiers of the Scottish regiment of General Colyaer deserted from the fortified town of Maastricht. All three of them were relatively young: Thomas Volum was twenty-three years of age, William Mackrabe was twenty-two, and Samuel Dean was only eighteen. They had served with General Colyaer for only a month when they decided to run. Three officers pursued them on horseback. William was caught near the small town of Bree in the Prince Bishopric of Liège, and brought back to Maastricht 'under beautiful promises'.[36] Thomas and Samuel had already reached Bree, and proved harder to catch. They had taken refuge in the church, and only agreed to return with their officers when an explicit promise was made that the death penalty would not be applied. Their pursuers agreed, but when they lined up their captives to bring them back to the regiment, 'as much as one hundred people' armed with 'sticks and forks' gathered at the town gates, insisting that the deserters were free within the jurisdiction of Liège. Only when the crowd was convinced that the runaways returned voluntarily did they let the officers and their captives go. This proved to be a fatal mistake. At their return in Maastricht, all three deserters were court-martialled and hanged within less than a week of their capture, leaving the population of Bree 'to the utmost surprised and perturbed'.[37]

In his commentary on the case, Boomhouer took the officers to task for the cruelty displayed in their actions. From his point of view, a particularly sore point in the case was the fact that the officers had gone back on the promises made to the fugitives in order to lure them back to Maastricht where they could be put on trial. But there were other circumstances that made the instant execution of the three young soldiers stand out. First of all, they were sentenced to death in peacetime, not in time of war. Secondly, they had run after only a month of service, which could have been a cause for leniency.[38] Thirdly, the officers risked antagonizing the local population of one of the important catch-net areas of recruitment for the States' Army by employing such cruelty. But on one point, Boomhouer could not fault the officers: by bringing the three deserters to death, they had in fact remained within the boundaries of military regulations, which, according to the sentence, were prescribed to counter desertion 'always with every rigour in order to make an example for others'.[39]

However, as Boomhouer was quick to point out, the sentence was misleading for suggesting that the death penalty was singularly applied in such cases. Boomhouer illustrated this on the basis of a second case of three young deserters from the same regiment.[40] These desertions took place in 1727 when General Colyaer's troops were garrisoned in Namur, which had the additional benefit of showing the Namur-based Boomhouer in the role of the humane prosecutor who pleaded in favour of the defendants. Again, the captured deserters were young, and had only recently been recruited. After a night of apparent heavy drinking, John Cambel (20), Charles Macqueleen (18) and John Macqueleen (19) had found the courage to go to the city walls, where they bound two ropes together in order to make their descent. The youngest, Charles Macqueleen, went first, but before the others could follow they were discovered by a corporal Christoffel Warnier. The two Johns flew back to their barracks, where they pretended nothing had happened. Charles climbed back over the wall and returned to his barracks the same night. Being discovered, they were brought in front of the garrison's Court Martial, a body consisting of six officers and presided over by the garrison commander or his representative.[41] Initially, these officers were inclined to have all three put to death. However, Boomhouer held a long plea for moderation. The core argument was that the three defendants had returned of their own volition to the barracks, thereby limiting their crime to the harbouring of an intention to desert, rather than actual desertion. But there were other mitigating circumstances as well:

> On top of this comes into consideration the youthfulness of the three captives . . .; and further, that they have only served for three Months, and that the third, *John Macqueleen*, over and above this was pressed into the army; yes, that *John Cambel*, and *Charles Macqueleen*, do not understand any other language than the language of the Scottish Highlands, and therefore were not aware of the Military Articles, nor therefore understood the danger of their actions.[42]

Boomhouer's plea convinced the judges of the hardly less cruel sentence of holding a lottery between the three defendants to hang only one of them, and inflict corporal punishment on the others. This did not satisfy the procurator, who asked for an appeal to the States General. The States General sent the request to the Council of State, the highest authority in military affairs. This body finally overturned the death sentence. Instead, it prescribed regimental correction or running the gauntlet for three days on end for John Cambel and Charles Macqueleen and for one day for John Macqueleen. Despite the fact that a higher judicial body prescribed a lighter sentence, the Court Martial, clearly not pleased by this outcome, sought to mete out the maximum amount of violence that could be wielded under the circumstances. Making use of the fact that the Council of State's decision had not specified how often the three soldiers should run the gauntlet it ordered the first two to undergo this severe form of physical punishment four times each on the three days, and the latter the unusually cruel amount of eight times on one single day.[43]

It might seem strange, after these two cases of which the outcome was either death or severe physical punishment, to point out that the terror that could be applied to discipline deserters was not without limits. Nevertheless, this is important in order to understand the juridical grounds on which the Council of State went against the judgement of the Court Martial and at least partially pardoned the three defendants in the second case. Despite the fact that the Military Articles demanded execution in all cases, jurisprudence acknowledged that mitigating circumstances in fact did exist. A legal commentary on the 1590 and 1705 military articles published in 1716, just after the War of the Spanish Succession when problems in regular troop payments abounded, explained that the death penalty was unjustified for deserters 'who had not received their payment, nor could obtain it after complaining to the Captain at the appropriate time'. The reason for this was:

> Because all agreement is made on this condition, *I will keep my promise, if another keeps his*. If now I am not given my pay, so I am not obliged to be a soldier. . . . Which has to be understood in the following way: that he [the soldier] who is lying in garrison, should complain with the Colonel or Commander. If he does not get a hearing, and does not succeed to provide for his upkeep by work or begging, so he is free to leave, provided he does not seek employment with the enemy.[44]

Significantly, this text emphasized that military employment, like other forms of contractual service, did rest on an agreement of mutual obligations, even when once both parties had entered into the agreement their relationship was defined as unequal. A similar emphasis on the contractual limits to the application of desertion clauses can be found in another important juridical commentary from the second half of the eighteenth century. Here, it was emphasized that the harsh punishment for those who went absent without leave could only be justified in a context where soldiers entered the army of their own volition, harking back to the judicial fiction that in contrast to slavery, bond service was the voluntary and temporary subjection of the servant to his master 'since where no engagement and obligation exists, there can neither be a breach of engagement; So it should be clear to everyone that I speak here only of Soldiers who enter employment voluntarily, and not of those who are pressed into service, which is not customary with us.'[45]

Boomhouer, in his treatment of the two cases cited above, clearly showed that he shared these notions. Adding to these, he also cited Roman law to make clear that in judging deserters courts should take account of circumstances such as 'Rank, the Payment, the Place, the Post that was deserted, the prior Walk of life, the number, and the length of absence'.

> Because it is well possible, that today someone is forced into military service, and tomorrow, even before he has drawn any pay, he already leaves the army; or that he walks away without notion or sense, or out of Stupidity, or through any other Coincidence; and whoever sentences such people to death, would most certainly sin against Natural Reason and his own conscience.[46]

In part, these eighteenth-century texts relied on a fiction of free recruitment and lawful treatment that never came near the realities of impressment, trickery, abuse of power, violence and deceit characterizing officers' behaviour towards ordinary soldiers. Nevertheless, they did have some bearing, however limited, on the outcome of appeal processes, as the 1727 desertion case demonstrates. It is important to notice that these authors did not primarily argue for a change in attitude out of a growing sense of humanitarianism. Boomhouer still favoured the use of mutilating physical force to maintain military discipline. For example, in *Miles Desertor* he argued against the abolition of the practice of cutting off the nose and ears of soldiers who defected to the enemy, countering religious objections to the disfiguring of faces by stating that the likeness to God resided in the soul, not in one's profile.[47] The prime concern of these authors was to provide a juridical basis for military authorities to respond to desertion in a more pragmatic fashion than the Military Articles allowed for, reserving the use of naked terror mainly for those cases in which they perceived desertion to threaten directly the fighting spirit of the troops in battle, or the integrity of the army itself.

Shifting legal attitudes reflected a practical need of the state for a more flexible approach. Faced with massive desertion on the one hand and the immediate need for large numbers of recruits due to the immanence or actuality of war on the other, the States General issued general pardons for deserters who returned to their units of their own accord in 1688, 1701, 1703, 1704 and 1708. Even more significantly, in 1726 a peacetime general pardon was announced in order to assist in a new round of recruitment, and this pardon remained valid until 1 March 1772.[48] During the War of the Spanish Succession courts martial had still customarily condemned to death deserters who did not voluntarily return to their units. However, in the long period of armed peace that followed, lighter sentences started to become customary, though they never fully replaced horridly violent forms of punishment. Severe corporal punishment, such as running the gauntlet, remained part of the standard repertoire of military courts.[49] In the second half of the eighteenth century, when the prescribed sentence for desertion was changed to lifelong forced labour, authorities often chose to reduce punishment. A special role in this was reserved for the *stadtholder*. The custom was developed to put all court-martial verdicts up for pardoning by William V, and with few exceptions this meant that sentences for deserters were lowered at his discretion. The motive for this might have been political, strengthening the illusion of a 'special relationship' between the late *stadtholder*s and the army rank and file.[50] Nevertheless, this further widened the space for negotiation for soldiers caught running.

Leaving the army in the late eighteenth century: Some quantitative indicators

Court-martial cases in the Dutch Republic show desertion to be by far the most frequent offence committed by common soldiers in the eighteenth century.[51] Analysing late-eighteenth-century *stamboeken* (soldiers' registers) provides even better insight into the staggering frequency of this form of illegal exit. Each regiment was required to maintain a *stamboek* registering the details of a soldier's career, such as the date of joining the army, duration of the soldier's contract, actual length of service and form of exit from the army. Thus, these registers contain very accurate information on the number of soldiers who either left their regiments through discharge, obtaining passports or through desertion. In addition, the *stamboeken* contained such important personal information as the age at which soldiers were recruited, their place of origin, their height, and in many cases their professional training.

Unfortunately, only twenty-seven of these *stamboeken* have been preserved for the eighteenth century. Seventeen of these deal with the period after 1770. On the basis of *stamboeken* from the final decades of the eighteenth century, Sander Govaerts has collected a sample of 773 soldiers recruited to the (Dutch) States' Army from the Dutch-speaking regions of the Prince-Bishopric of Liège.[52] Of these, 102 had joined the army for an unlimited term (i.e. for life). The rest had signed contracts from a minimum of twenty-one months to a maximum of 196 months, with an average length of employment of 82.5 months or almost seven years. Focusing on the soldiers from this important area of recruitment has the advantage of showing the patterns of leaving the army among a relatively homogeneous group for whom, at least when garrisoned close to the Southern Netherlands as was the case for most of these regiments, the geographic and infrastructural possibilities of escape were approximately similar. Also, the sample cuts across individual army units, and the divide between infantry and cavalry. The obvious disadvantage is that the sample does not allow for comparisons between Dutch-speaking natives and non-Dutch-speaking outsiders, such as the Scottish soldiers mentioned in the previous section. This could have had some impact on the willingness of authorities to apply the ultimate punishment, although of course even when Dutch speaking, these soldiers from Liège should still be considered outsiders to the Republic.

Of the 773 soldiers in the sample, 489 ended their service within the period of time recorded in the *stamboeken*. Table 4.1 gives an overview of how these 489 soldiers ended their careers with their regiments. As this table shows, almost exactly half (49.9 per cent) of the soldiers who left the army in those years did so either through desertion or through negotiation before they had served out 50 per cent of their contracts. Figure 4.1 gives the

TABLE 4.1 *Ways of ending service, final decades of the eighteenth century*

Way of ending service	Frequency (N)	Frequency (%)
Desertion	199	40.7
Permit (> 50 per cent of term served)	158	32.3
Permit (< 50 per cent of term served)	45	9.2
Permit from a contract for life	13	2.7
Death	49	10.0
Other	25	5.1
Total	489	100

Source: Database Sander Govaerts

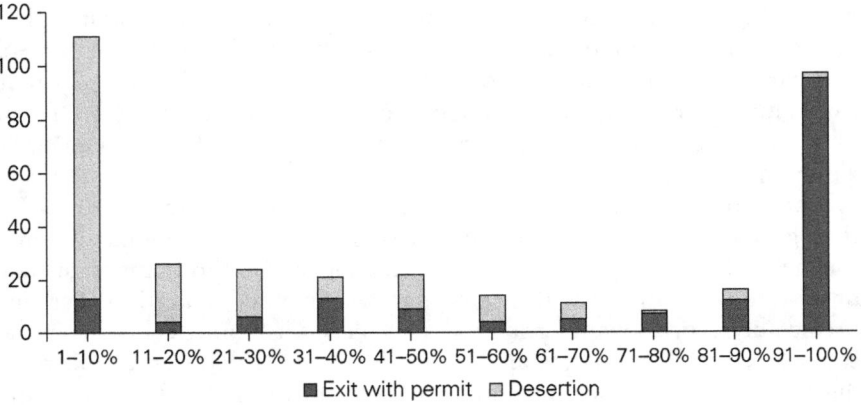

FIGURE 4.1 *Frequency (in numbers) of first-term soldiers with a fixed-term contract leaving the army through desertion or permits as a function of the percentage of the contractual term served*
Source: Database Sander Govaerts

frequency of the two main ways of leaving the army as a function of the proportion of the contractual period served. It shows that desertion was overwhelmingly the preferred option for those in the early stages of their employment by the army, having served 30 per cent of their time or less, with a strong emphasis on the first 10 per cent period of the contract (usually less than a year). But it also shows that from an early stage of the contract onwards, negotiating one's way out of service became an option.

An interesting group among those are the thirteen soldiers who obtained a passport to leave the army during the very first months after being recruited. Most of them left the army after a couple of months, but Francis Tommessen, Hermanus Mulenars and Francis Beckers were released from service within their first month, after having signed up for 55, 56 and 78 months respectively.[53] All three of these cases took place in the peace year 1786, and it seems to be no coincidence that in contrast to these cases, only two new recruits were allowed to leave at such an early stage at a time of war or impending war.[54] Unfortunately, we do not know whether these soldiers in return for their passports were made to pay a fine, or at least pay back their *handgeld*, the advance on wages received at the time of recruitment. However, early release in at least some cases was considered a way to get rid of individuals who after joining were deemed not suitable for the army. Admittedly at a later stage of his career, Gerardus Simons was released with a permit after serving twenty-eight of his thirty-six months, in order 'to improve the unit'.[55] If a passport allowed captains to release unruly or incompetent recruits while claiming compensation, this must have been an attractive alternative in a situation in which such high numbers of early recruits actually managed to run away. Of the total group of almost 200 deserters, eighteen deserted after one month of service or less, having no prior experience in the army. Of these, only two returned to their units, voluntarily or otherwise. Hendrik Slingers ran away from his unit within less than half a month in the war year 1781. After two months, he returned, was pardoned and transferred to a different unit, only to desert again after two and a half months, this time taking along his arms.[56] Jan van den Reyden ran away three days after his recruitment, and returned to his unit after eleven months.[57]

Apart from the stage in a soldier's career, another obvious question of timing was of great influence on the patterns of running or lawfully leaving: the incidence of war years and peace years. Figure 4.2 shows the frequency of desertions and exits with passport in wartime and peacetime. Perhaps predictably, they show desertion to have reached its numerical peaks in the early war years 1781 and, to an even greater extent, 1793. At the same time, during these war periods the number of soldiers allowed to leave the army with a permit over time decreased to very low numbers.

While the figures recorded in the *stamboeken* do not give the concrete stories of running that can be gathered from court cases and other legal texts, they still do tell one story to great effect: the story of deserters' overall

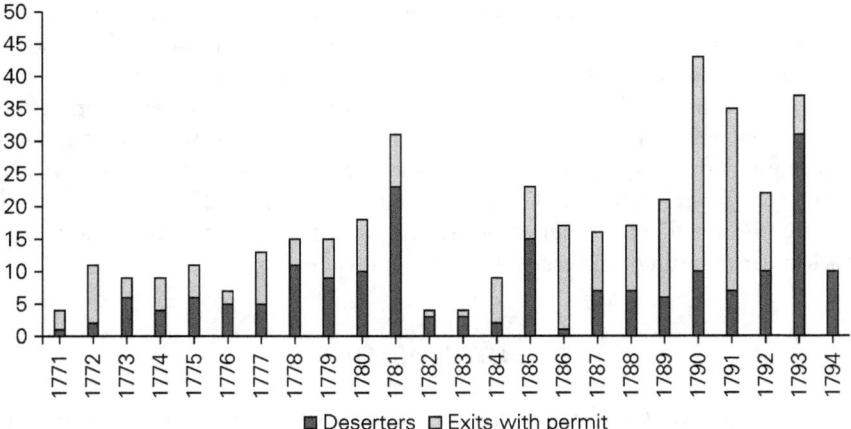

FIGURE 4.2 *Frequency (in numbers) of peacetime and wartime exits from the army, 1771–94 (based on sample group)*
Source: Database Sander Govaerts

success. Only a small minority of forty out of the almost 200 were caught or returned voluntarily. Only in two cases do the *stamboeken* note a lifelong forced labour sentence 'with the wheelbarrow'. However, neither of these two persons was marked down in the registers as an actual deserter. A symbolic death penalty was pronounced over twenty-four deserters who were not caught. Their names were 'written on the gallows', signalling that they had forfeited their lives. However, in the seven cases where these soldiers returned to the army at a later stage, they received a pardon and were re-engaged. One deserter drowned in Breda.[58] The other soldiers lived and were re-engaged. That does not mean they did not receive any punishment: 'corrections' meted out within the regiment such as running the gauntlet might not have been noted in the *stamboeken*. Nevertheless, these records do make clear that the large majority of deserters managed to escape any form of punishment. And even for those who were captured and who might have received physical punishment, this did not necessarily bind them to their units more effectively. For Joseph Beyloes and Cornelis Frissen, as for seventeen of the others who had deserted and returned to their regiments, the experience had proven to be an object lesson in the possibilities of running. They showed their gratefulness for their pardons by deserting again at a later stage.[59] Interestingly enough, quite a number of soldiers deserted or re-deserted after having received a temporary permit to leave their units. Of the almost 200 deserters, thirty-two (or 15 per cent) were soldiers who did not return to their units after being absent with leave. The majority of them had obtained temporary permits to work elsewhere.

As the previous sections outlined, the terms of employment as well as the military-judicial framework under which soldiers worked set severe limits to their freedom and put many formal restrictions on their mobility beyond the symbolic cannon-shot from camp. However, as both the shift in legal attitudes, as well as the figures from the second half of the eighteenth century show, in reality the boundaries for moving out of employment were often more permeable. Desertion was endemic and the authorities often felt constrained for pragmatic reasons from putting into practice the extreme stringency of military law. The brutal punishment meted out in exemplary cases could not keep soldiers from seeing running away as a real and viable option for escaping oppressive military contracts.

Conclusions

As is well known, Candide's escape from the army did bring him outside the reach of the military authorities, but not into 'the best of all possible worlds'. Rather, the free use of his legs brought him to one site of injustice after another on a travel across continents, in which he confronted religious fanaticism and persecution, the cruelty of Suriname slavery and the horrors of war at sea. The story can serve as a reminder that Candide's real-life colleagues who ran away from the States' Army did not run away into freedom. In all likelihood they were bound for careers in different armies, navies or other working environments where they were subject to low pay, strict discipline or ruinously unhealthy working conditions.

Nevertheless, the high percentages of success for eighteenth-century desertions and the reluctance of military authorities in the Dutch Republic to implement the ultimate punishment during the second half of the eighteenth century does tell an important story. Despite the fact that the Dutch were pioneers in introducing draconian military laws that were uniform in demanding death for all runners, the realities of soldiers' mobility defied the stringency of military law. Military authorities as well as writers of juridical textbooks had to grant the notion that, as servants, soldiers did not only have obligations but possessed rights as well, in theory even including the right to run away when they had been victims of impressment or when their captains did not hold to their end of the bargain. While the Military Articles did not recognize mitigating circumstances for deserters, eighteenth-century commentaries did adopt the idea that there were fundamental differences between desertion in peacetime and wartime, at an early stage after recruitment or after a long time of exposure towards military discipline, as a young man or as a seasoned soldier. The 1748 resolution of the States General that replaced the death penalty for peacetime desertions with lifelong forced labour, although in all likelihood partly inspired by the *stadtholder*'s political ambitions, was a further recognition that the circumstances under which desertion took place did matter.

As the 1723 and 1727 case studies cited by Boomhouer show, officers and Court Martials in the eighteenth century could and did resort to deadly violence in answer to desertion. While after 1748 the practice of pardoning deserters became more widespread, this did not preclude severe physical punishment within army regiments. Nevertheless, the late-eighteenth-century *stamboeken* show that soldiers ran away in large numbers. Over 40 per cent of the soldiers recruited in the Dutch-speaking areas of the Prince-Bishopric of Liège who left the army between 1770 and 1795 did so as deserters. Only one fifth of these deserters returned to the army, mostly of their own volition, and of them approximately half deserted again. In successfully reclaiming their 'privilege of using one's legs', they undercut the notion of the military contract as an unbreakable bond.

Notes

1 In the course of a tutorial at the University of Amsterdam, Sander Govaerts provided me with essential input for this chapter. I owe him many thanks for liberally allowing me the use of the database that he compiled as part of this tutorial. I thank Marcus Rediker and the editors Jeannette Kamp and Matthias van Rossum for their comments, and the fellow participants in the ENIUGH-session on comparative histories of desertion in the Dutch empire for a highly stimulating exchange. Responsibility for the way their suggestions were handled remains entirely with the author, giving them the full freedom to run from my conclusions temporarily or permanently.

2 Voltaire, 'Candide of Het optimisme', in Voltaire, *Filosofische vertellingen* (Amsterdam: Van Gennep, 2003), pp. 153–236, pp. 156–7.

3 Ibid.

4 Cf. Frank Tallett, *War and Society in Early-Modern Europe, 1495–1715* (London and New York: Routledge, 1992), p. 116.

5 E.g. Herman Ketting, *Leven, werk en rebellie aan boord van Oost-Indiëvaarders (1595–1650)* (Amsterdam: Aksant, 2005) and Matthias van Rossum, *Werkers van de wereld. Globalisering, arbeid en interculturele ontmoetingen tussen Aziatische en Europese zeelieden in dienst van de VOC, 1600–1800* (Hilversum: Verloren, 2014).

6 Erik-Jan Zürcher, 'Understanding Changes in Military Recruitment and Employment Worldwide', in Erik-Jan Zürcher (ed.), *Fighting for a Living: A Comparative Study of Military Labour 1500–2000* (Amsterdam: Amsterdam University Press, 2013), pp. 11–42, p. 27.

7 Jan Lucassen, 'Labour and Early Modern Economic Development', in Karel Davids and Jan Lucassen (eds), *A Miracle Mirrored: The Dutch Republic in European Perspective* (Cambridge: Cambridge University Press, 1995), pp. 367–409, pp. 394–6; Jan de Vries and Ad van der Woude, *Nederland 1500–1815. De eerste ronde van moderne economische groei* (Amsterdam: Balans, 2005), p. 703.

8 David W. Galenson, 'The Rise of Free Labor: Economic Change and the Enforcement of Service Contracts in England, 1351–1875', in John A. James and Mark Thomas (eds), *Capitalism in Context: Essays on Economic*

Development and Cultural Change in Honor of R.M. Hartwell (Chicago and London: University of Chicago Press, 1994), pp. 114–37; Catharina Lis and Hugo Soly, 'Labor Laws in Western Europe, 13th–16th Centuries: Patterns of Political and Socio-Economic Rationality', in Marcel van der Linden and Leo Lucassen (eds), *Working on Labor: Essays in Honor of Jan Lucassen* (Leiden and Boston: Brill, 2012), pp. 299–321.

9 Erika Kuijpers, 'Labour Legislation at a Developing Labour Market: Holland 1350–1600'. Paper submitted to the European Social Sciences History Conference, Lisbon, February 2008.

10 Lucassen, 'Labour', pp. 369–76; Erika Kuijpers, *Migrantenstad. Immigratie en sociale verhoudingen in 17^e-eeuws Amsterdam* (Hilversum: Verloren, 2005).

11 Lis and Soly, *Labor Laws*, 317.

12 Pepijn Brandon, *War, Capital, and the Dutch State (1588–1795)* (Leiden and Boston: Brill, 2015), Chapter 3; Pepijn Brandon, 'Accounting for Power: Bookkeeping and the Rationalization of Dutch Naval Administration', in Jeff Fynn-Paul (ed.), *War, Entrepreneurs, and the State in Europe and the Mediterranean* (Leiden and Boston: Brill, 2014), pp. 151–69.

13 This distinction between core and periphery, for example, is central to the interpretive model used by Jan Luiten van Zanden, *The Rise and Decline of Holland's Economy: Merchant Capitalism and the Labour Market* (Manchester: Manchester University Press, 1993).

14 Military discipline: Erik Swart, *Krijgsvolk. Militaire professionalisering en het ontstaan van het Staatse leger, 1568–1590* (Amsterdam: Amsterdam University Press, 2006), pp. 108–9. The workhouse: Pieter Spierenburg, 'The Sociogenesis of Confinement and its Development in Early Modern Europe', in Pieter Spierenburg (ed.), *The Emergence of Carceral Institutions: Prisons, Galleys and Lunatic Asylums 1550–1900* (Rotterdam: Erasmus Universiteit, 1984), pp. 9–77, p. 24. Immigration controls: Dienke Hondius, 'Access to the Netherlands of Enslaved and Free Black Africans: Exploring Legal and Social Historical Practices in the Sixteenth–Nineteenth Centuries', *Slavery & Abolition* 33:3 (2011), pp. 377–95.

15 Sailors: Van Rossum, *Werkers*. Children and apprentices: Elise van Nederveen Meerkerk and Ariadne Schmidt, 'Between Wage Labor and Vocation: Child Labor in Dutch Urban Industry, 1600–1800', *Journal of Social History* 41:3 (2008), pp. 717–36, pp. 725–7. Housemaids: Rudolf Michel Dekker, 'Getting to the Source: Women in the Medieval and Early Modern Netherlands', *Journal of Women's History* 10:2 (1988), pp. 165–88, pp. 167–8. Contract labourers: Ruud Beeldsnijder, '*Om werk van jullie te hebben*'. *Plantageslaven in Suriname, 1730–1750* (Utrecht: Universiteit Utrecht, 1994), p. 34 and Karwan Fatah-Black, 'Suriname and the Atlantic World, 1650–1800', Dissertation, Leiden University, 2013, Chapter 5.

16 Alessandro Stanziani, 'Beyond Colonialism: Servants, Wage Earners and Indentured Migrants in Rural France and on Reunion Island (c. 1750–1900)', *Labor History* 54:1 (2013), pp. 64–87, pp. 66–7.

17 This can be seen from the large collection of labour contracts for the Dutch West Indies in the Amsterdam Notary Archives, categorized by S. Hart and his

students. SA, Notariële Archieven, collectie S. Hart, nrs. 433–4. On the role of Amsterdam and Rotterdam merchants as intermediaries in large-scale labour migration to the Americas, see Marianne S. Wokeck, *Trade in Strangers: The Beginnings of Mass Migration to North America* (University Park, PA: The Pennsylvania State University Press, 1999), especially Chapter 3.

18 J.A. Schiltkamp and J. Th. de Smidt, *Plakaten, ordonnantiën en andere wetten, uitgevaardigd in Suriname 1667–1816*. Deel I: 1667–1761 (Amsterdam: Emmering, 1973), pp. 166–9, pp. 381–4, pp. 666–75; J.A. Schiltkamp and J. Th. de Smidt, *Plakaten, ordonnantiën en andere wetten, uitgevaardigd in Suriname 1667–1816*. Deel II: 1761–1816 (Amsterdam: Emmering, 1973) pp. 1066–75.

19 Ibid., pp. 1066–7.

20 Swart, *Krijgsvolk*, p. 53; David Parrott, *The Business of War: Military Enterprise and Military Revolution in Early Modern Europe* (Cambridge: Cambridge University Press, 2012), p. 156; Petra Groen (ed.), *De Tachtigjarige Oorlog. Van Opstand naar geregelde oorlog 1568–1648* (Amsterdam: Boom, 2013), pp. 162–70.

21 Swart, *Krijgsvolk*, pp. 65–6.

22 'Artikelbrief 13 August 1590', reprinted in J.W. Wijn, *Het krijgswezen in den tijd van Prins Maurits* (Utrecht: Hoeijenbos, 1934), pp. 548–9.

23 Ibid., p. 549.

24 Ibid.

25 Ibid., p. 553, article 46.

26 For their role in the military revolution, see Geoffrey Parker, *The Military Revolution: Military Innovation and the Rise of the West, 1500–1800* (Cambridge: Cambridge University Press, 1988); Geoffrey Parker, 'The Limits of Revolutions in Military Affairs: Maurice of Nassau, the Battle of Nieuwpoort (1600), and the Legacy', *The Journal of Military History* 71:2 (2007), pp. 331–72. For the disciplinary revolution, Calvinism and state formation: Philip S. Gorski, *The Disciplinary Revolution: Calvinism and the Rise of the State in Early Modern Europe* (Chicago: University of Chicago Press, 2003), p. 75; Marjolein 't Hart, *The Dutch Wars of Independence: Warfare and Commerce in the Netherlands 1570–1680* (London and New York: Routledge, 2014), pp. 62–5. For primitive accumulation: Peter Linebaugh and Marcus Rediker, *The Many-Headed Hydra: Sailors, Slaves, Commoners, and the Hidden History of the Revolutionary Atlantic* (London: Verso, 2000), p. 32; Peter Way, 'Class-Warfare: Primitive Accumulation, Military Revolution and the British War-Worker', in Marcel van der Linden and Karl Heinz Roth (eds), *Beyond Marx: Theorising the Global Labour Relations of the Twenty-First Century* (Leiden and Boston: Brill, 2014), pp. 65–87.

27 Michael Sikora, 'Change and Continuity in Mercenary Armies: Central Europe, 1650–1750', in Erik-Jan Zürcher (ed.), *Fighting for a Living: A Comparative Study of Military Labour 1500–2000* (Amsterdam: Amsterdam University Press, 2013), pp. 201–41, p. 219.

28 Olaf van Nimwegen, *'Deser landen crijchsvolck': Het Staatse leger en de militaire revoluties 1588–1688* (Amsterdam: Bakker, 2006), pp. 52–8.

29 Petrus Pappus van Tratsberg, *Corpus juris militaris, Waer in begrepen 't Hollandts Krijgs-Recht en Articul-Brief* (Utrecht: Dirck van Ackersdyck, 1663), p. 118.

30 A developed system of permits to move outside the direct vicinity of the plantations was a central part of Suriname labour regulations. E.g. 'Reglement voor plantagebedienden' 1759, Schiltkamp and De Smidt, *Plakaten Suriname* I, pp. 666–75.

31 A summing up of the many different forms of permits and passports, as well as the development of regulation connected to them, can be found in Johan Dibbetz, *Het groot militair woordenboek* (The Hague: Jacobus van den Kieboom, 1740), pp. 500–3.

32 Falsifying passports remained a tested means of escape for unfree or semi-free labourers. In a very different but still connected context, the former slave Frederick Douglass attached great significance to mastering his former master's handwriting, which allowed him to forge a passport and thus obtain his freedom. Frederick Douglass, *Narrative of the Life of Frederick Douglass, an American Slave: Written by Himself* (London: H.G. Collins, 1851), p. 43.

33 Swart, *Krijgsvolk*, p. 67.

34 Johan Boomhouer, *Miles desertor ofte verhandeling van de desertie, met noodige aanmerkingen en rechtsgronden verklaart en opgeheldert tot dienst der militairen* (The Hague: Fredrik Boucquet, 1731).

35 M.L. Dorreboom, *'Gelijk hij gecondemneert word mits deezen'. Militaire strafrechtspleging bij het krijgsvolk te lande, 1700–1795* (Amsterdam: Cabeljauwpers, 2000), p. 246.

36 Boomhouer, *Miles desertor*, p. 8.

37 Ibid., p. 9.

38 Boomhouer explicitly cites 'the youth and the short time that they are in service' as reasons for leniency. Ibid., p. 16.

39 Ibid., p. 12.

40 Ibid., pp. 17–65.

41 Dorreboom, *Militaire strafrechtspleging*, p. 60.

42 Ibid., pp. 38–9.

43 Ibid., pp. 64–5.

44 Gerh. Feltman, *Articul-Brief voor de militie der Vereenighde Nederlanden. Met aanmerkingen* (The Hague: Paulus Scheltus, 1716), p. 117.

45 Joh. Jac. van Hasselt, *Verhandelinge over de straffe van de kruiwagen, waar mede de ruiters, dragonders, soldaten en alle anderen in dienst van den staat der Vereenigde Nederlanden zynde, tot Sergeanten en Wagtmeesters incluys, die van hunne Compagnien deserteren, hedendaags worden gestraft* (Arnhem: Jacob Nyhoff, 1769), p. 23.

46 Boomhouer, *Miles desertor*, voorrede.

47 Ibid., p. 139.

48 Dorreboom, *Militaire strafrechtspleging*, p. 170.

49 Dorreboom, *Militaire strafrechtspleging*, pp. 246–7.

50 Ibid., p. 257.

51 Ibid., Annex IV.

52 Govaerts' sample is based on *stamboeken* for seventeen regiments that can be found in the National Archive in The Hague (henceforth NA), Archief Raad van State, nos. 1949, 1950, 1952–1958, 1962, 1965, 1968, 1973, 2017, 2023, 2024 and 2028. His data have been modified by me to better allow for quantitative comparisons, and to trace differences between wartime and peacetime patterns of leaving the army. The large majority of the soldiers in the sample were recruited between 1770 and 1795, but a handful of soldiers who served extra-ordinary long periods had already entered service in the late 1730s. All individual career tracks mentioned in this section are taken from these entries in the *stamboeken*.

53 NA, Archief Raad van State, no. 1968, fol. 27, fol. 29 and fol. 30.

54 These two were Libertus Hermans, who left the army with a passport after only one-and-a-half months of service in 1780, and Thomas Opteind, who received a permit to leave after three-and-a-half months in 1793. Significantly, both were young when they signed up, 19 and 18 respectively, and both served in a cavalry unit. NA, Archief Raad van State, no. 2023, fol. 302, and no. 2028, fol. 54.

55 NA, Archief Raad van State, no. 2024, fol. 57.

56 NA, Archief Raad van State, no. 1953, fol. 288 and fol. 330.

57 NA, Archief Raad van State, no. 955, fol. 195.

58 This soldier was Peeter van Dal, who deserted in 1791 but was caught and court-martialled. NA, Archief Raad van State, no. 2024, fol. 126.

59 For Joseph Beyloes: NA, Archief Raad van State, no. 1958, fol. 145 and fol. 151. Cornelis Frissen: NA, Archief Raad van State, no. 2023, fol. 448.

Atlantic and Maritime Asia

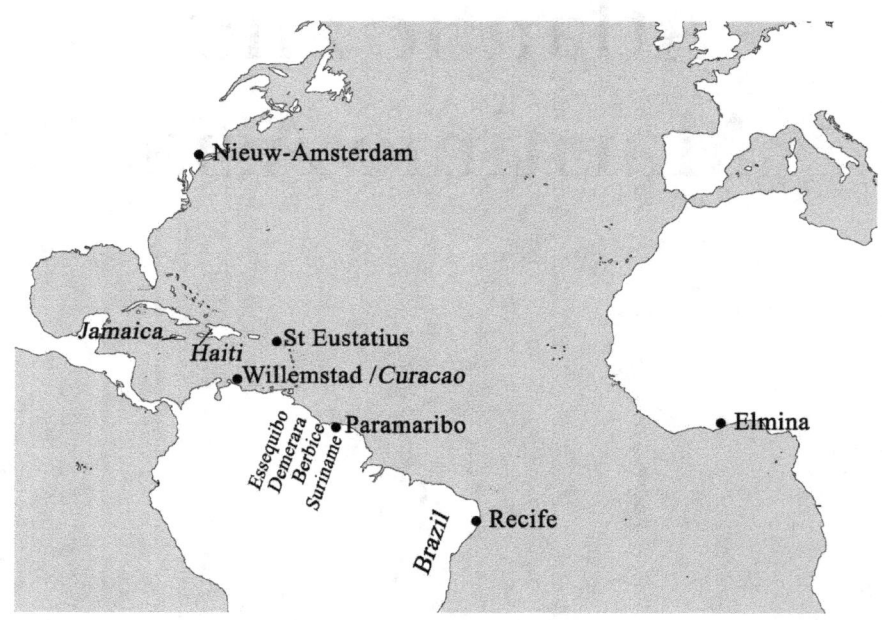

ILLUSTRATION 4 *Map of North and Middle Atlantic (Erik Odegard).*

5

Desertion by Sailors, Slaves and Soldiers in the Dutch Atlantic, c. 1600–1800

Karwan Fatah-Black

Introduction[1]

Desertion was ubiquitous in the Dutch Atlantic, but surprisingly does not figure prominently in the historiography. By deserting, slaves, sailors and soldiers in the Dutch Atlantic challenged the discipline and authority that was central to colonial projects. The scale and intensity of desertion co-determined the development of the Dutch presence in the Atlantic. My tentative exploration of the topic of desertion in this chapter starts by discussing its scale, secondly the types of desertion (individual and collective, overt and covert) and lastly the opportunities and obstacles that deserters faced. Doing so, this chapter presents an overview of desertion in the Dutch Atlantic and hopefully will be a first step to exploring this issue and its implications further.

By challenging definitions of loyalty and territory, desertion played an important role in the formation of empires. This chapter shows that desertion by slaves, soldiers and sailors subverted the designs of the Dutch state and companies in the early modern Atlantic.[2] In doing so, deserters shaped how the institutions of the Dutch empire developed overseas. To desert, sailors, soldiers and slaves had to imagine a future for themselves in an area beyond the boundaries set for them from above. They also bridged linguistic, territorial and cultural boundaries, while creating new loyalties, exchanges and cultural practices. This was not only through their own movement.

Running away often forced their former superiors to establish lines of communication and even negotiation with the areas the deserters moved to or through.

Recent scholarship has established that the Dutch presence in the Atlantic 'mattered more than was long assumed', to quote the cautious words of Gert Oostindie and Jessica Roitman at the end of a five-year project investigating the Dutch Atlantic. They also argued that it was not easy to define the Dutch Atlantic; 'even ascertaining what territories constituted' it 'is difficult in the extreme'.[3] We can divide the early modern Dutch Atlantic into two periods that differed greatly in the scale of military engagement and the role of free trade (versus the chartered West India Company). The first period runs from 1600 to 1670 and involves the incursion of the Dutch in Northern Brazil, the conquest of West African forts, small settlements in the Caribbean and the Guiana Coast as well as New Netherland in North America. In the second period, from 1680 to 1795, the Dutch held on to small strategically placed trading colonies, primarily Elmina on the Gold Coast, Curacao, St Eustatius and plantation colonies on the Guiana Coast, Suriname, Berbice, Essequibo and Demerara. In this second period the armies were much smaller and, except for the Maroon Wars, less engaged in lethal combat.[4]

In the Dutch Atlantic historiography, desertion as defined in this volume is only discussed when studying slaves and slave revolts, rarely when looking at other subordinates.[5] Quite recently sailors' agency in reshaping the world overseas is beginning to receive some attention and in the future hopefully also soldiers' resistance will be included.[6] This chapter only focuses on the act of desertion, and as a result consciously leaves out the communities of runaways that were formed, such as the Curacao logwood communities, cacao planters in Coro, Maroons in Suriname and pirate ships. By studying the act of desertion we can learn more about the expectations people had about the Atlantic world, their lives in general, what they understood as acceptable and unacceptable restrictions on their working life, and the risks they were willing to take when serving their superiors.

Desertion has always been a challenge for commanders during military operations. Overseas expansion by merchant empires also introduced this challenge to the realm of sea transport and proto-industrial working environments like the mines and plantations in the nascent Atlantic world. Movements of labourers to Africa and the Americas involved chains and contractual bonds that were rarely open to formal renegotiation during a person's enslavement, the course of a ship's voyage or the term of military service. Coercion and violent punishment was near-universal in these working environments. When taking a view 'from below', the fear of being lost at sea in an unseaworthy ship or under an incompetent captain must not have been dissimilar to the anxiety when facing a more powerful enemy or going to battle under a hapless commander.

From the mid-seventeenth to the eighteenth century, common sailors, low-ranking soldiers and enslaved plantation labourers were found in proximate and similar working environments. Although the work they did was dissimilar, in practice they could be subjected to quite similar work and overlapping working environments. For example, sailors and soldiers could sometimes be engaged for what was regarded as slave work, slaves served on ships as sailors but were also serving as soldiers, and those recruited as soldiers could be engaged as sailors and vice versa.[7] This is not to say that this was accepted by the workers involved. Especially using sailors and soldiers for what they regarded as work that should be done by African slaves could spark revolt. It does, however, illustrate that the higher levels of the colonial hierarchy were willing to use their subordinates interchangeably regardless of formal contracts or ideas about race.[8]

The overlap and proximity of the working environments and the similarity in the relationship between master and subordinate resulted in similarities of restrictive measures against desertion found on plantations, ships and fortresses. Subtle differences aside, the size of the workforce, the operating hierarchies, common punishments, enforced working hours as well as restrictions on their movements were similar for soldiers, sailors and plantation labourers. Ship crews, plantation workforces and army units ranged from at least ten to at most 200 or occasionally 300 men – or men and women in the case of plantations. Despite the (often ideologically motivated) emphasis on the differences between freedom and slavery, these working environments present a continuum rather than a polar opposition between enslavement and contract. From the late eighteenth century onwards the commonalities in size and operation slowly but surely disappeared in the wake of ever-increasing emphasis on the difference between freedom (understood as mediation by the market and regulation through contracts) and enslavement.[9] This, however, should not hinder the present-day historian's perspective on the coercion inherent in transoceanic labour relations in the Atlantic world, even if they were formally mediated by the market and regulated by contracts.

Scale of desertion

How big a problem was desertion for the Dutch authorities in the Atlantic world? Based on information gathered from the existing literature and primary source material it is safe to say that it was common for workers to desert and that it was quite cautiously registered by administrators of ships, army units and plantations. As the administration for slaves, sailors and soldiers differed, it proves difficult to give overall desertion rates comparable between these three categories. For sailors the desertions are not counted per year, but per voyage. The desertion rates for soldiers are mostly per annum; although sometimes there is precise recruitment and desertion data, there is not always accurate information on the size of the unit from which they deserted. Reconstructing size would be possible, but not in the scope of this present preliminary investigation. For slaves in Suriname there is a body of literature available, which provides rough indications per year for several periods. A guesstimate of the overall average of desertion for the entire Dutch Atlantic in the early modern period would most likely put the annual desertion rate at 5 per cent of the contracted workforce. It stands to reason that this rate rose during periods that saw direct military confrontation. For the enslaved, desertion rates were decidedly lower.

Sailors

The crew on the merchant fleet of the Middelburg Trading Company (MCC) can serve as a good entry point to study desertion patterns for sailors in the Dutch Atlantic. The rich archival material of the MCC is registered as a UNESCO Memory of the World for the company's role in the slave trade. Many of its voyages, however, were not slaving voyages per se, but were trading or smuggling expeditions to the Mediterranean and the Americas. One caveat in using the data of the MCC is that it contains proportionally far more smuggling and slaving voyages than the entire commercial shipping of the Dutch. Zeelandic shipping in general was more high-risk because the economically more powerful shipping companies from Amsterdam operated the less risky shipping connections. It stands to reason that sailors were more eager to leave a ship engaged in high-risk activities, although the opposite could be argued based on the greater access to alternative sources of income and opportunities for career making. On the Atlantic voyages of the MCC there were 10,294 registered voyagers and 568 cases of desertion (5.5 per cent). This figure was slightly lower than the overall figure of the MCC, which had a registered desertion rate of 5.9 per cent (see Table 5.1).

TABLE 5.1 *Death and desertion of seamen in the service of the MCC (including non-Atlantic voyages)* *

	N	Percentage
Deserted	700	5.9
Deceased	923	7.8
Number of seamen's voyages (including multiple voyages per person)	11,789	

Source: Poortvliet database.

*The terms w*eggelopen, gedeserteerd, absent* and *gedrost* were all counted as desertion. The actual desertion and death rates are very likely to have been higher. The data for some ships appears to be incomplete and the table depends on the correct and uniform entry of data into the database.

The deserting crew members on Atlantic voyages of the MCC were typically low-ranking common sailors born in urban centres at some distance from the place of recruitment, but not too far away. The more loyal elements in the crew were the recruits who had been born at less than 60 km by land route from Middelburg, which includes the island of Walcheren as well as the island's vicinity in the province of Zeeland. Those higher up in the hierarchy and the seamen who had been born further away (more than 160 km) from Middelburg, and so likely to have travelled further to enter the trade, deserted less than the average crew member. Sailors, cooks and their mates as well as artisans such as coopers were deserting far more often than the others on board. The top layers of the hierarchy as well as the surgeons and scribes on board rarely appear to have abandoned their post (see Table 5.3). Those who deserted from the MCC were not only men hired in Europe. People who joined the service of the company in the Caribbean were few in number, but they overwhelmingly decided to desert before they served out their contracts.

It does not come as a surprise that common sailors deserted more often than other professions on board the ship: conditions on board were bad and their skills were easily transferable to other merchant companies. So even if they had little to gain, they had even less to lose by seeking employment on another ship. In contrast, sailors who had a more personal investment in a

TABLE 5.2 *Desertion by MCC seamen in the Atlantic, 1721–98**

Function	Employed	Deserted (excl. absent)	Percentage
Cook's mate	60	5	8
Sailor	5,542	457	8
Second cooper	94	6	6
Corporal	156	9	6
Boatswain's mate and sailmaker*	94	5	5
Cook	240	10	4
Second carpenter	153	5	3
Boatswain	220	6	3
Boy	735	10	1

Source: Poortvliet dataset.

*Only functions are shown here if the MCC employed at least ten people in that function or combination of functions on Atlantic voyages (to Africa and/or the Americas), and if at least five people deserted while in that function.

TABLE 5.3 *Seamen who did not desert Atlantic voyages of the MCC ordered by rank*

Function	Voyages with the MCC
Captain	240
First mate	252
Second mate	231
Third watch	191
Master	14
Surgeon	43
Second surgeon	17
Bottler's mate	22
Secretary	20
Boatswain / sail maker	20
Tamboer	13

Source: Poortvliet dataset.

voyage, either because they were part of Zeeland's social fabric or because they had travelled a long way to join the company, deserted less. This is supported by the geographical spread of the desertion. Of the people born close to Middelburg (less than 60 km by land route, which includes the entire island of Walcheren) only 2 per cent deserted. This is much less than people who were born at some distance from the town (more than 60 km but less than 160 km), who had a desertion rate of 10 per cent. Lower desertion rates are also found for people who were born further away in Germany or Scandinavia; their desertion rate of 5 per cent is more or less in line with the average rate of desertion (see Appendix).

Soldiers

The armed forces of the Dutch were, like the sailors, recruited from all over North-Western Europe. In the first half of the seventeenth century the size of the armies deployed in the Atlantic was far greater than in the eighteenth century when territories were consolidated and restricted to smaller areas. The Atlantic War between the united Iberians and the Dutch Republic involved very large armies, somewhere between 35,000 and 40,000 soldiers and sailors on the Dutch side.[10] Wim Klooster notes the stark contrast between the armies of the Dutch in the Netherlands itself who rarely mutinied, and those in Brazil, where mutiny and desertion appear to have been greatly undermining the effectiveness of the armed forces. There were no fewer than eight Portuguese companies made up of deserters from the Dutch armies.[11] Those who did not join the Portuguese menaced the armies, much like escaped slaves, by raiding foraging expeditions.[12]

The organization of payment overseas was notoriously unreliable and so was the arrival of ships that were supposed to provision the troops.[13] The brutal first phase of Dutch conquest, in which they openly sought to fight the Iberians, went hand in hand with mutiny and desertion.[14] Providing accurate figures for the number of deserters is impossible because the administrators in Brazil left out many deserters from their registrations. This enabled them to collect the income of dead or missing soldiers for their personal gain.[15] Soldiers typically deserted just before or during battle. In the Atlantic, we also see significant numbers of soldiers escaping the service before arriving in the colony overseas. In 1633, for example, 13 per cent of the recruits had deserted the armed forces of the Dutch West India Company before they had reached their destination in Brazil.[16] In the voyages to Suriname between 1696 and 1795 1.3 per cent of the company recruits deserted. The majority of these desertions took place between 1760 and 1765 and almost half of the soldiers left while in Great Britain.[17] In those years the British were short of soldiers and did not hesitate to complete their troops by requisitioning men from other ships. This means that these desertions did not necessarily happen voluntarily, but because they were pressed into British service while out in the port. This also happened on board ships. Between 1760 and 1762 no fewer than twenty-four soldiers were taken off their Dutch ship *en route* to Suriname to come to work for the British.

Overall desertion rates for soldiers in the colonies vary between different locations. Between 1700 and 1755 a total of 697 men were recruited to serve in Curacao, including twenty-eight men who had been recruited on the island directly. The army owed much of the loss of its manpower to death: 295 men died during their service – particularly during their first year (166 men). The number of soldiers lost through desertion was considerably lower: seventy-six (almost 11 per cent of the recruits). Sixteen soldiers left their service legally before the end of their contract. For another seventeen men it is not clear whether and how they left service. This means that only a total of 293 soldiers completely served their contract. The number of men that survived their service with the WIC in Curacao was almost equal to those who died.[18]

St Eustatius is located halfway across the string of Caribbean islands that runs from Cuba to the South American mainland. From the island, one can easily reach the nearby islands. In the eighteenth century, especially during the American War of Independence, its importance as a nodal point in the Atlantic world increased quickly. The WIC had a small garrison stationed there and it appears that there was a rather flexible labour market for European soldiers, quite possibly from nearby islands, amending the Statian garrison. The flexibility of this labour market is also reflected in the desertion patterns from the island. The data shows a small, but constant number of desertions (see Table 5.4). At the same time a surprising number of requests for dismissal were granted. The garrison did not seem to be understaffed and soldiers from all over Europe were recruited on the island to replace the vacancies.[19]

Suriname was by far the largest plantation colony in the Dutch Atlantic, and military deployment differed greatly from St Eustatius. At its height in the 1770s there were about 60,000 enslaved workers in the colony. As will be discussed later, many of these slaves managed to escape the plantation areas and settle in maroon communities. These maroon communities were the greatest military threat to the colony. Assaults from competing European powers occurred only rarely, while maroon assaults were becoming more regular towards the middle of the eighteenth century.[20] The armed forces were primarily there to fight the maroons and guard the plantations. Definitive desertion rates for Suriname have not yet been calculated, although it would be possible to do so with the available source material.

Soldiers looking to go to another European colony and stationed at the two main Surinamese fortresses, Fort Zeelandia and Fort Amsterdam, had the best chance to desert successfully. The most adverse conditions were met during the deadly campaigns in the marshlands and forests as well as in the outposts along the *Cordonpad*. This *Cordonpad* was a 100-km-long path around the plantation area that was hacked through the jungle with posts at regular intervals to prevent maroon incursions. The most complete figures are from the 1740s, when 785 new soldiers were recruited to serve in Suriname: 220 soldiers died in the colony and 40 deserted (5 per cent).

TABLE 5.4 *Deaths, desertions and dismissals of military personnel on St Eustatius, 1769–74*

	1769	1770	1771	1772	1773	1774
Number serving at the end of the year	50	51	47	–	48	44
Deaths	2	2	3	–	2	4
Desertions	2			–	1	2
Banishments	1	1	1	–	2	4
Dismissals		4	7	–	10	3

Source: NA, NWIC, 1201, A–E. Data for 1772 is missing.

TABLE 5.5 *Recruitment and desertion by soldiers in Suriname and Curacao, 1700–55*

	Suriname			Curacao	
	Soldiers recruited	Desertions	Deaths (incl. executions)	Soldiers recruited	Desertions
1700s	535	17	145	95	17
1710s	492	20	223	136	30
1720s	403	0	68	101	9
1730s	835	4	193	229	7
1740s	785	40	220	135	13
1750s	1,676	22	646		

Sources: M. Lohnstein, *De militie van de sociëteit c.q. directie van Suriname in de achttiende eeuw* (Velp: unpublished, 1984), pp. 91 and 119; Han Jordaan, 'De vrijen en de Curaçaose defensie, 1791–1800', in Han Jordaan, Henk den Heijer and Victor Enthoven (eds), *Geweld in de West: een militaire geschiedenis van de Nederlandse Atlantische wereld, 1600–1800* (Leiden: Brill, 2013), p. 141.

Slaves

Slaves were by far the least mobile of the three groups studied in this chapter. Enslaved Africans were bound to their owner, which, in a plantation economy with absentee-ownership, meant that they were bound to the ground they tilled. This resulted in three forms of desertion. Firstly, what is traditionally known as *grand marronage*: the wholesale escape from the plantation with the intention to stay away and build up life elsewhere. Secondly, the more common *petit marronage*: being absent from the plantation temporarily, but with the intention to return to it. Thirdly, we can distinguish what Hoogbergen has called 'step-by-step marronage'. In such cases slaves absented themselves from the plantation and settled nearby in the *kapuweri*, the thick brushes that grew where provisioning grounds had been abandoned, often behind plantations. This enabled the escapee to visit his (it was predominantly a male practice) friends and family at night and share in the plantation's provisions. Over time this could develop into groups that would move away from the plantation, which would then be classified as *grand marronage*.[21] Flight was by far the most common form of resistance by slaves on plantations in Suriname.

Research by Rénie van der Putte and Hoogbergen provides detailed data on the number of escaping slaves and the number of returnees. It is estimated that between 1779 and 1792 on average 93 per cent of the runaways were male. In the period 1767 to 1802 there were 6,228 registered escaping slaves. In that same period there were also 3,089 returnees and therefore 3,139 (50.4 per cent) who stayed away.[22] While the number of escapes remained the same in

TABLE 5.6 *Resistance on plantations in Suriname, 1750–99**

	Maroon	Uprising/attack	Mass *marronage*	Strike	Conspiracy
1750s	26	10	3	1	1
1760s	10	4	4	1	
1770s	32	1	1	3	1
1781, 1784 and 1789	7	2	1	1	
1795 and 1799		1	5		

Source: Alex van Stipriaan, *Surinaams contrast roofbouw en overleven in een Caraïbische plantagekolonie, 1750–1863* (Leiden: KITLV Uitgeverij, 1993), pp. 446–8.

*The original table in the book by van Stipriaan registers the incidence ordered per year and by plantation. Instances of mass *marronage* are counted if more than 10 per cent of the slave force of a plantation was involved. For the 1780s and 1790s only incomplete data is available.

the nineteenth century, the return rates increased drastically.[23] Given these numbers, Hoogbergen states that in the eighteenth century the desertion rate will have been about 0.5 per cent, much lower than that of soldiers and sailors. It stands to reason that the social ties of plantation slaves kept them from abandoning their working environment. After all, escape from the plantation did not only mean that they left a brutal system of exploitation, but also the place where they lived, had family and arguably more of a life than sailors had on board ships or soldiers in their barracks, forts or outposts. Even if it was proportionally rare for slaves to escape, the difference between sailors, slaves and soldiers might be less significant if we were to compare the data on escaping slaves for the same age and sex as that of the average soldiers and sailors.

Individual and collective desertion

The preferred mode of desertion for soldiers and sailors seems to have been in pairs, most likely because this gave an advantage over fleeing alone, without becoming a group that was easily noticed. Slaves predominantly fled alone (34 per cent of the cases), but fleeing in pairs was a close second at 21 per cent.[24] In terms of planning, execution and impact, we can clearly distinguish between individual and collective desertion. The reasons behind individual desertions varied: they ranged from the wish to avoid combat, escape debt, avoid punishment or to simply seek a better life elsewhere. The same motivations could apply to collective desertions as well, although collective desertion was often a final (desperate) act at the end of a series of attempts at collective resistance.

Individual deserters often relied on support by fellow soldiers, slaves and sailors, or on people providing support along the way. Although they were not a collective, also individual deserters relied on information networks and a shared understanding among those in that particular working environment of the possibilities offered by escape. Seemingly individual escapes might have been the only option open to groups of people, since geographies did not always allow for more than a small number of individual desertions in rapid succession. For example, in Curacao, the deserters from the navy ship *Ceres* in 1795 all took similar routes off the island in quick succession, rather than one big departure.[25] It remains guesswork whether such small numbers of successive desertions were plotted together, a copying of examples or simply a similar assessment of limits and possibilities by several people in the same workplace. Whatever the case might have been, the top of the hierarchy understood that individual desertions could be a sign of impending collapse of discipline. Even small numbers of individual desertions could quickly undermine army units. After the desertion of two soldiers, Governor van Hoogenheim of Berbice remarked that this was 'quite possibly the spearhead of a larger mutiny'.[26]

In the context of plantation slavery, the distinction between individual and collective escape was similar to that on ships and in army units. For slaves *petit marronage* was often an individual act more akin to absence than desertion. Episodes of *grand marronage* were often individual as well. Okanisi Maroons typically refer to themselves as *Lowéman*.[27] This name derives from the Dutch *loop weg man* or *wegloper* meaning runaway. In the oral tradition the *lonten* (flight) is sometimes treated as an individual ordeal during which the refugee was tested, travelling a long distance through unknown terrain to reach safe areas where others had settled before. On this journey the refugee could be helped by spirits or birds to find a safe haven.[28]

TABLE 5.7 *Size of groups of escaping slaves in Suriname, 1767–1802* *

Size of escaping groups	Number of slaves	Percentage
1	2,118	34
2	1,308	21
3	846	14
Between 3 and 10	1,569	25
More than 10	355	6
Total	6,196	100

Source: Rénie van der Putte, 'Surinaamse "Weglopers" van de Jaren 1767–1802', *OSO: Tijdschrift voor Surinamistiek* 24:2 (2005), p. 278.

*Note that inconsistencies in the number of escapees provided by van der Putte have been corrected.

Collective desertions are closely related to collective forms of resistance, such as work stoppages and mutinies. In the case of collective desertions from army units and ships, they were often the last stage of a process of negotiation between the men and their commander. On plantations this was the same, although here a retreat into the forest could also herald the start of negotiation between slaves and the plantation director. For collective desertion it seems useful to distinguish covert desertion plots and the mass desertions that take place as part of a revolt or mutiny and are undertaken in full view of the commanders or captain. Not only was collective desertion a problem for the commanding officer because it quickly thinned the ranks, but it was also an expression of his failure to have authority over the troops.

A good example of the collapse of an army unit due to the lack of legitimacy of the commander authority in the eyes of the soldiers occurred during the standoff between the Portuguese and the Dutch on São Tomé in 1642. The fortress to which the Dutch had retreated before the ceasefire was located near the city of São Tomé. On the same day that the negotiations were opened, 18 November 1642, a reconnaissance mission by twenty-two Dutch soldiers was intercepted and killed to the last man. Friendly relations between the Dutch and the Portuguese were initiated on that same day, which included the cajoling of the Dutchman Jan Coenders by the Portuguese Lourenço Pires, who gave Coenders' wife a nice set of golden earrings and a necklace. The spectacle must have bewildered the Dutch soldiers who had just lost twenty-two of their comrades. Given the ceasing of hostilities the men were now allowed to walk into town and buy food and supplies, a freedom that resulted in a steady stream of desertions. On 1 December, twenty soldiers and a sailor left. On 4 December, a captain and a sergeant left and even Coenders' *vaandrig* left. The Portuguese answered the request to return the troops with the remark that soldiers seek profit, just like merchants – referring to the lack of morality of the Dutch because they did not serve a god-ordained king but a republic of traders. More than forty soldiers left, leaving Commander Coenders with only eighty men in his fort.[29] The next year the fort began to deteriorate quickly, and the batteries were in a state of disrepair because the carpenters had deserted as well.[30]

A lack of ascendance could also result in overt collective desertion, as happened in 'white man's grave' Elmina on the Gold Coast. In Elmina, Eurafrican *Tapoeyer soldaten* formed the backbone of the WIC's armed forces. After the WIC was liquidated and its overseas possessions were taken over by the Dutch State there were several conflicts between the soldiers and local officials. Natalie Everts describes an incident of 5 December 1798 when twenty armed soldiers walked out of the gates of the fortress in protest. Soon after, fifteen soldiers from the redoubt at Coenraadsburg did the same. The men protested against the default payment of their salary, the rising prices of provisions and their increasing debts. The action was stopped because the men were disarmed by the King of Elmina.[31]

Similar to the waning trust of soldiers in their commander was the fear of sailors that their captain was unskilled, took too many risks, that the ship would not survive the next crossing, or that the ship would not be able to leave port at all. In December 1790 and January 1791 many crew members of the MCC ship *Standvastigheid* (meaning steadfastness) deserted after it had to seek shelter in Dover after a difficult crossing out of Zeeland.[32] Lack of confidence in the ship was also very likely the reason behind desertions and a mutiny from the Dutch naval vessel *Medea* in 1795 and 1796. The mutiny ended with the mass discharge of the crew, several of whom re-entered Dutch service aboard the still seaworthy *Ceres*.[33]

Overt collective desertions or walk-outs were also seen aboard ships where a group of sailors had access to a sloop and could leave the main ship easily. Such overt collective desertions typically followed a stalemate during a mutiny and seem to be an ad hoc and collective response. The MCC ship *Don Luis*, on a disastrous voyage in which it had initially been accompanied by the *Don Carlos*, saw an episode of overt collective desertion in the face of a failing voyage. On 25 December 1725, part of the crew, which had been murmuring, striking and deserting in the preceding months, sabotaged the cannons on board and demanded to be brought to a Spanish ship nearby.[34]

The constant movement of sailors going to shore to fetch firewood and fresh water as well as to trade along the coast was conducive to desertion. A spontaneous episode of overt collective desertion occurred in 1757 aboard the *Prins Willem de Vijfde*, a slave ship of the Middelburg trading company under the command of captain Adriaan Jacobsz. The voyages of the ship were ridden with difficulties. On 19 October 1757, a sloop with trade goods went to shore. When the sloop returned in the afternoon the sailors demanded to eat before unloading the vessel. The crew came into conflict with the cook, demanding to be fed. Abraham Janse, from Bergen in Norway, threatened to kick the cook and cursed loudly. The first mate, alarmed by the ruckus, told the Norwegian either to shut up or be sent ashore. He repeated the order to unload the sloop before getting their food. But the sailors refused. Eleven of them packed their things and stepped back into the sloop and left, no longer wanting to serve on the *Prins Willem de Vijfde*. The captain asked a *mafoeke* (African broker) to retrieve the crew, which he did, assisted by a group of Africans. After having found the deserters, the Africans beat the deserters, chained them and locked them in a small house where goods and slaves were kept. The Africans were paid five rifles, two barrels of gunpowder and eight barrels (*kelders*) of Dutch gin to guard the deserters.[35] The next day the captain went ashore to interrogate them. The men were surrounded by 'three hundred negroes with loaded rifles'.[36] Punishment of the deserters was mild: six were taken back into the service and five were beaten by the Africans and transported to Cabende on the Angolan coast.

For slaves overt collective desertion was less common, although work stoppages took the form of slaves walking off the plantation and waiting until their demands were met. In 1828, all the slaves of the Potribo plantation

ILLUSTRATION 5 *Slaves working in the fields (Suriname), anonymous, circa 1850. Collection Rijksmuseum Amsterdam, NG-2013-22-19.*

walked off, except for the elderly and the children. They went on strike until the plantation director was fired.[37] According to Alex van Stipriaan, this form of protest became the dominant type of 'desertion' in the nineteenth century and, in contrast to the *grand marronage*, was aimed at enforcing piecemeal reforms. Van Stipriaan writes that slaves regularly left work to move to the edge of the plantation, or just outside it.[38]

In contrast to the overt collective desertions, covert collective desertions demanded more extensive plotting. Some permanent flight by enslaved Africans from the plantations occurred in smaller or larger groups as the outcome of a revolt or a plotted escape, rather than individual attempts to join up with a maroon community.[39] The oral tradition of the Okanisi mentions the use of *obiya* (guiding spirits or talismans), carried altars and other ways to seek help from Sweli Gadu and other spirits as an important characteristic of the collective desertions. To what extent these religious practices were developed during flight or were already part of the religious tradition on the plantations is uncertain. It seems likely that black overseers, who were sometimes also *lukuman* (seers), had an important role in preparing flight.[40]

It must have been a pleasant (albeit hazardous) pastime for soldiers, sailors and slaves to discuss options for desertion with comrades while keeping watch at an outpost, sitting around below deck or cutting sugar cane. Soldiers discussed desertion both in the barracks as well as during their watch. If such casual conversations developed into more concrete plans the group of conspirators needed a way to ensure loyalty. Signing bonds of trust, for example, was a way to do so. Two elements stand out in these bonds: their circular form and their leadership. Groups of soldiers made lists or circles when deciding on a course of action or choosing a leader.

In the 1688 revolt against van Sommelsdijck, 150 mutineers stood in a circle and chose the German trumpet player as their leader.[41] Also in the desertion during the Berbice revolt in 1763 the deserters stood in a circle to swear loyalty.[42] This was sometimes put down in writing, as happened with the desertion in 1684 under van Sommelsdijck as well as with the desertion from Fort Nieuw Amsterdam in 1747. This was dangerous, but also a way to keep the plot safe by giving all involved a strong interest in keeping the plot and the document secret. If the document were to fall in the wrong hands everyone would be compromised. In the end, the main difference between on the one hand the desertion by individuals or pairs and on the other hand the desertion in groups seems to be that the group desertion often followed episodes of revolt or mutiny.

Opportunities and obstacles

The difference between sailors and soldiers on the one hand and slaves on the other is most pronounced in the outcome they sought in deserting, and in line with that, the strategies they used to overcome geographical challenges. Plantation slaves in the Dutch Atlantic were less mobile than the sailors and soldiers. The political geography of the plantations and colonies was important in determining the success of deserters. Natural and political borders were important factors determining the outcome of desertion attempts. These borders were different for sailors, soldiers and slaves.

Environmental factors

The availability of rugged and nearly impenetrable terrain was both an obstacle and an opportunity for deserters. Especially for escaping slaves, the possibility to form larger maroon groups was strongly determined by the availability of both mountains and forests.[43] This can easily be observed in Suriname, Jamaica and the Haiti interior. The presence of indigenous groups or 'pacified' maroons could impact on the ease of escape. Fleeing from the plantation was more difficult in Guyana where the indigenous population were keen on capturing fugitive slaves. From the 1760s onwards, it also became more difficult to escape from Surinamese plantations once the established maroon groups signed a peace treaty obligating them not to accept new refugees and extraditing newcomers to the colonists.[44] Even before the peace treaty maroons were not always welcoming. Conflicting African identities or suspicion towards creolized slaves could prevent cooperation and integration of new refugees into established groups. Those exceptions aside, the presence of other maroons made flight and survival easier and more likely.

The Surinamese environment also offered opportunities to Europeans, although they were clearly not keen on escaping over land, and they were also rarely successful when they tried. In 1733, three French deserters from Cayenne passed through Suriname and asked to continue their westward voyage to reach Berbice. It never came to that because they were killed by a group of indigenous men.[45] Also the escape by soldiers in Suriname in 1684, discussed above, failed to succeed. Another attempted escape over land occurred in 1763, when soldiers were marching from Suriname to suppress a slave revolt in neighbouring Berbice. After encountering hardship along the way they mutinied and decided to try and make their way to the Orinoco River, which was Spanish territory. When they attempted to join the rebels that they had come to suppress, twenty-eight of the soldiers were executed on the spot by the rebels and the thirteen remaining men were enslaved.[46] Plantation slaves clearly had more luck when escaping overland. An important reason might be that they were able to join established predecessors, or at least benefit from their experience.

Geopolitical factors

In the revolt against van Sommelsdijck in Suriname in 1688 the goal of the deserters was said to have been to sail to the Dutch Republic to get a hearing for their complaints. This was rare, since deserters mostly tried to make their way into non-Dutch areas once they deserted. The competitive political geography of the Atlantic shaped the way desertion occurred in this region and could be used by authorities as a political weapon during imperial conflicts. Catholic nations, for example, encouraged slaves in Protestant colonies to run away by promising them freedom if they converted.[47] The English loyalists also used escaping slaves to weaken the thirteen rebellious colonies as did the French during their (temporary) abolition of slavery. For soldiers and sailors desertion almost always implied the crossing of imperial boundaries. Maroons placed themselves beyond the reach of European empires, and this was sometimes also attempted by Europeans, for example by turning to piracy. However, it should be noted that pirates often sought allegiance and protection from colonial governors of competing empires. Escape by boat was one of the very few options people had if they were uncomfortable with the prospect of life in the marshes and forests of the backcountry. Regular inter-imperial shipping clearly benefited desertion in such cases. A good example are the slaves on Curacao for whom escape by boat was the only option, and one that was increasingly used in the eighteenth century when shipping between the Dutch colony and the Spanish Main increased.[48]

Networks of support and solidarity

As was noted in the section on collective and individual desertion, deserters often had to rely on support, also if they fled alone. If deserter(s) did not plan a hostile take-over of a ship, they needed connections and trust to get safely on board a vessel and be hidden during inspections. When the States of Zeeland ruled Suriname (1667–82) there were many desertion attempts by the colony's soldiers. The governor complained that the number of soldiers dropped steadily, simply because many were sick and died, but also because they hid on outgoing ships. Governor Versterre complained about captains who were wilfully protecting deserters. During an inspection of an outgoing ship, a governor reported, 'when the sergeant tried to look a bit longer [for stowaways], the captain ordered him [the sergeant] to make haste, or he would adjust his sails and take him away as well.'[49]

If no helpful captain was available, a hostile take-over was the only way to procure a ship. Such action obviously needed bonds of trust among deserters so as to be willing to use force to subdue the crew of the prospective ship for the escape. In 1747, the 25-year-old illiterate soldier Michel Harder from Hamburg had been stationed in the garrison at Fort Nieuw Amsterdam, but was now detained in Fort Zeelandia. He spilled the beans on a desertion plot after the investigators reminded him of his punishment several months earlier for another desertion plot he had been part of. At that previous incident the rumour that a French privateer was sailing in the estuary of the Suriname River had triggered Harder and seven others to attempt an escape. Now, with a new desertion plot in the making, Harder decided to tell on his fellow soldiers. This plot was again triggered by a foreign ship, this time an English barque mooring close to Fort Nieuw Amsterdam. The soldiers tried to get some forty to sixty men to sign a document that would serve as a bond of commitment to the plot. Their plan was to disarm those soldiers unwilling to sign, tell the officers to keep quiet, take provisions and arms from the storehouse, and escape.[50]

Plots that included the hostile take-over of a ship demanded a more sizeable group of conspirators. The scale of the plot demanded solidarity not only to keep everyone quiet, but practically to organize the escape. Harder and his comrades who had plotted their escape on a foreign ship in 1747 from Suriname made a plan to ensure that those who could not swim across the moat of Fort Nieuw Amsterdam would be carried by their comrades. The fortresses were not only designed to keep enemies out, but also to keep soldiers in. Another problem for the soldiers were the cannons on the fort, which were able to fire on them during their escape. The plan was, therefore, to sabotage the cannons, after which the men would take a barge to bring them to the English barque and sail off.[51] The magnitude of the plot is striking, although only a small group of ringleaders were charged for the conspiracy. There was a clear overlap between the ringleaders of the first and second attempt at desertion.

Solidarities among deserters were forged in the face of bitter prospects. The choice of either of the competing empires does not seem to have played a big role in the decisions made by the deserters, but was rather a result of the ease of reaching either one. As one deserter allegedly said 'brother, this here is a bad land, what are we doing here any longer?'[52] This was not a politically driven betrayal of the colony or 'cowardice' in the face of impending violence, but indifference to the priorities of the colonial armed forces and the future they offered. Part of this was the fact that debts were increasingly encumbering soldiers so long as they did not get promoted. Debt was a good reason to switch sides for individual soldiers. When a soldier was trapped by high debts, crossing the border into the enemy's hands could be an easy way out. A Dutch Governor Temminck wrote in 1725 that soldiers in Suriname were 'eagerly longing for regime change'.[53] A hostile take-over would release them of their debts, since the soldiers 'were primarily those who were naively debauched or could never enter any service in other ways'. These men were oppressed 'by the unbearable burden of the *zielverkopers*'.[54] And so, when a hostile assault by a foreign power would face the colony these soldiers 'would have nothing to lose but the debt of the *zielverkopers*'.[55] Changing imperial borders, therefore, did not necessarily mean that the soldiers had to move; not moving and allowing a foreign take-over could have the same desired effect.

Prevention and control

In the long distances of water that were crossed during colonizing and trading ventures the actual threat of a military confrontation was small and even in the fortresses endless time was spent without even sighting the enemy. The abundance of time and open space created many opportunities for escape for subordinates. The authorities in the Atlantic had several tools at their disposal to prevent this. Since desertion was often born out of hopelessness it helped those in power to offer opportunities for career making and other ways to prevent despair. The Dutch admiralty made sure that debts would not become insurmountable.[56] The promise of future victory and glory was used in the case of soldiers, although not for slaves and sailors. A common method of prevention used for plantation slaves, soldiers and sailors was the creation of rules and regulations to ensure their isolation from their immediate surroundings. The moats and walls of the renaissance fort kept assailants out, but also kept soldiers (who often could not swim) in. Furthermore, the extradition treaties, especially with non-European neighbours, created a barrier around the plantations and the forts by making the hunt and capture of escapees mutually beneficial for the colonists and the surrounding communities.

Brutal punishment was the fate of many who failed in their attempted desertions. In 1684, during the rule of Governor Cornelis van Aerssen van Sommelsdijck, a group of soldiers made a plot to escape, first with a canoe and later over land to the French colony of Cayenne. To this end they signed their names in a circle. Soon after, part of the group changed their mind and the signatures were burned. This change of heart might have scared some of the others because they made their escape in a hurry.[57] Both the deserters as well as the others who had chosen to dissolve the plot, but failed to inform their superiors, were all condemned to death. The leader, Pierre Malarbe, was executed by hanging, the others by rifle fire. Before the execution they could decide by lot which three of them would be buried in the ground.[58] This course of events was typical of the reign of the ruthless Governor van Aerssen van Sommelsdijck. Under his rule an unprecedented number of both Europeans and indigenous Americans were executed.

Van Sommelsdijck was intent on introducing forced labour from whatever source he could find to build up the colony. Desertion shook the core of the vision he had for the colony. Van Sommelsdijck also arranged that convicts from Holland were to be shipped to the colony to work on building the defences. A group of these European convict labourers escaped 'their enslavement' by taking several vessels and trying to make their way along the Guiana Stream to the Orinoco. Van Sommelsdijck sent his son on an expedition to retrieve the men.[59] Van Sommelsdijck's obsession with hard labour and discipline was also what brought his rule, and life, to an end. He was shot dead while charging – on his own and with a drawn sabre in his hand – at a group of disgruntled soldiers who had come to his palace to complain about the forced labour they had to perform and their reduced rations. Together with some artisans, the soldiers who shot van Sommelsdijck took control of the colony's fortress. After being in control of the fortress the group tried to resolve the ensuing stalemate between them and the civilian militias by taking control of a slave ship and attempting to make their way from the colony. This failed and the men were overpowered.[60]

Superiors could prevent desertion also in less directly brutal ways. Keeping hope alive by offering a bright future somewhere over the horizon was an important way to prevent desertion. When all hope was lost, slaves, sailors and soldiers more readily abandoned whatever it was they still had and sought their freedom. For slaves, possibilities for a career or simply a respectable and fulfilling life on a plantation could be a great motivator to stay; more than for soldiers and sailors, having families and family connections raised the stakes for desertion. Keeping the black overseers on plantations (*basya* in Sranan) in check was crucial when it came to preventing desertion. If a black overseer's position was threatened he could in turn use his powers and connections to quickly destabilize the entire plantation. *Basyas* often functioned informally as gatekeepers allowing or barring visitors (maroons or relatives) to visit the plantation and regulating informal trade. The eighteenth-century traveller J.D. Herlein noted about slaves going to nearby plantations to visit their partners that this made them *loopagtig en diefagtig* – prone to escaping and thieving.[61] When a *basya* felt dishonoured or was obstructed in his plans by the plantation manager he could choose to escape, having enough influence on the plantation to take prominent people with him. Also, if for example field slaves felt unbearably oppressed by the *basya*, and did not see a future for themselves under his command, they could decide to escape.[62]

Providing career opportunities was not the only instrument employed to prevent desertion in the case of sailors and soldiers. Providing a regular income and preventing excessive debts among the crew were also important instruments of control. Heavily indebted soldiers or sailors had more to gain by crossing into another empire's territory and join the service there. In the early 1770s a document was compiled advising the local government of Demerary on how to conduct itself with regard to desertion and other practical matters such as regional trade and defences. Experiences from Suriname and Curacao were cited as examples on how to deal with desertion. Appended to the letter was an example of a soldier's wage administration and an example of the regular payment throughout the year.[63] Navy administrators as well were urged to prevent excessive debt.[64] Failure to do so resulted in some massive episodes of desertion as well as mutinies against the administrators of debts on board navy ships.[65]

Suspicion of unfamiliar men was encouraged by authorities in their attempts to prevent smuggling and deserting. In Paramaribo, the presence of men suspected of coming from ships that remained down river, outside the colony, resulted in a call 'forbidding any inhabitants to converse with such seamen'.[66] Complaints had been made by captains from Holland that despite the regulations regarding the lodging of seamen, 'sailors regularly deserted or went into hiding until their ships sailed out and subsequently established themselves in the colony'.[67]

More than suspicion, authorities could mobilize outright hostility in their attempts to curb desertion. It can be argued that 'othering' an enemy not only served to ease their killing, but also to prevent desertion from the ranks to the 'other'. In the multi-ethnic Dutch forces, blaming the French within the ranks and characterizing them as deserting cowards served the same purpose. The message from the officers was clear: if you desert then you are no better than those Frenchmen in the unit. Unsurprisingly, the few Frenchmen present were more likely to desert.[68] Dutch-led iconoclastic furies by an amalgam of Europeans in Brazil against the Catholic 'other' has been argued to have been a direct response to desertions in the ranks of the Dutch West India Company's forces.[69]

Conclusion

This chapter has given an overview of the scale of desertion in the Dutch Atlantic, the ways in which people deserted (in groups, alone, openly or secretly) and the countermeasures taken by those in power. Low-ranking soldiers and sailors deserted regularly. Soldiers deserted from all the different places where they were stationed. It seems that none of the outposts, forts or garrisons in the Dutch Atlantic were free of occasional desertion, and neither were the units on their way to the colonies. Sailors deserted at a similar rate to soldiers. Due to the availability of a very complete set of data it is possible to establish a relationship between origins and desertion rates among the crew of merchant ships. Slaves deserted much less than both sailors and soldiers. Despite the horrific conditions on the plantations, they might have felt they had much to lose when leaving behind relatives. The mid-way option of hiding in the *kapuweri* provided an alternative whereby a refugee from the plantation could be free and continue to be in contact with those still in slavery.

Overall we can conclude that deserting was relatively easy, but surviving afterwards proved more challenging. In the colonial context preventing desertion became a priority beyond the battlefield for companies and states since labour was scarce while hostile competitors were omnipresent. Escape was often a final measure after negotiations with superiors proved to be fruitless. The response by those in power was to increase the reach and jurisdiction of the state, to deem absence immoral and to extend national loyalty to the economic sphere, thereby contributing a small but important element to what would develop into full-blown nationalism in the nineteenth century. In the case of the enslaved, who were largely excluded from definitions of national belonging, their acts of rebellion and desertion contributed to suspicion against people of colour.

Looking at the three categories of workers (slaves, sailors and soldiers) shows us that the early modern European expansion not only opened vast geographies to European states and companies, but also created a range of possibilities for those working for these states and companies to get away and find a better future. The early modern plantations were places on which the lives of slaves were so meagre that leaving the plantation to settle in the rugged interior most likely did not mean a deep fall in the standard of living.

For soldiers and sailors the stark contrast between high levels of desertion among the lower ranks and its virtual absence among the higher ranks also shows that the combination of benefits for the higher ranks as well as the options for promotions prevented their desertion.

Summing up, desertion by subordinates in the Dutch Atlantic seems to have been determined by three structural factors. First, the lack of opportunities for lower ranks within working environments to develop meaningful working lives, a condition that was worsened by the omnipresence of debt and for slaves few opportunities for manumission. There was also a distinct lack of personal interest to tie low-ranking subordinates to the Dutch colonial project. Instead, brutal punishment of insubordination resulted in episodes of desertion by people who literally tried to save their skin, either individually or collectively. The main geographical determinants of desertion in the Dutch Atlantic were the lack of urban spaces into which deserters could 'disappear'. Coupled with a lack of adequate control over borders and border areas, the act of escape was eased, and simultaneously provided plenty of opportunities for inter-imperial border-crossing.

Appendix

TABLE 5.8 *Desertion of MCC seamen related to their place of birth*

	Place	Recruits	Deserters	Desertion (%)	Distance (km)
	Middelburg	1,260	33	3	0
	Vlissingen	1,346	20	1	7
	Veere	160	4	3	8
	Arnemuiden	28	0	0	14
	Westkapelle	40	2	5	15
Birthplaces (close to) Middelburg	Goes	84	4	5	23
	Sluis	67	3	4	26
	Zierikzee	122	2	2	30
	Brugge	75	3	4	48
	Gent	46	4	9	60
	Average			2	0–60

Birthplaces at medium distance	Bergen op Zoom	56	2	4	62
	Tholen	27	2	7	66
	Oostende	185	15	8	73
	Antwerpen	27	6	22	80
	Rotterdam	127	11	9	95
	Dordrecht	61	4	7	100
	Brussel	33	4	12	108
	Leiden	26	3	12	114
	Duinkerken	83	14	17	115
	Amsterdam	193	18	9	153
	Average			10	60–160
Faraway birthplaces	Groningen	50	1	2	330
	Bremen	83	2	2	448
	Hamburg	131	8	6	553
	Scotland	28	5	18	555
	Lubeck	45	2	4	615
	Holstein	37	1	3	640
	Flensburg	37	2	5	669
	Stralsund	42	2	5	795
	Stettin	58	4	7	865
	Kopenhagen	62	3	5	871
	Gothenburg	50	1	2	1,096
	Danzig	121	3	2	1,189
	Drammen	29	2	7	1,266
	Stavanger	68	5	7	1,390
	Koningsbergen	46	2	4	1,400
	Stockholm	146	7	5	1,492
	Bergen (Norway)	29	2	7	1,578
	Average			5	>160

Source: Poortvliet database; Google Maps walking routes. Ports with more than 25 recruits and deserters.

Notes

1 Thanks go to Matthias van Rossum and Jeannette Kamp for setting this stimulating challenge. People who have clearly contributed to the research for this chapter are Hans Schwartz who manages the data at www.zeeuwengezocht.nl and provided me with the data collected by P.F. Poortvliet as well as Martijn Houweling, Martijn Heijink and Hans Welling who pointed me to further desertion cases in the archive of the Middelburgse Commercie Compagnie and Suriname Company (Sociëteit van Suriname).

2 John Gabriel Stedman, *Narrative of a Five Years' Expedition against the Revolted Negroes of Surinam, in Guiana, on the Wild Coast of South America, from the Year 1772 to 1777* (London: J. Johnson & J. Edwards, 1796); Wim Hoogbergen, *The Boni Maroon Wars in Suriname* (Leiden: Brill, 1990); Frank Dragtenstein, *'De ondraaglijke stoutheid der wegloopers': marronage en koloniaal beleid in Suriname, 1667–1768* (Utrecht: BSS, 2002); Richard Price, *The Guiana Maroons: A Historical and Bibliographical Introduction* (Baltimore, MA: Johns Hopkins University Press, 1976). Soldiers have received far less attention; exceptions to this rule are: Bruno Romero Ferreira Miranda, 'Gente de Guerra: origem cotidiano e resistência dos soldados do exército da companhia das índias ocidentais no Brasil (1630–1654)' (PhD, Leiden University, 2011); Marjoleine Kars, 'Policing and Transgressing Borders: Soldiers and Cross-Cultural Relations in the Berbice Slave Rebellion, 1763–1764' (presented at Multiculturalism, Religion and Legal Status in the Dutch Colonial World, 1600-1960, Baltimore County, Maryland, 2009); M. Lohnstein, *De militie van de sociëteit c.q. directie van Suriname in de achttiende eeuw* (Velp: unpublished, 1984). In the volume on Dutch military power in the Atlantic, especially the article by Han Jordaan, information is provided about desertion: Han Jordaan, Henk den Heijer and Victor Enthoven (eds), *Geweld in de West: een militaire geschiedenis van de Nederlandse Atlantische wereld, 1600–1800* (Leiden: Brill, 2013).

3 Gert Oostindie and Jessica V. Roitman (eds), *Dutch Atlantic Connections, 1680–1800* (Leiden: Brill, 2014), pp. 1–21.

4 Gert Oostindie and Jessica Vance Roitman, 'Repositioning the Dutch in the Atlantic, 1680–1800', *Itinerario* 36:2 (2012), pp. 1–21; Jan de Vries, 'The Dutch Atlantic Economies', in Peter A. Coclanis (ed.), *The Atlantic Economy during the Seventeenth and Eighteenth Centuries: Organization, Operation, Practice, and Personnel* (Columbia, SC: University of South Carolina Press, 2005), pp. 1–29; Piet C. Emmer and Wim Klooster, 'The Dutch Atlantic, 1600–1800: Expansion without Empire', *Itinerario* 23:2 (1999), pp. 48–69.

5 Key publications regarding slave desertions and rebellions in the Dutch Atlantic exist primarily for Suriname and Curacao. For Suriname: Stedman, *Narrative*; Price, *The Guiana Maroons*; Sandew Hira, *Van Priary tot en met De Kom: De geschiedenis van het verzet in Suriname, 1630–1940* (Rotterdam: Futile, 1982); Dragtenstein, *De ondraaglijke stoutheid*; Frank Dragtenstein, 'De opstand op Palmeneribo, 1707', *OSO: Tijdschrift voor Surinamistiek en het Caraïbisch Gebied* 23:2 (2004), pp. 214–35; Hoogbergen, *The Boni Maroon Wars*; Alex van Stipriaan, *Surinaams contrast: roofbouw en overleven in een Caraïbische plantagekolonie, 1750–1863* (Leiden: KITLV Uitgeverij, 1993); Peter Meel and

Hans Ramsoedh, *Ik ben een haan met een kroon op mijn hoofd: pacificatie en verzet in koloniaal en postkoloniaal Suriname: opstellen voor Wim Hoogbergen* (Amsterdam: Bert Bakker, 2007). For literature on Curacao: A. Paula, *1795: de slavenopstand op Curacao: een bronnenuitgave van de originele overheidsdocumenten* (Curacao: N.A., 1974); Linda M. Rupert, 'Marronage, Manumission and Maritime Trade in the Early Modern Caribbean', *Slavery & Abolition: A Journal of Slave and Post-Slave Studies* 30:3 (2009), p. 361; Artwell Cain, *Tula: de slavenopstand van 1795 op Curaçao* (Amsterdam and The Hague: NiNsee Amrit, 2009); Wim Klooster and Gert Oostindie, *Curaçao in the Age of Revolutions, 1795–1800* (Leiden: KITLV Press, 2011).

6 Promising examples of how the study of soldiers could be developed are offered by Kars, 'Policing and Transgressing Borders' and Ferreira Miranda, 'Gente de Guerra'.

7 For the military history of the Dutch Atlantic: Jordaan et al. (eds), *Geweld in de West*; Christopher Leslie Brown and Philip D. Morgan, *Arming Slaves: From Classical Times to the Modern Age* (Yale: Yale University Press, 2006). For slaves working as sailors in the regional trade of Curacao: Rupert, 'Marronage'. For sailors doing the same work as slaves: Karwan Fatah-Black, 'Slaves and Sailors on Suriname's Rivers', *Itinerario* 36:3 (2012), pp. 61–82. Also, building fortresses was done by African slaves, European convicts and soldiers alike.

8 In Berbice in 1763 soldiers revolted because there were no slaves to cut the way through the bushes and the soldiers were forced to do this work themselves. Kars, 'Policing'. A mutiny breaks out when slaves on board the slave ship are helping to lift the anchor alongside the sailors. Zeeuws Archief (ZA), Middelburgsche Commercie Compagnie (MCC), *Journaal van Het Fregat Prins Willem de Vijfde, Reis Afrika-Suriname, 1751–1753*, entry 20, inv.nr. 968.

9 Frederick Cooper, Thomas Holt and Rebecca Scott, *Beyond Slavery: Explorations of Race, Labor, and Citizenship in Postemancipation Societies* (Chapel Hill: University of North Carolina Press, 2000).

10 Wim Klooster, 'Marteling, muiterij en beeldenstorm: militair geweld in de Nederlandse Atlantische wereld, 1624–1654', in Han Jordaan, Henk den Heijer and Victor Enthoven (eds), *Geweld in de West: een militaire geschiedenis van de Nederlandse Atlantische wereld, 1600–1800* (Leiden: Brill, 2013), p. 338.

11 Ibid., pp. 336–7.

12 Ibid., p. 320.

13 Ferreira Miranda, 'Gente de Guerra'.

14 Klooster, 'Marteling'.

15 'Memorie door den Kolonnel Artichofsky, bij zijn vertrek uit Brazilië in 1637 overgeleverd aan Graaf Maurits en zijnen Geheimen Raad', *Kroniek van het Historisch Genootschap gevestigd te Utrecht* 25, nr. 5, V (1869), pp. 326–8.

16 Ferreira Miranda, 'Gente de Guerra', p. 96.

17 Lohnstein, *De militie*, p. 102.

18 Han Jordaan, 'De vrijen en de Curaçaose defensie, 1791–1800', in Han Jordaan, Henk den Heijer and Victor Enthoven (eds), *Geweld in de West: een*

militaire geschiedenis van de Nederlandse Atlantische wereld, 1600–1800 (Leiden: Brill, 2013), p. 141.

19 Nationaal Archief (NA), Archief Nieuwe West-Indische Compagnie (NWIC), *Militaire soldijboeken van Sint Eustatius over de jaren 1769–1779*, inv.nr. 1201, A–E.

20 Dragtenstein, *De ondraaglijke stoutheid*.

21 Hoogbergen, *The Boni Maroon Wars*, p. 9.

22 Rénie van der Putte, 'Surinaamse "Wegloopers" van de Jaren 1767–1802', *OSO: Tijdschrift voor Surinamistiek* 24:2 (2005), pp. 276–88.

23 Van Stipriaan, *Surinaams contrast*, p. 278.

24 Van der Putte, 'Surinaamse "Weglopers"', pp. 276–88.

25 Karwan Fatah-Black, 'Orangism, Patriotism, and Slavery in Curaçao, 1795–1796', *International Review of Social History* 58:21 (2013), pp. 1–26.

26 Kars, 'Policing and Transgressing Borders'.

27 Now commonly referred to as Okanisi, they are also known as Aukaners, Ndyuka or in the colonial period *bevredigde bosnegers van Achter Auka* (the pacified bush negroes of Achter Auka).

28 Wim Hoogbergen and Bono Thoden van Velzen, *Een zwarte vrijstaat in Suriname: de Okaanse samenleving in de achttiende eeuw* (Leiden: KITLV Press, 2011), chapter 4.

29 Klaas Ratelband, *Nederlanders in West-Afrika 1600–1650: Angola, Kongo En São Tomé* (Zutphen: Walburg Pers, 2000), pp. 177–8.

30 Ibid., p. 179.

31 Natalie Everts, 'Krijgsvolk in Elmina: Asafo, garnizoen en Tapoeyerkwartier, 1700–1815', in Han Jordaan, Henk den Heijer and Victor Enthoven (eds), *Geweld in de West: een militaire geschiedenis van de Nederlandse Atlantische wereld, 1600–1800* (Leiden: Brill, 2013), p. 91.

32 ZA, MCC, 20, 1070–1.

33 Fatah-Black, 'Orangism'.

34 Ruud Paesie and Hubregt Kempe, *Voor zilver en Zeeuws belang: De rampzalige Zuidzee-expeditie van de Middelburgse Commercie Compagnie, 1724–1727* (Zutphen: Walburg Pers, 2012), pp. 164–5.

35 ZA, MCC, 20, 984, Scheepsjournaal 19 oktober 1757.

36 ZA, MCC, 984, Scheepsjournaal 20 oktober 1757.

37 Van Stipriaan, *Surinaams contrast*, p. 279.

38 Ibid., pp. 418–19.

39 Dragtenstein, *De ondraaglijke stoutheid*.

40 For the religious experiences during flight: Hoogbergen, Van Velzen, *Zwarte Vrijstaat*. The position of the *basja* in relation to religious services is discussed in Natalie Zemon Davis, 'Judges, Masters, Diviners: Slaves' Experience of Criminal Justice in Colonial Suriname', *Law and History Review* 29:4 (2011), pp. 925–84.

41 Jan Jacob Hartsinck, *Beschryving van Guiana, of de Wildekust in Zuid-America*, vol. 2 (Amsterdam: Gerrit Tielenburg, 1770), p. 652. Original:

'vertoonde zich eerlang op de Fortresse honderd vyvtig Man in de wapen, wanneer zy een ronde kring sloegen en uit het midden van hen een Oversten verkozen zynde een Hoogduitsch Trompetter (die, eenige maanden te vooren, wegens Desertie gevonnisd was, om geharquebuseerd te werden'.

42 Ibid., p. 426. Original: 'Vervolgens sloegen zy een kring en zwoeren met opgestooken Vingeren malkander getrouw te blyven, onder bedreiging, dat zo een van hen wilde wegloopen zy dezelve op staande voet zouden doodschieten.'

43 Price, *Maroon Societies*, p. 5.

44 Eric Jagdew, *Vrede te midden van oorlog in Suriname: Inheemsen, Europeanen, Marrons en vredesverdragen, 1667–1863* (Paramaribo: Anton de Kom Universiteit, 2014), p. 477.

45 Ibid., p. 863.

46 Kars, 'Policing and Transgressing Borders'.

47 See, for example, the escape across imperial boundaries by slaves from Curacao. Rupert, 'Marronage'. For conflicts about deserting soldiers and West India Company servants see: Ratelband, *Nederlanders in West-Afrika*; Henk den Heijer, *Goud, ivoor en slaven: Scheepvaart en handel van de Tweede Westindische Compagnie op Afrika, 1674–1740* (Leiden: Walburg Pers, 1997).

48 Linda M. Rupert, *Creolization and Contraband: Curaçao in the Early Modern Atlantic World* (Athens, GA: University of Georgia Press, 2012), pp. 96–7.

49 Letter of Pieter Versterre, 10 April 1676 in: *Zeeuwse archivalia uit Suriname en omliggende kwartieren, 1667–1683*.

50 NA, Hof van Politie en Criminele Justitie en voorgangers, in Suriname, 1669–1828 (Politie), 1.05.10.02, 938, film 544.

51 Ibid.

52 NA, Politie, 938, f. 544. Original: 'broeder t is hier een slegt land, en wat sulle wij hier langer doen?'.

53 Lohnstein, *De militie*, p. 95.

54 Ibid.

55 Ibid.

56 Accountants on board navy ships were ordered not to encumber sailors with too much debt. This was done explicitly as a measure to prevent their desertion. Marc van Alphen, *Het oorlogsschip als varend bedrijf. Schrijvers, administratie en logistiek aan boord van Nederlandse marineschepen in de 17de en 18de eeuw* (Franeker: Van Wijnen, 2014), p. 56.

57 *Copije Criminele Actien Voorgevallen in de Colonie van Zuriname. Sedert Het Gouvernement Van Sijn Excelentie Den Heere van Sommelsdijck Beginnende Met Den Den Jaere 1683, 1683 November 16 – 1684 November 20* (Paramaribo, 1684), NA, Sociëteit van Suriname, 1.05.04.01, Overgekomen Brieven en Papieren, inv.nr. 212, folios 159–64. Original: 'in een ronde geteijcent' and 'hebben haere hanttijckeninge verbrant'.

58 Ibid. The condemned deserters were Pierre Malarbe, Guillaume Le Moor, Pierre Cretien, Paul Broques, Antoine Duval, Jean Le Clair, Philip Meijer,

Frans Aelbreghts, Isaacq de Vreede, Moyse Adojer, Jacques Dasoulle, Jacques Laff and Francois Neveu.

59 Hartsinck, *Beschryving*, pp. 649–50. 'Deese Woeste Hoop, het lui leeven gewoon, beslooten, zich hunner Slaverny te ontslaan, en hadden dien einde zich weeten van hunnen boeijens te verlossen; hier toe aangemoedigd door de geringen Bezetting, hun bestaan gelukte, en zy begaven zich met eenige Vaartuigen op de vlucht naar de rivier Orinoque'.

60 Ibid., pp. 651–71; Gerard W. van der Meiden, *Betwist Bestuur: een eeuw strijd om de macht in Suriname, 1651–1753* (Amsterdam: Bataafsche Leeuw, 2008), pp. 57–59.

61 J.D. Herlein, *Beschryvinge van de volk-plantinge Zuriname: vertonende de opkomst dier zelver colonie, de aanbouw en bewerkinge der zuiker-plantagien. Neffens den aard der eigene natuurlijke inwoonders of Indianen; als ook de slaafsche Afrikaansche Mooren; deze beide natien haar levens-manieren, afgoden-dienst, regering, zeden* (Leeuwarden: Meindert Injema, 1718), pp. 96–7.

62 Klinkers, *Op hoop van vrijheid*, pp. 43–44.

63 NA, Verspreide West-Indische Stukken, 1.05.06, inv.nr. 141. *Memorie Bij Forme van Missive Concerneerende Diverse Poincten van Voorzieninge Aan Den Directeur-Generaal En Raden van Demerary Af Te Zenden, Betreffende de Handel Aldaar, Het Voorkomen van het Deserteren En Ontvluchten Der Soldaten En Slaven, de Rechtspraak, Het Bestuur, de Aanleg van Verdedigingswerken* (1772).

64 Alphen, *Het oorlogschip*.

65 Fatah-Black, 'Orangism'.

66 Bylaw 413, March 29, 1743, *Plakaatboek* 503.

67 Bylaw 783, April 4, 1778, *Plakaatboek* 943–53. Original: 'aan alle ingesetenen geinterdiceert van met gene soodanige scheepslieden eenige conversatie te hebben.' '. . . ons klagten zijn ingekomen van de Hollandsche schippers op deeze colonie navigeerende en thans alhier ter rheede leggende, dat niet jegenstaande onze voorzieninge ten opzigte van 't logeeren of ophouden van scheepsvolk, 'er dikwils matroosen of andere van hun volk van hunnen scheepen of uit hun dienst alhier deserteeren en zich schuylhouden tot dat hun schip is vertrokken vervolgens sig hier etablisseeren.'

68 Lohnstein, *De militie*.

69 Klooster, 'Marteling'.

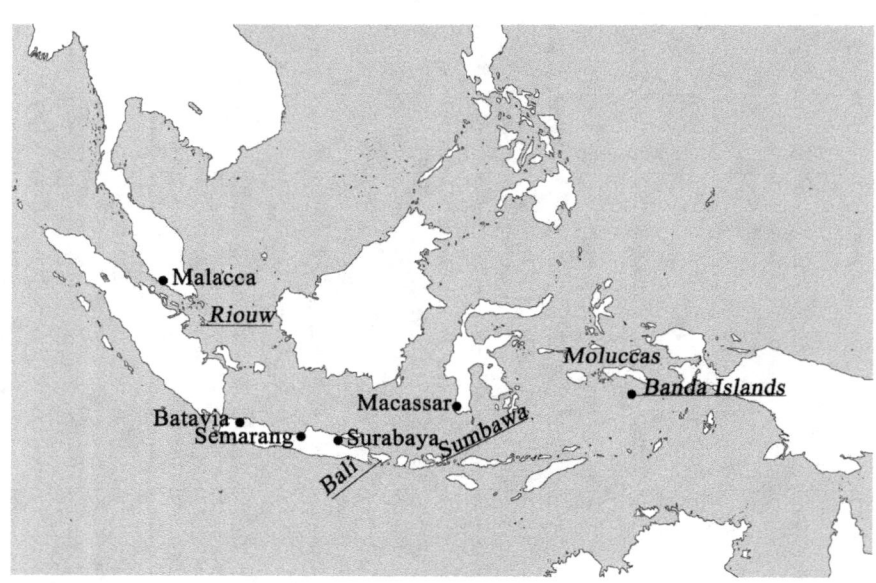

ILLUSTRATION 6 *Map of Southeast Asia (Erik Odegard).*

6

'Working for the Devil':

Desertion in the Eurasian Empire of the VOC

Matthias van Rossum

Runaway crews

If you want to take him, you will have to take me [on] too![1]

Responding to the claims of two Company officials, the English private captain Scott drew his sabre in a rage. He refused to hand over his mate, who had deserted from the VOC (Dutch East India Company) a year earlier. The evening before, Scott's vessel had been brought up by a *panchalang* in order to have their passes inspected at Malacca. The following day, 21 March 1784, the ship was inspected by two VOC officials, Captain Abo and *sjabandaar* Van Papendrecht, the harbourmaster of Malacca. Arriving on board, Captain Abo recognized one of the crew members as 'a sailor who had deserted from his ship at Queda on the 7th of May, 1783'.

The situation was tense. Abo asked 'this sailor for the reason of his desertion'. The sailor replied, according to the captain, 'that he was now sailing under the English flag as a mate and that he had nothing to do with him anymore'. Abo continued his interrogation by questioning the reason 'why the flag was taken down just before our arrival'. The flag 'was damaged', the sailor replied.

In the meantime, the 'armed crew' of the VOC was stationed on deck, 'according to the customs of war'. The *sjabandaar* asked Captain Scott to provide his pass, but he declared 'to have no pass'. The demand was repeated, this time with the explicit statement 'that they had come to inspect his papers, and that the captain claimed the mentioned sailor as a servant of the Company, belonging to the equipage of his ship, and since he, Scott, did not have a pass, he could not protect him'.[2]

Although surrounded by Company soldiers, Scott responded as if he was insulted.[3] By drawing his sabre, he signalled that he was prepared to defend his crew member and his honour as a captain. The *sjabandaar* answered calmly, asking 'whether he knew what he was doing'. Now Scott 'rose his sabre in order to strike at us', as Captain Abo declared. The soldiers drew their sabres and daggers, but before they could strike, Abo grabbed Scott and prevented him from attacking. Scott dropped his sabre and was arrested together with his eleven crew members.[4]

The mate was interrogated before the Court of Justice of Malacca, where he declared himself to be Johannes Kodij from 'Cathan'. He confessed that he had previously been employed as a sailor on the ship of Captain Abo. 'In the service of the Dutch Company' he was known 'under the name of Pieter Zwart'. Lying before Queda, Johannes deserted during an expedition to shore with his captain. There he 'hid himself in the woods until the ship departed'. After this, he returned to Queda, where he was employed by Captain Scott 'as a mate with a wage of fifty rupees per month'.[5]

Engaging in a world where formal boundaries were continuously transgressed, Scott sent out multiple vessels along the ports of South and Southeast Asia, trading tin, rice, opium and other goods. His vessels were claimed to have 'used the Portuguese flag during the war as well, but [they] again sailed under the English flag after the news was received about the truce'.[6] For more than a year, Johannes worked for the English private trader. Sailing south along the west coast of the Malayan Peninsula, they went from Queda to Selangor. From there they sailed to Bengal. The voyages of Johannes under Scott continued 'along the Malayan coast' to Malacca and Riouw. In these Dutch-controlled ports, the English vessel was denied access. This did not prevent Scott from 'going to shore' in Riouw, 'buying goods' and 'receiving a lot of people from shore'.[7]

The crews of Scott's vessels were just as audacious as his trading activities. On board the vessel before Malacca, at least, the runaway sailor Johannes was not exceptional. An interrogation of five other members of the crew testifies to the high level of mobility and endless opportunities. The first to be interrogated was Imandie, a 'Moor' and resident of 'Naoer' (Naora, Bengal), who declared that he had worked on a Portuguese ship named *St Maria*, before he had taken service with Captain Scott as a sailor 'for twelve rupees a month'.[8] The second crew member to be interrogated was a 'native from Bengal' called Maart. This must have been his slave name as he declared that he had been a slave of a citizen from Java named Pieters. Travelling with his master from Malacca, their ship had been captured by the English, who set him free on Queda, stating 'that he could go wherever he wanted'. As he 'was free, and had no means of subsistence, he had taken service with Captain Scott as a sailor for seven rupees a month, in whose service he had been for more than a year now'.[9]

They were accompanied by Poese de Rozairo from 'Masanbiko' (Mozambique), who said he had been a sailor on a 'Moorish ship, sailing under a Portuguese flag, taken by the French near Aceh'. From there, he travelled to Queda and took service with Scott for seven rupees per month. The fourth deponent, Mira Fakkier, resident at Madras, stated that he arrived at Selangor with an English vessel and took service with Scott about a month ago for two Spanish reals. The interrogation was concluded with the statement of Gregorius Jeremias 'from Oejong Sala', who declared that he 'had been taken from his place by the Malayans and was sold on Queda'. After he 'had bought his freedom, he engaged into the service of Captain Scott for seven rupees per month'.[10]

Forgotten histories

The case of Captain Scott defending his runaway mate and the rest of his assorted crew provides a remarkable insight into the early modern world of work, mobility and dissent. Although often irregular or at the margins, workers and runaways created their own local and global connections through desertion, smuggling and other (illegal) activities that authorities found hard to control. Desertion was a crucial strategy for workers trying to avoid hardship or improve their lot. As the case of Captain Scott indicates, workers could easily find other opportunities for work. Specific parts of the early modern global economy may have been more suitable for this. Sailors, slaves and others could, for example, find work in the intra-Asiatic shipping of small private merchants (the so-called *country trade*), dominating the Indian Ocean trade from the last quarter of the eighteenth century onwards.[11] Soldiers and artisans found work under the Mughals and in other armies. European trading companies tried to control the desertion of their own personnel, but simultaneously relied on the sometimes large-scale recruitment of runaways from their competitors.

From early seventeenth century until the middle of the eighteenth century, the Dutch East India Company was the biggest of the European trading companies operating in Asia.[12] The Dutch East India Company (VOC) has been referred to as one of the first multinationals, employing thousands of European and Asian sailors, soldiers, artisans and other workers in different parts of the world.[13] Within this VOC empire, desertion was a structural phenomenon.

In the period 1680–1794, at least 14,649 of the 737,448 workers recruited in Europe were recorded in the *Scheepssoldijboeken* as having deserted.[14] Another 61,309 were registered as having left the service of the Company by being absent, missing or for reasons unknown.[15] This means that more than

10 per cent of the workforce recruited in Europe went missing, of which at least 4 per cent were through desertion and absence. It is important to note that these numbers only provide information on the workers recruited in the Dutch Republic for which the administration of personnel has been preserved. The exact incidence of desertion among the entire European and Asian personnel of the VOC throughout the seventeenth and eighteenth centuries remains uncertain. Even less is known about the destinations of these workers, and the outcome of their attempt. In short, we often know too little of what happened to them. Specific cases, like the one of Johannes Kodij, sometimes provide a glimpse of the lives of runaway workers.

The stories of deserters and other travellers frequently remind us that the VOC and its workers did not operate in isolation, nor did they arrive from Europe in a barren economic landscape. On the contrary, just as in Europe, the VOC was able to recruit workers in well-developed maritime and military labour markets throughout Asia. The VOC was a state as well as a capitalist enterprise. It mobilized labour and created ties of globalization on an almost unprecedented scale. The VOC shipped highly diverse crews of Dutch, Germans, Scandinavians and other Europeans to Asia, employing them in its overseas settlements and its sizable intra-Asiatic shipping. Similarly, the Company employed Indian, Chinese and Javanese sailors on ships on intra-Asiatic routes and for (maritime) work in and around its settlements. Indian sailors were, for example, employed as rowers and sailors for work on the river, the roadstead and the various work islands of Batavia. The Company employed Javanese, Malayan, Buginese and other Asian soldiers throughout its empire, using a 'divide and rule' system by shifting troops between the different parts of Asia.

The Asian world not only offered opportunities for trading companies, but provided them for their workers as well. Often bound by contract or other forms of coercion backed up by law, many workers ran from their work and working environments throughout early modern Europe and Asia. They did so with varying motives, ranging from avoiding prosecution or escaping the brutal working discipline in the service of European trading companies, to leaving in the hope of finding better jobs and payment. Whether running from injustices or from Justice, these runaways hoped for the alternative opportunities in lively and well-developed Asian regions, or for the opposite: the attractive silence of other largely uncontrolled terrains.

This chapter traces patterns of absence and desertion among workers employed by the VOC, showing that workers of the VOC had both incentives and opportunities to remain absent or to desert. Absence and desertion were defined as illegal acts for anyone in the service of the VOC, either bound by contract, through direct coercive mechanisms (slavery and convict labour) or through legal constraints on mobility. This chapter employs various methods and sources to study the general dynamics of absenteeism and desertion in the Republic and overseas. First, overall desertion rates and patterns will be traced for European contract wage workers through the use of the *VOC Opvarenden* database, containing data on personnel recruited in the Republic and their end of contract ('date', 'place' and 'reason').[16] Second, various other archival sources, especially legal and administrative documents from the VOC archives, will be employed to trace overall patterns of desertion by European and Asian sailors, soldiers, artisans and slaves en route from Europe to Asia and after arrival in Asia – mainly Batavia. Doing so, it provides insight into the dynamics of desertion developing around the intercontinental infrastructure of the empire of the VOC, focusing on the Dutch Republic, Batavia and the intercontinental shipping of the VOC. Throughout its Asian empire, including its sizable intra-Asiatic shipping network, the VOC was also confronted with large-scale desertion (see Chapter 8 on South Asia). Desertion was a structural phenomenon, related to the constraints, problems and opportunities encountered by VOC workers, as well as workers' strategies. From a broader perspective, therefore, this chapter aims to contribute to our understanding of the position of working people within the historical dynamics of imperialism, economic development and early modern globalization.

ILLUSTRATION 7 *Singalese soldiers in the service of the VOC and representatives of the King of Kandy, Jan Brandes, 1785. Collection Rijksmuseum Amsterdam, NG-1985-7-1-8.*

The Devil's Empire: Company labour around the globe

The empire of the Dutch East India Company spanned the globe, connecting Europe, Africa and Asia. With formal headquarters located in the seven Chamber Cities in the Dutch Republic, the overseas empire stretched from the Cape of Good Hope to India, Sri Lanka and the Indonesian archipelago. A strong presence in coastal settlements was combined with large territorial possessions in Sri Lanka (Ceylon), Java and several other parts of the Indonesian archipelago. The Company maintained trading offices in a region ranging from the Persian Gulf to China and Japan.[17] As the nodal point between the intra-Asiatic and the intercontinental shipping networks, Batavia became the actual centre of this empire. As the supreme body responsible for the political and practical management of overseas affairs, the Raad van Indië ruled from here. Other important settlements, such as Colombo, at times attempted to establish a more or less independent position from Batavia.[18]

The presence of the Company throughout its Eurasian empire demanded large numbers of sailors, soldiers and other workers engaged in transport, construction, maintenance, warfare, control and the production of goods. The VOC engaged these workers mainly through four types of labour relations: casual wage labour, contract wage work, slavery and obligated labour services (corvée or tributary labour).[19] Convict labour, the fifth type of labour relation, was less significant in respect to the size of workforce involved, but played a crucial role in enforcing discipline and control.

Casual wage labour was employed in Asian settlements, for example for transport work in Batavia, where so-called *coolies* were employed in loading and unloading ships and carrying goods in and around warehouses.[20] In the Dutch Republic, casual wage labour was employed in the shipyards and for transport work.[21] Casual wage workers, such as the *coolies* of Batavia and the Amsterdam shipwrights were able to come to work on a daily basis, and were also able to stay away without the threat of (criminal) punishment. These workers, however, formed only a small portion of the Company's workforce (as shown in Table 6.1).

The VOC preferred contract wage labour and other labour relations in which it was able to exercise more control over its workers. Most Asian sailors and soldiers, and almost all of its European workers were recruited through wage labour contracts.[22] In addition, slaves were bought and used mainly for local transportation and other work in and around the settlements.[23] Throughout the VOC empire, small numbers of convicted workers were employed for general kinds of work, such as the work in the rope factory of Edam and in the *gemene werken* of the various settlements.[24]

TABLE 6.1 Revised estimates of the number of workers directly employed by the VOC

	1625	1687–8	1700	1753	1780
European workers					
Dutch Republic	2,000	3,000	3,000	3,000	3,000
At sea Europe-Asia	3,200	6,000	7,000	10,000	9,000
At sea in Asia	1,555	4,000	3,802	3,054	1,282
Ashore in Asia and Africa	2,945	11,551	13,481	20,101	15,523
Total Europeans	9,500	24,500	27,500	36,000	29,000
Free Asians					
Shore workers*	?	3,605	[300]*	[1,000]*	[550]*
Asian sailors at sea	[150?]	[150?]	[250]	1,000	1,300
Asian soldiers	?	[7,000?]	[10,000?]	[12,000?]	5,229
*Asian and African slaves***	[ca 4,000?]	[ca 6,000?]	[ca 7,000?]	[ca 7,000?]	[ca 7,000?]
Total Asians and Africans	[ca 6,000?]	[ca 17,000]	[ca 18,000?]	[ca 21,000?]	[ca 14,000?]
Total VOC personnel	[ca 15,000?]	[ca 42,000?]	[ca 45,000?]	[ca 57,000?]	[ca 43,000?]

Source and original estimate: Jan Lucassen, 'A Multinational and its Labor Force: The Dutch East India Company, 1595–1795', *International Labor and Working-Class History* 66:2 (2004), p. 15.

* Asian shore workers 'under contract' of the Dutch East India Company, therefore excluding all casual wage workers hired on a daily basis to work, for example, in loading and unloading ships. The number of Asian sailors working 'on land' in Batavia (but often administered in 'sea muster roles') is added to the number of shore workers mentioned by Lucassen.
** This category concerns slaves owned (and possibly also hired) by the VOC, but excludes workers performing obligated labour services on Ceylon and later Java.

Obligated labour services were in use especially in agricultural production, transportation and military work in and around settlements on Ceylon and later increasingly in rural Java. These workers are not included in the reconstruction of the VOC workforce as they were not directly employed by the Company, but it must have concerned thousands of workers, who were obligated to work for the VOC at least part of the year, sometimes even up to a third.[25] They were confronted with Company rule, enforcing the obligated labour services, such as the so-called *oeliam*-duties, which included work by *coelies* (carriers, general workers) and *lascorins* (soldiers).

Despite the important differences in the position, treatment, (career) opportunities and (self-)perception of these different types of workers, the workers in these labour relations had one crucial element in common. They were all obligated to adhere to the Company, resulting from varying legal arrangements restricting their mobility and dictating the labour effort these workers were obligated to perform, as well as its duration, conditions and compensation. The specific legal arrangements were different, varying from contract, to conviction, to obligated labour services, and slavery. And such differences were significant. The clear and pressing legal and physical constraints, however, could show remarkable comparisons. In contrast to casual wage workers, workers engaged through contracts, slavery and corvée could all be sentenced to convict labour for labour offences, such as absence, desertion, theft, revolt and other criminalized acts. The coercive element might be evident for slave, tributary and convict labour relations, but this is not always evident for contract labour. This type of labour relation could be technically categorized as 'free' labour as one is free to leave *before* and *after* engaging in the contract. Although one could argue about the role of deception, debts and coercion in recruiting and maintaining workers, it is most important to realize that these workers were in any case not free *during* the contract period.[26]

Most of the workers engaged through contract wage labour had contracts ranging from three to eight years. Only Asian sailors sometimes seem to have been recruited for contracts with the range of one year.[27] The labour relations involved were mainly characterized by a combination of relatively free or semi-free recruitment with strict legal and physical enforcement of the working contract. Contract workers were subject to Company law, with judicial procedures conducted by the various Councils of Justice of the Asian settlements or, in the case of lesser offences and temporary decisions on board ships, by a council of ships' officers. Refusing to work and other acts of disobedience were punished physically by (petty) officers, but could also be prosecuted through the legal system. All kinds of acts related to work and to social interaction in and around working environments, such as disobedience, theft, smuggling, violence, deviant sexual behaviour, absence and desertion, were punished frequently.[28]

Defining desertion: A view from Batavia

In this world of contracts and coercion, walking away from a job was illegal for workers in the most important labour relations under the Company – contract wage labour, slavery and obligated labour services. Desertion (*desertie*) was used as a concept not only for military labour, but also for maritime and other workers. In the Court of Justice of Batavia it was used against European sailors, soldiers, boatswains, cooks, carpenters, etc. It was also used for runaway Asian sailors. For slaves and convicts, the Court of Justice often employed the accusation of *fugie*.[29] In other places, the Court of Justice sometimes simply equated *desertie* and *fugie* in their accusations against runaway employees.[30]

Synonyms such as *drossen* were used as well. The use of the word *drossen* is interesting as it was used in cases against runaway European sailors, soldiers and artisans as well as in cases against fleeing slaves.[31] For convicts kept in chains, the act of running away was often called *verbreken van ketting*, the breaking of chains. In the trial against the convicted slave Kintar of Java in 1748 this was explicitly linked to *fugie*.[32] The same accusation of *fugie en verbreken van ketting* was formulated against European convicts, such as Lodewijk Rek from The Hague, who fled the artisans quarter where he was stationed as a convict in 1744.[33]

The employment of such synonyms for different types of workers indicates the common character of the act: criminalized walking away from work. A cluster of categories was used to refer to this act commonly known as desertion, *desertie*, *drossen* and *fugie*. One other important category that was related to these terms, but was understood and treated as something distinctly different, was the notion of *absentie* – absence. This was mostly understood as *temporary* absence from the workplace, ranging from one night to days, weeks and even months. In settlements such as Batavia this was a very common offence.

It is difficult to make a clear distinction between temporary and permanent escape from work or workplace. Absent or deserting workers sometimes decided to return to the Company. Sometimes runaways were brought in by Company soldiers or through contracts of exchange with other trading companies. In these instances, the difference between temporary absence and permanent desertion was often a matter of interpretation. When runaway workers were able to stay out of the hands of the Company, there were similar problems. The result can be traced in the administration of personnel, where the Company used various categories for employees who became untraceable physically or administratively: *weggelopen* (deserted), *vermist* (missing) and *laatste vermelding* (last reference).[34]

The VOC struggled with exactly these distinctions, not only in its administration, but in implementing its rules as well. In the early seventeenth century, various ordinances placed harsh punishments upon the offence of desertion, including corporal punishment and annulment of payments.[35] For slaves, a clear distinction was made between *domestique straffen*, private punishment by the slave owner for small domestic crimes, and *criminele straffen*, criminal punishment by the Court of Aldermans and the Court of Justice. Short periods of absence were seen as 'domestic offences' and could be punished within the household or workplace by the slave owner or overseer. Such punishments often entailed a severe beating of the slave, while he was bound to a pole that stood in the courtyard for this purpose (often referred to as the *paal*). Longer periods of absence, regarded as *fugie* or *drossen*, were dealt with through criminal law.

For contract workers, the Company made a similar distinction between employees who had been absent for a short period and employees who had been absent for longer periods, in general for more than a month. Only in the case where a servant had been absent for less than a month, and had not committed any other crimes, such as theft, violence or otherwise, was he sentenced to only a physical punishment. Cases that involved longer absence or other crimes were dealt with by a period of *kettingarbeid* (convict labour) or more severe punishment.[36]

The punishment for absence could be harsh as well. For the absence of eight nights, it was demanded in January 1730 that the sailor Pieter Ellernisse from Veere be punished with half a day on the *houten paard* – the 'wooden horse' – and be put in jail for three days, receive a severe beating and pay a fine of one month's salary. Pieter was acquitted, however, because he could prove that he 'went to shore with the permission of his first mate'.[37] Punishments were more severe when a sailor missed the departure of his ship during his absence. Jan Cornelis from Delft, for example, had been absent for five nights and missed his ship to Banda in February 1730. The punishment demanded against him was a public beating, a fine of ten months wages, and incarceration 'in chains' for six months in order to perform convict labour. In response to Jan's declaration, in which he claimed he had been ill, the Court ruled that he would first be brought to the hospital. After recovery, Jan was punished with a severe beating and sent back to the Republic.[38]

The distinction between desertion and absence remained problematic. In 1738, for example, an ordinance was issued which announced that Indian sailors who were convicted of desertion would no longer be punished with imprisonment or with the death penalty, but only with a physical punishment. In the 1760s the ordinance caused confusion in the trial before the Court of Justice of Batavia dealing with the runaway sailor Baboe from Bengal. After an absence from his work at the wharf of Batavia for the period of one and a half years, Baboe tried to sail out of the city at night to serve on an English vessel.[39] The officer in charge of the case against the sailor, the *waterfiscaal* Maurits Theodorus Hilgers, concluded that Baboe was 'a servant of the Company and therefore a subject of the Dutch State'. At the same time, he concluded, it seems that 'the desertion of Moor sailors in the service of the Company is not considered as a major offence', referring to the ordinance of 1738 prescribing that Indian sailors were 'not to be punished with death or other capital punishment, but with a *laarsing* or other domestic punishment'. Accordingly, Hilgers demanded Baboe should be punished with 'a beating behind the City Hall'.[40]

The Court of Justice upheld a different interpretation of the ordinance of 1738 and made a distinction between *absenteeren* and *wesentlijk deserteren* – 'absence' and 'actual desertion'. The Court sentenced Baboe to two years of convict labour on the island of Edam, where he would have to work in the rope factory. The ruling in this case led to the renewal of the regulation on the punishment of runaway Indian sailors in June 1760. The distinction between absence and actual desertion, as made by the Court of Justice, gained a prominent place in this ordinance. Deserters who engaged in the employment of foreign trading companies or ships were punished with convict labour in the rope factory of Edam; Indian sailors who had only been absent would 'as usual' be punished with a severe public beating.[41]

Remaining absent in the Dutch Republic

In the Dutch Republic, *absentie* had a completely different meaning. For the crews ready for departure to Asia, this was not a mere temporary absence from the workplace, but absence at the moment of the departure of the fleet. This meant that absent workers destined for service in Asia actually missed their ship. This made absence at the moment of departure effectively the same as desertion. These cases of absence were taken very seriously and were dealt with, for example, by making retrieved runaways work on board without wages.[42]

The levels of absence of VOC employees at their time of departure in the Dutch Republic changed over the eighteenth century, increasing strongly from 1745 onwards. In general, these levels of absence were not strongly related to the regions of origin of workers from Europe. Absence was higher among workers originating from outside Europe, mainly the West and East Indies. And towards the end of the seventeenth century (between 1687 and 1694) there was a temporary rise of absence among workers originating from the direct hinterland of the Republic and from Scandinavia and the Baltic area.

Two important factors seem related to the level of absence in the Dutch Republic and its remarkable rise. First, the relation between occupation and absence. Absence was especially high for workers recruited in lower occupations, such as soldiers, young sailors, sailors, boys and others. Second, the relation between absence and debt. This relation was not the same as the impact of debt on desertion – as debts could lead to a higher rate of desertion. In the case of absence in the Republic, on the contrary, absence was lower for workers with debts to the Company. This needs explanation. At their recruitment in the Dutch Republic, workers could sign a *maandbrief*, a letter

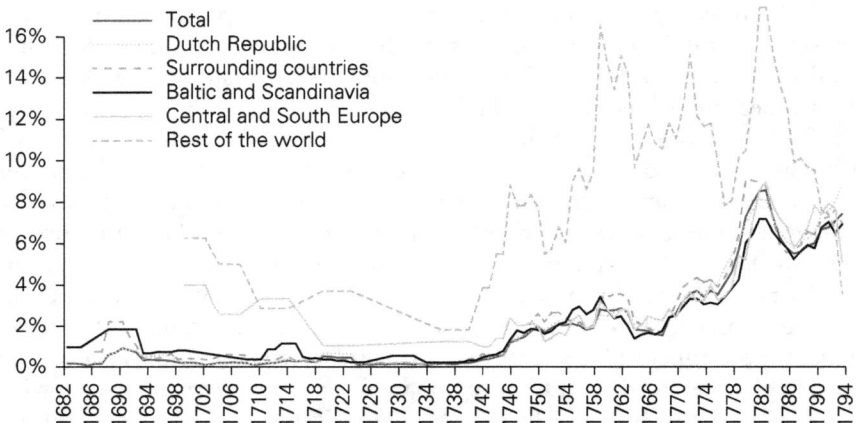

FIGURE 6.1 *Absence of VOC workers at departure from Republic (percentages, five-year averages)*

entitling relatives to a regular payment of a part of the worker's wages while he was overseas, and a *transportbrief*, a letter of debt arranging the payment of one specific sum of money from the wage account of the worker to either a relative or someone else. Both payments were only performed after the VOC employee had earned enough salary (on his account) during his service overseas. The *transportbrief* had priority over the *maandbrief*. In cases where workers had both a *maandbrief* and a *transportbrief* it was possible for the *transportbrief* to be assigned to either family or to debtors such as intermediaries in the recruitment and provisioning of clothing and equipment.

The *transportbrief* was mainly used as a payment for debts made by the worker before his departure. Recruitment intermediaries such as boarding-house masters, hawkers and provisioning specialists would make sure to claim the *transportbrief* of the worker. The *transportbrief* served as payment for the equipment and services provided. These recruitment intermediaries sold the *transportbrief* for a price lower than the actual value of the letter, but high enough to compensate costs and deliver some profit. The buyers of the *transportbrief*, so-called *ceelkopers*, speculated on a reasonable rate of return from the payments on the letters of workers they bought. Workers who only signed a *transportbrief* – and no *maandbrief* – seem to have used this as a way to pay off these intermediaries, other debt or to gain direct access to cash for other purposes. It is not likely they used it as a payment for relatives, because the *maandbrief* was a better way to transfer wages to them. If a *maandbrief* was signed, an additional *transportbrief* may have served for family purposes. The use of a *transportbrief* without assigning money to relatives through a *maandbrief*, however, indicates the involvement

TABLE 6.2 *Share of VOC employees with* transportbrief, *but without* maandbrief *(percentage)*

	All recruits	Absent in Republic	Deserted overseas
1680–1700	53%		61%
1700–1720	57%	50%	74%
1720–1740	65%	61%	82%
1740–1760	76%	10%	91%
1760–1780	81%	5%	96%
1780–1800	60%	1%	80%

Source: VOC Opvarenden (2012).

of intermediaries in the recruitment process. Foreign workers, often arriving in Amsterdam and other Chamber Cities without the necessary contacts and knowledge, were naturally more dependent on such intermediaries and were more vulnerable to the possible malpractices that were used against them.

This system of debts and *transportbrieven* does not provide a full explanation in itself. The eighteenth century witnessed a strong increase in the level of absence as well as in the level of workers with only a *transportbrief* (and no *maandbrief*). The level of workers with only a *transportbrief* rose from between 50 and 60 per cent around 1700 to somewhere between 75 and 85 per cent in the period 1740–80.[43] The coinciding rising levels of absence and debt indicate an increase in the role of recruitment-related intermediaries as well as the changing character of the recruitment processes.

This indicates the full explanation for this phenomenon: recruiters started exercising more control over the recruit, making sure that their indebted workers were on board at the moment of departure, and thus securing their payment through the *transportbrief*.[44] Until 1740, levels of debt of absent workers indicated via the *transportbrieven* were fairly similar to the average. This changed in the 1740s as levels of absent workers with debts dropped significantly at the same time as the level of *overall* absence increased. The increased role of recruitment intermediaries coincided with increased control of these intermediaries over workers using *transportbrieven* as a form of payment. The indebted recruits traced through the *transportbrieven* had a relatively high level of presence as recruitment intermediaries secured their boarding.

The recruitment system in Chamber Cities such as Amsterdam underwent significant changes in character, developing into a system with more deceitful and violent characteristics, resulting in rising levels of both absence and debt.[45] Studying VOC recruitment patterns, J.R. Bruijn signalled the increasing scarcity of qualified sailors for the VOC and the Dutch Navy in the 1740s and 1750s.⁴⁶ The crisis of recruitment in the 1740s, however, was not only a question of the shortage of skilled labour. Examples of riots related to the recruitment of sailors and soldiers indicate changing dynamics in the recruitment industry and the violent ways through which boarding-house masters secured their business.

The *volkhouder* Jan van Swol, for example, had around 300 persons in his boarding house at the Zeedijk in Amsterdam in 1754. A fight broke out between the men of the boarding-house master and his 'clients', who complained about the food. Some of the angry recruits were arrested, but the others took over the boarding house and declared that 'they had made the house into an imperial free city, and that everyone was allowed to enter and leave freely'.⁴⁷ This was a reference to the level of coercion and control that was inherent to many of the boarding houses. Walking away was not allowed. Some boarding houses may have had more resemblance to a prison than a guest house. A few years later, 'a few hundred Noors or Juts' attacked a boarding house in Amsterdam, because the boarding-house master 'did not want to release some of their mates'. They confronted the 'servants or overseers' who worked for the widow who owned the house. After that, the '*zielverkopershuis*' at the Zeedijk was completely plundered, everything in the house was destroyed, the porcelain cabinet thrown on the ground, a clock smashed, and even the parrots were killed'. Furthermore, the sailors 'freed everyone who was locked up and chased them out of the house'.⁴⁸ These cases are telling, not only for the changes in the labour markets, but also for the (collective) responses by sailors.

Jumping ship in Europe and the Atlantic

VOC workers not only remained absent in the Republic, but also deserted during outward-bound voyages in Europe and in the Atlantic, and after their arrival in Asia. For the workers recruited in Europe, it is possible to trace the numbers and patterns of desertion via the VOC Opvarenden database. This database does not include the Asian and European workers recruited in Asia. Personnel that went missing or deserted were registered as *weggelopen* (deserted), *vermist* (missing) or *laatste vermelding* (last reference). The ambiguity in these categories makes it difficult to provide a precise reconstruction of the total number of deserters of the employees recruited in the Republic. The category of workers registered as *weggelopen* provides a minimum that might underestimate the real desertion rates. Workers that were retrieved after desertion and sentenced by the Court of Justice were registered as *gestraft* (convicted) together with employees convicted of other crimes.⁴⁹ Some deserters may also have been registered as 'missing' or with 'last reference', but these categories also contain workers that had not deserted, but went missing, for example, during a storm or a military conflict.

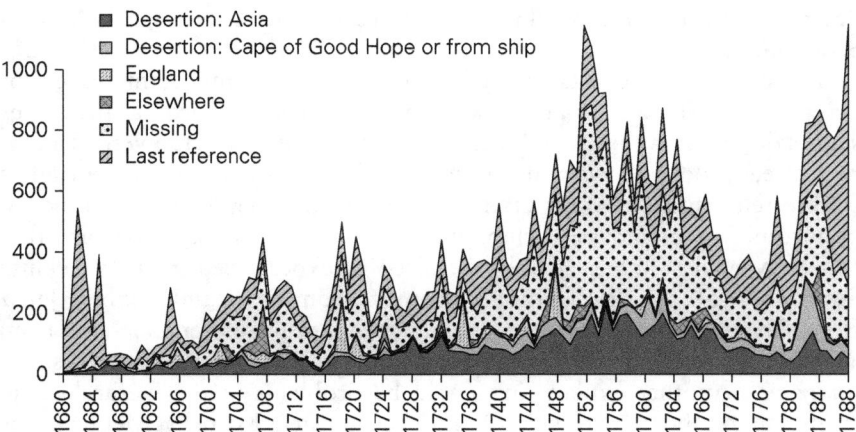

FIGURE 6.2 *VOC employees recruited in the Dutch Republic, deserted and missing, 1680–1788*

On outbound ships, desertions occurred along the European coast as well as in the Atlantic. These desertions during voyages were more dependent on the concrete opportunities that occurred and occurred more irregularly. Desertion was only possible in situations where ships came close to land or other vessels, collecting water or halting for blockades, wars or disasters. The ship *Sint Andries*, for example, sailed from Amsterdam to Asia 'via Cape Verde and S. Paulo de Luanda' in 1677.[50] This enabled the soldier Lourens Specx from Den Bosch to desert on 3 November. On 11 March 1680, the sailor Pieter Wit from Stockholm deserted, after his ship *Huis te Zilverstein* had been lying before Portland (England) for almost three weeks.[51]

Desertions on outward-bound voyages were not only individual acts, but could be collective as well, varying from a single group to longer-lasting waves of desertions. In the spring of 1693, at least 32 workers deserted from the outward-bound fleet as it was held up at Portsmouth (England) from January until late April due to the Nine Years War. On 17 February, the gunner Jan Isbrantse from Texel and the quartermaster Jacob Poul from Oosthuizen deserted from the ship *Agatha*. Perhaps they ran together with the sailors Pieter Bartelse from Utrecht, Jacob van Leewen from Maarseveen, and Gerrit Dirckse and Andries Pieterse from Amsterdam, who deserted from the ship *Nichtevecht* on the same day. The sailor Leendert Claase from Potbroek also deserted that day from the ship *Faam*. Two weeks later, on 2 March, the sailors Doede Tierties from Leeuwarden and Claas Theunise de Bijl from Naarden deserted from the ship *Nichtevecht*. Three gunners from Amsterdam, Meijndert Roelants, Warnar Dircxe and Jacob de Braa decided to run from the ship *Faam* two days later. Later in March, petty officers Sent Arentse from Amsterdam and Daniel Ros from Copenhagen deserted from this vessel. On 20 March, six sailors deserted from the ship *Agatha*. The desertions continued in April until the fleet continued its voyage to Asia via Scotland.⁵²

The islands and coasts of the Atlantic were also important places for desertion. During a stop at Santiago, one of the Cape Verde Islands, four sailors deserted on the same day from the ship *Azië*. The Cape Verde Islands might seem too isolated and unattractive for deserters, but as the islands were often visited by ships taking in fresh water, they provided sufficient opportunities to find new employment. It is interesting, therefore, that this crew of deserters probably consisted of experienced men. Jan Hansz Swart from Stockholm, Anthonij Thomasz from Delft and Lubbert Jansz from Groningen were gunners (*bosschieters*), while Barent Pietersz from Waasbergen, probably Waesberg near Zottegem, was an able-bodied sailor (*matroos*). Another explanation could be problems in the hierarchy and treatment on board the ship *Azië* – the master, Kornelis Meppel, was 'disrated' during the voyage.⁵³

Finding their way: Desertion rates in Asia

The number of workers deserting from Company service in Asia was higher and showed a more stable trend than the number of workers that remained absent during departure in the Dutch Republic or jumping ship in the Atlantic. Workers deserted as a response to very different situations, ranging from harsh conditions to career opportunities. The Company complained that 'despite the punishments against desertion', employees 'did not mind to leave the service of the Company and to engage into foreign service'. Desertion could vary significantly regionally. Some regions seemed less favourable, but desertion could take on a considerable size nevertheless. Especially in economically thriving areas, providing alternative opportunities of employment, the level of desertion was high. The complaints of the Company concerned mainly regions such as 'Bengal, Coromandel, Ceylon, Malabar, Surat, Sumatra's Westcoast and Malacca, as being places where desertion to foreign nations is the most frequent and easiest.'⁵⁴

The desertion rate based on the VOC Opvarenden database shows an absolute minimum of the share of deserters of the workers recruited in the Dutch Republic *per departure cohort*. In the eighteenth century, annually at least some 100 to 200 workers recruited in the Dutch Republic can be traced to have deserted at the Cape or in Asia. The total numbers of desertion must have been much higher. In 1759, for example, the total number of deserters from the settlements in Surat, Coromandel and Bengal amounted already to some 200 employees.⁵⁵ The absolute numbers of desertion by employees from Europe indicate a relation with wars, leading to waves of desertion especially towards the end of the War of the Austrian Succession (1740–48), the Seven Years War (1756–63) and the Fourth Anglo-Dutch War and its aftermath (1780–84).

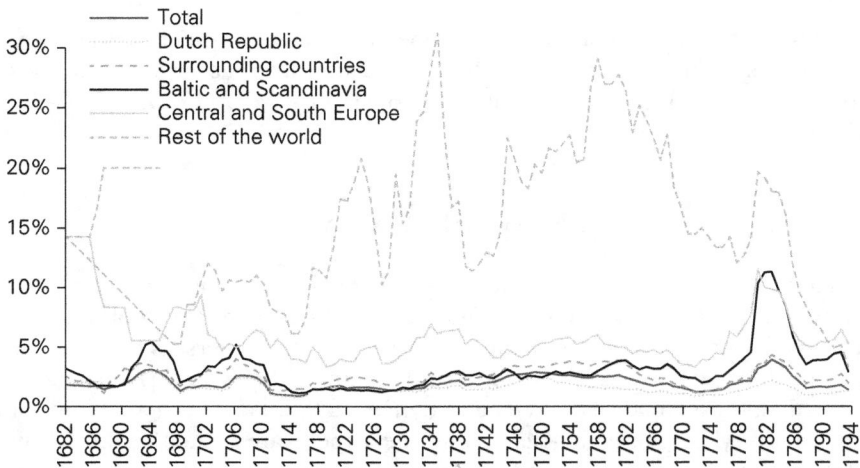

FIGURE 6.3 *Desertion rate of VOC workers per departure cohort from Republic (five-year averages)*

The differences between workers from different regions of origin indicate a relation between the place of origin and the tendency to desert. Employees from the Dutch Republic were less likely to desert than foreign employees. These differences increased during the second half of the eighteenth century. The desertion rate for Scandinavian and Baltic workers is rather high. This does not only seem to be related to notions of loyalty. Skills and experience especially may have played a role here. The need for labour in Asia by both European trading companies and Asian employers concerned skilled labour especially. Scandinavian and Baltic sailors were often skilled maritime workers. The Company tended to recruit them as experienced sailors, for example in the position of gunner.[56] In Asia, these sailors often made careers rather quickly or could try to make use of their advantageous position by deserting and finding better employment.[57]

The difference between Dutch and Scandinavian workers is all the more remarkable when compared to differences between desertion rates of workers originating from within the Dutch Republic. As patronage networks strongly influenced career opportunities within the VOC, it might be expected that workers from the smaller Chamber Cities would be less likely to desert. Especially upon recruitment in the Dutch Republic, local patronage was an important factor in appointments for captains, officers, petty officers and specific functions within the lower ranks. The overseas local patronage networks crucial to the many appointments needed for replacing (petty) officers and their mates on the ships and forts in Asia were more open to foreigners and other Dutchmen. The workers of Chamber Cities, however, were not significantly less likely to desert. Even when excluding Amsterdam, as a large city that was perhaps more open to foreigners, the desertion rates of Chamber Cities were higher than the Dutch average in some periods (1680–1700; 1750s) and only slightly lower in others (1700s; 1720–40; 1770s).

Escaping Batavia

Deserters did not just run during voyages or at the fringes of the VOC empire. In a way similar to the situation in the Dutch Republic, workers also remained absent and deserted Batavia, the heart of the overseas empire. The acts of desertion by slaves, sailors, soldiers and other workers in Batavia show many resemblances to the basic dynamics that have been analysed for the Atlantic (Karwan Fatah-Black) and the Cape (Kate Ekama). Three main types of desertion also occur here. Absence or temporary disappearance was an important phenomenon for contract workers, such as soldiers, sailors and artisans, as well as for slaves in Batavia. Individual desertions – successful or failed attempts – were common, and often related to work grievances, alternative economic opportunities, conflicts, avoidance of punishments, etc. Collective forms of desertion were regularly undertaken by (small or medium-sized groups of) sailors and soldiers, and especially by slaves.

The large size and busy character of Batavia, however, gave way to a set of specific dynamics that were less likely to occur in and around smaller settlements. Just as in other places, of course, many runaways fled the city of Batavia, escaping to overseas destinations, to inland Java or neighbouring cities such as Bantam. Simultaneously, many deserters remained close to the city or did not leave the city at all, hiding in the anonymity of the outer city. As will become apparent later in this chapter, the environment had a strong impact on the destinations and survival strategies of deserters.

So how then did these dynamics of desertion work out in practice? Let us first take a closer look at the desertions aimed at escaping the city. These could be both individual and collective acts. Despite the control the VOC tried to exercise over the port of Batavia, sailors and other workers were reported to desert on ships. Some deserters tried their luck as stowaways on VOC ships. The sailmaker Egbertus Schravers from Amsterdam, for example, deserted from his ship *Middelwout* by hiding on the chialoup *De Deka* that was destined for Bengal. He made sure to remain in hiding until the ship 'was far at sea' and the first mate 'had started his prayers'.[58] Foreign vessels seemed a better option. Especially English, Portuguese and other European ships provided ways out. For the deserters who would be retrieved by the VOC, the recruitment in foreign service, however, added to the severity of the offence. This did not necessarily discourage sailors. The English vessels that regularly visited Batavia were especially attractive to deserters. In 1682, the sailor Marcus Jansz Wolf was accused of having spoken – while being drunk – of plans to desert and recruit with the English.[59]

Another opportunity was the employment in the local shipping of Asian, Eurasian and *burgher* owners. Especially for the Asian sailors of the Company this was an attractive alternative. In the late eighteenth century, it was decided with regard to Indian sailors that 'the absentees and deserters are never allowed back into the service, in order to prevent them from serving for some time on private vessels, for higher wages'.[60] The Javanese sailors that were recruited as sailors by the VOC in the 1780s were perhaps even more inclined to desert. Officials from Semarang advised on measures to prevent the desertion of Javanese sailors in Batavia. The desertions were partly related to the conditions of work under the VOC – with solutions dealing with problems in payments, supplies and treatment – but were also related to the experience of the sailors. In Batavia it was argued that it was especially the 'newlings', who were not yet accustomed to the work and conditions.

In the second half of the 1780s, the VOC had begun to employ local Javanese rowers in the harbour, complaining that they often 'ran or remained absent' after 'having been used in that service for one or two days'.[61] These local rowers may have returned to their places of origin, like the Javanese sailors on intra-Asiatic shipping, who were probably recruited in northeast Java. At the same time, it is very well possible that these sailors and rowers simply ran to other employers. The desertions seem related to the high demand for labour in the reviving maritime industry after the Fourth Anglo-Dutch War. The captains of private vessels, where conditions and payment were supposed to be better, complained 'equally about the desertion of that people'.[62]

Sometimes it is difficult to distinguish whether the desertion and recruitment with foreign vessels was voluntary or that coercion played a role. In 1746, a group of seven workers was brought before the Court of Justice on the charge of desertion.[63] They came from different vessels, but may have been familiar to each other through family and friendship relations, or perhaps just via socializing and drinking. The sailor Willem Jansz from Amsterdam was the only deserter of this group providing a more detailed account that did not revolve around drunken escapades. While preparing goods for a Company ship at Onrust, he had witnessed an English vessel with someone called Willem Everhard. The sailor Jansz claimed that they had both been in the 'armseniersweeshuis' in Amsterdam – probably referring to the Almoners' Orphanage (Aalmoezeniersweeshuis). Everhard had become a sailmaker 'in the service of the English' on the ship *Herder*. Requesting Everhard to bring him to the island of Kuiper, Willem Jansz declared he had been brought to the English ship *Faem* instead, where he was locked in 'the bread storage'.

The others provided accounts that were less detailed and seem to indicate that they were out drinking together before their – possibly coerced – transfer to an English vessel. The boatswain's mate Cornelis Jans from Wolgast and sailor Marten van der Klugt from The Hague served on the ship *Vrijheid*. Marten may have been family of Laurens van der Klugt from The Hague, serving as sailor on the ship *Nieuwland*, together with quartermaster Pieter Jansen from Kristiansand and sailor Anthonij Laros from Bordeaux. These five sailors claimed that, after having been drunk in Batavia 'in the company of some English sailors', they had woken up on an English ship. There they had been prevented from leaving, being locked up every time a Dutch vessel approached. The soldier Jan Christiaen Paul from Berlin, stationed on watch at the Diestpoort, one of the city gates, did not mention any sailors, but claimed that he had been drinking *arak* with the French cooper of the English vessel before being taken away.

The argument of drunkenness was often used by VOC employees that were faced with criminal charges. Of course, a large share of the conflicts and offences did indeed occur during or after drinking. At the same time, drunkenness was often mobilized as an excuse – in this case, for not resisting the transport to the foreign vessel. VOC courts were not always easily convinced by this defence. In this case, the prosecutor was only convinced after he had seen proof of a letter which was sent by the sailors to the commander of the island of Onrust upon the return of the vessel to Batavia. Explaining that they had been sailing on the English vessel 'against their will', the letter had been reason to retrieve the sailors from the ship. It remains uncertain whether this was true or was a successful strategy to return into VOC employment without punishment. In the case of the latter, it seems doubtful whether the desertion had actually taken place through abduction – as taverns, *warongs* and public places were common places for recruitment, they may very well have been tempted by the promise of higher wages on an English vessel.

Recruitment networks not only seduced European and Asian contract workers to run from Batavia, but directed themselves at slaves as well. In 1749, for example, the Court of Justice dealt with a large group of slaves who had deserted from the VOC and from private slave owners. The slaves testified that they had been approached by the VOC sergeant Baries and Captain Aboe, who promised them positions as soldiers in one of the native regiments that were to be sent to Surat. Baries approached most of the slaves in the outer city, near the Utrechtse Poort, and invited them into his house 'in order to chew some *pinang*' – a recreational drug. Some of the slaves were actively persuaded to leave their house or Company workplace. Others had first deserted independently before entering into contact with the sergeant and captain. The Buginese slave Batjoe, for example, had 'already been deserting (*drossen*) for six months'.[64]

The urban jungle

Batavia was not only a place workers ran away from. Batavia was a sprawling metropolis and an attractive environment for deserters. The population of Batavia grew from more than 65,000 in 1690 to over 170,000 in 1780. While the 'inner city' became less populated, the 'outer city' grew rapidly (from 50,000 in 1690 to over 160,000 in 1780).[65] The outer city was a lively world with residential areas (*campongs*), markets, gardens, sugar mills and other workplaces. This offered many opportunities for runaways. This strongly influenced desertion strategies. Successful desertion attempts were not dependent on the ability to escape the urban environment. This reduced to need to plan escapes to countrysides, forests or hills carefully or with large groups of deserters. Especially for slaves and other Asian workers, the size of the city meant they could desert individually first. After desertion, runaways could remain in the city, but needed to stay away from places and neighbourhoods where they could easily be recognized. This resulted in strategies of slaves, but also soldiers, sailors and others escaping their workplaces and households, avoiding specific areas in the city, and trying to make a living on one's own or joining a group of deserters later.

European runaways could sometimes hide for months without being caught. Christoffel Karus from Danzig, a smith working on the island of Onrust, disappeared for a month, probably in or around Batavia. He was not prosecuted for desertion, only for absence.[66] After his participation in various illegal activities had been uncovered, the quartermaster Jacob Hoffhuisen fled with 'an inland vessel' from Surabaya via Semarang to Batavia. There he was able to remain fugitive 'as a *drosser*' for four months.[67]

The open-hearted, somewhat desperate account of Phillip de Bertherand from Luxemburg, a sailor on the ship *Casteel van Tilburg*, provides an insight into the possibilities in and around Batavia. The value of this deserter's narrative is difficult to assess, because it was Phillip himself who returned to the Company and confessed to the act of sodomy, claiming to 'deserve punishment'.[68] In July 1759, he declared before the Court of Justice of Batavia that he had been absent for eight nights, wandering 'near or on the so-called *drosserspadt* [deserters' road] between the posts of Rijswijk and Noordwijk' – two military stations in the hinterland of Batavia, amidst the rice and sugar fields.[69] He claimed to have 'requested various boys [referring probably to slaves] to go with him in order to perform that vile and evil act [referring to sexual acts between men]'. Phillip claimed that he was only able to convince two of them, 'not knowing who these boys were or where they belonged to'.[70]

After having roamed around on the *drosserspadt*, Phillip went back to the city. In a Chinese drinking house, near the Rotterdam Poort, at the corner of the road to Antjol, he met 'a European' named Jan, who claimed to be a carpenter in the artisans' quarter. They went to a *warong* (eating house) near the Utrechtse Poort. During the rest of the day, Jan and Phillip wandered around, talking about the possibility of 'both having a girl tonight'. Jan answered, according to Phillip, 'yes, that is impossible now, because neither of us has money to get girls'. In the evening, Jan had taken him to 'an empty and decayed house behind the Roua Nova'. Jan forced the door, saying 'this is where I am home'. Phillip declared that they had slept together. The next day Jan went 'into the city' – referring to the inner city of Batavia – promising to return 'outside' as soon as he had found something to 'live on' from a friend. Jan did not return. 'Alone and without money', Phillip decided to turn himself in with the Company 'as a deserter' and confess his 'godless ways to the judge'.

Europeans were by far a minority in the urban sprawl of Batavia, but the stories of European deserters that remained in and around the city indicate that it was possible to survive and remain undiscovered for a considerable period of time. For European runaways it seemed more difficult to go into the smaller and European dominated 'inner' city. They could walk almost publicly, however, in and around the larger and highly populated 'outer' city. This also seemed the case for Asian runaway contract workers. The 'Moor' sailor Baboe from Bengal 'decided to desert after his recovery from the Moor hospital'. He was able to 'roam around here and there' making a living out of casual work for a year and a half. This meant he was also able to be 'in the city', where he was recruited by the Bengali boatswain of an English vessel. He was discovered only while trying to leave Batavia, passing his former colleagues at the rowers' quarter.[71] The 'Moor sailor' Ramiam from Bengal was convicted in 1747 after an absence of some three years.[72] A year before, the Bengali sailor Fakiera was convicted for having been absent from his position in the artillery for over two years.[73]

Although the measures of control were much stronger for Asian slaves and ethnic groups associated with slaves that were deemed violent and dangerous, such as Buginese and Balinese, the outer city and its surroundings offered many opportunities to disappear into the anonymity of city life. Some slaves ran away individually after a conflict. Manto from Maccassar, the slave of the bookkeeper Jan Jacob Tenpezel, for example, 'deserted because his master did not want to give him *pinang* money' – a small allowance that was sometimes provided by slave owners. He remained in the city and slept on 'a bamboo *digge digge* or bench that he found on the sidewalk of a *warong* near the river'.[74] Manto did not last long as he was held up by some *kaffers* – helpers of the bailiff.

Other slaves fled together, such as the Buginese slave Badjoe and the Balinese female slave Julia, both slaves to the widow Baillet. They were not only charged with *fugie*, but also with theft.[75] As a way to provide for one's livelihood, theft was a common crime for runaway slaves. It also created new ties between runaways, slaves and local inhabitants. In 1788, the runaway Baroedien from Batavia, former slave of the carpenter Stephanus Butor from Batavia, was brought before the Court of Justice on the charge of 'stealing and selling a horse, vagabonding and roaming' around the hinterland of the city. An accomplice, named Satar, was charged with 'housing and maintaining' him.[76]

Larger groups of runaway slaves were sometimes more bold in their survival strategies, often mixing desertion with theft and various forms of violence. In 1760, a group of runaways faced these charges before the Court of Justice of Batavia. The ethnic background of the slaves seems to have been an important factor: all the slaves were 'from Boeton'. These Butonese slaves came from a range of different owners – 'Moors' (Indians), Chinese and Europeans or Eurasians. Robo had ran away from his owner, the Moor Nina Poele, Galand from the inland Christian Johannes, Kula and Compepe from the Moor Mochama Mika Lebe, Sieuwma alias Cabolos from the Malay Ali, October alias Palessa from the corporal Schoppenhouwer, and Coneke from the widow Vermehr. The Indian and Chinese owners lived throughout Batavia: in the 'southern outer city' ('suijder voorstad'), just outside the Utrechtse Poort and in the Chinese *campong*.[77]

In the very diverse but heavily populated Batavia, 'ethnicity' or 'origin' seems to have been a more important factor, also for slaves and runaways. As evidence for the Cape of Good Hope and other cities indicates, this is in contrast to the more open character of runaway groups in smaller and medium-sized settlements of the VOC (as indicated in Chapter 7 by Kate Ekama). The large size of the slave population, rising from 26,000 in the late seventeenth century to more than 40,000 towards the end of the eighteenth century, may have been crucial in creating this difference. Various ethnic groups were large enough to maintain social interaction and ties based on, for example, language, origin or religion.

Privately owned slaves could be employed in workplaces, houses and gardens, but were also frequently rented out to others or to the Company. Through various ways, therefore, they could interact and make alliances with Company-owned slaves. In 1730, several Company-owned slaves from Timor fled the artisans' quarter. They met each other again outside the city and were joined by Jacob from Timor, slave of the messenger Rudolph Coster. It seems that Jacob had taken care of some weapons: 'a musket, a bayonet, a cutlass, gunpowder and bullets'. They roamed around in the hinterland of Batavia until they were caught by some Javanese.[78]

Theft could be an important part of survival strategies. The Balinese slave Salomon of the *burgher* Bouman, who had fled the artisans' quarter after he had been convicted of theft, was found two months after 'he had silently entered the house' of some inland citizens. Salomon himself claimed that he had 'returned from the *bovenlanden* to the city in order to bring bananas to an acquaintance'; unable to find the house, he entered the house of inland citizens to ask for some directions.[79] At the same time, the accusation of theft was an important means to add to the severity of the charges of runaway slaves.

One of the crucial dynamics that set Batavia apart from smaller settlements and cities was the active and often rather uncontrolled scene for the recruitment of contract and coerced labour. Two different ways of 'finding' labour power were important here. First, the widespread employment and possession of slave labour went together with a very lively slave trade to, in and from Batavia and its *ommelanden*. The practice of buying and employing enslaved labourers created its own dynamics of seduction, kidnapping and human trade.[80] Second, it seems that various (underground) recruitment networks were occupied with recruiting soldiers, sailors and other workers for Asian and European vessels, for armies (at least the VOC military), for the different industries in and around Batavia (agricultural production, the sugar mills, etc.), and for *coelie*-work. The need for labour – both contracted as well as casual – provided opportunities for runaways. In the vibrant outer districts and the surroundings of Batavia, runaway slaves had many opportunities for maintaining their livelihood, varying from working for wages in the fields and sugar factories, to trying to live through gathering food. The Buginese slave Sabar, for example, deserted after he was refused his freedom, despite having offered his owner fifty rixdollars for his manumission. After he was caught, he declared that he 'fled over land from Anke to Bantam with another six slaves of other owners' and that he 'had maintained himself with agriculture'.[81]

Not all of the runaways blended in the outer districts and rural environments of Batavia. In some cases, runaway slaves grouped together and formed gangs that posed a more serious threat to the existing social and economic order. In 1677, for example, it was reported from Crawang that a group of 300 deserters had attacked several villages in an attempt to take them over. The Company regularly sent out military expeditions to capture bands of runaway slaves.[82] In other instances, collective desertion took the form of revolt or mutiny. The Balinese slaves on the ship *Mercuur*, for example, managed to take over the ship, sailing it from the island of Edam, near Batavia, to the Sunda Strait. They remained fugitive for at least five days before the ship was sunk during the third attack by armed forces of the Company. It is most likely that some at least of the Balinese mutineers did manage to escape to nearby islands and the coast of South Sumatra.[83] The mutiny on the *Mercuur* was followed by a series of revolts of Asian slaves and sailors on board the Dutch East Indiamen.[84]

The combination of revolt and escape was not exceptional. In 1715, a group of Balinese slaves, employed on the island of Edam, was reported to have fled after having murdered some of the Europeans on the island in a revolt.[85] In 1743, slaves from South Sulawesi, illegally brought on board by VOC officers, revolted and killed an officer. The European crew abandoned the vessel and the slaves were able to reach a nearby island by running the ship ashore.[86] On the VOC ship *Meermin* in 1766, the slaves bought and transported for the VOC from Madagascar to the Cape of Good Hope rose up, took over the ship and forced the crew to run it ashore.[87] Similar uprisings were undertaken by convicts on the island of Edam (1772, 1781), but also on Robben Island (1751).[88] In the case of contract workers, such as European and Asian sailors and soldiers, revolts, mutinies and strikes could be used to bring forward and negotiate specific demands, but in several instances uprisings of contract workers seem mainly to have been related to attempts to flee Company hierarchy and control.[89]

Conclusions: A world of runaways

Jumping from one ship to another, at times breaking free from the bonds of previous labour obligations, the runaway crew of Captain Scott introduced at the beginning of this chapter captured the importance of mobility and labour, obligations and defiance, in early modern globalization. Leaving little information on the labour relations on the ship itself, it provides crucial information on its surroundings. The crew of Scott consisted of (former) slaves, sailors and deserters. Johannes Kodij – or Pieter Zwart – ran from a binding labour contract. Gregorius Jeremias 'from Oejong Sala' stated that he had bought his own freedom – after having been enslaved or made a prisoner of war. The slave Maart claimed to have been freed by his former master, a citizen from Java, but that statement may very well have been a functional lie. Facing the authority of the VOC as a fugitive slave was far from attractive; one could better pretend to be manumitted in that case. Either way, it transformed his situation from being bound to a master, to being 'free' and having 'no means of subsistence'.

Even though many workers were tightly bound to labour duties through *contracts* (European and Asian sailors, soldiers, artisans and others), *corvée* (workers on Ceylon, Java and elsewhere) and *property rights* (slaves), this did not prevent them from attempts to take their lives into their own hands. Escape was an important part of the work, survival and mobility strategies of early modern workers. Depending on the situation, escape could take many forms, ranging from temporary absence, to individual desertion, collective desertion and even armed uprisings and *marronage*. Desertion could be related to avoiding work obligations, escaping harsh working conditions, oppressive hierarchy and command. Desertion, however, could also be related to escaping prosecution, or be part of an attempt at social or geographical mobility.

Workers under the VOC deserted around the globe. This chapter traced desertion and absence along the core (intercontinental) infrastructure of the VOC empire, looking at workers running in the Dutch Republic, en route from Europe to Asia, and in and around the overseas imperial centre of Batavia. In the eighteenth century, the European workers recruited in the Dutch Republic remained absent after recruitment in growing numbers. This seems related to the increasingly violent and deceptive character of the maritime labour market in the Dutch Republic from the 1740s onwards. In the period 1680–1794, some 14,300 were absent at the moment of departure of their ships to Asia. Many other European workers deserted en route to Asia, running when ships anchored along the coast in the Channel or near one of the small islands in the Atlantic. European workers also deserted after arrival, and they did so throughout Asia. Of the 737,448 workers registered, at least 4 per cent left through desertion or absence. Many more went missing or were lost for reasons unknown (10 per cent).

It is important to note that Asian workers deserted in great numbers as well. The case of Batavia made clear that Asian sailors, soldiers and slaves ran from the VOC, but also from private vessels, slave masters, and so on. Workers deserted from Batavia, sometimes by hiding as stowaways on ships of the Company, but more often by finding work on one of the many European and Asian vessels. The act of desertion not only led to geographical mobility, but also to the transgression of legal and social boundaries. Runaway slaves fled by becoming soldiers or sailors. Others disappeared in the lively world of the outer city of Batavia and its rural environment, working for wages in the fields, factories and elsewhere, or sustaining themselves through gathering food, or even robbery and stealing. Runaways, especially former slaves, could at times also threaten the public order in Batavia and its hinterland. The VOC reacted by employing military power against bands of runaways and refining systems of social and public control (see Chapter 8 on South Asia).

Large cities created different dynamics with different opportunities and threats. Human trafficking could lead to abduction or forced recruitment. The existence of recruitment networks also meant opportunities – and social highways – to escape and find other employment. The large population of Batavia meant that dynamics of ethnicity and origin remained important, even for (runaway) slaves. In contrast to less densely populated areas, where ethnic categories tended to fade under social categories, collective desertion by slaves in Batavia seems to have been influenced by categories of ethnicity. Crucial also is the fact that the size of the city meant that desertion was not only aimed at leaving the city, but that disappearing and surviving in the urban jungle of Batavia was a real option for Asian contract workers and slaves, and even for Europeans. This also meant that one could more easily run away individually, joining groups of deserters only later.

Taking their lives into their own hands, the runaway slaves, soldiers, sailors, artisans and other workers freed themselves from the ties laid upon them by the Company, sometimes joining other trading companies or private traders, in other cases working in the fields and sugar factories, mingling in cities and local communities, or withdrawing into open and unexplored territories.

Notes

1 Translated from the Dutch original: 'die hem hebben wil moet mij ook neemen!' This could be interpreted as 'the one who wants him, will have to take me too' or 'will have to go by me'. Declaration of Kodij, British Library (BL), India Office Records (IOR)/R/9/21, Malacca Court of Justice, case 10.

2 Original: 'dat wij gekoomen waaren, om zijn papieren te willen zien; en dat den eerste ondertekenaar den voorn: matroos opeijschte als een Comps: dienaar, behoorende tot de Equipagie van zijn schip, wijl hij Scott geen pas hebbende hem geen bescherming kon verleenen.' Declaration of Abo and Van Papendrecht, BL, IOR/R/9/21, 10.

3 On violence and honour: Pieter Spierenburg, *A History of Murder: Personal Violence in Europe from the Middle Ages to the Present* (Cambridge: Polity Press, 2008); Nigel Worden, '"Below the Line the Devil Reigns": Death and Dissent aboard a VOC Vessel', *South African Historical Journal* 61:4 (2009), pp. 702–30; Nigel Worden, 'Public brawling, masculinity and honour', in Nigel Worden (ed.), *Cape Town Between East and West: Social Identities in a Dutch Colonial Town* (Hilversum: Uitgeverij Verloren, 2012), pp. 194–211.

4 Original: 'of hij wel wist wat hij deed'; 'waarop hij zijn houwer ligte om op ons in te kappen'. Declaration of Abo and Van Papendrecht, BL, IOR/R/9/21, 10.

5 Original: 'onder den naam van Pieter Zwart in den dienst van de Hollandsche Comp: geweest'; 'zig schuil gehouden had in het Bosch tot naar het vertrek van het schip'; 'als stuurman met 50 rop: besolding 's maands'. Declaration of Kodij, BL, IOR/R/9/21, 10.

6 Original: 'dat alle deze vaartuigen van hem Scot, geduurende den oorlog meede de Portugeeschen, dog na ontvangen tijding van wapenstilstand weder onder de Engelsche vlag hebben gevaaren.' Declaration of Kodij, BL, IOR/R/9/21, 10.

7 Original: 'dog dat hij veel volk van de wal aan boord gekregen hadt, die [hem] de gemelde goederen afkogten, begeevende capitein scot daar na met hun aan de wal ter ontvangst der contanten voor de verkogte goederen'. Declaration of crew, BL, IOR/R/9/21, 10.

8 'Naoer' presumably refers to Naora, near Kolkata. 'Moor' is often used in VOC administrations to refer to people from the Indian subcontinent or from 'Indian' communities in VOC settlements such as Batavia and Malacca.

9 Original: 'dat den Engels capitein hem op Queda vrijgelaaten heeft met zeggen te kunnen begeeven werwaarts hij wil en dat hij dus vrij zijnde en geen middel van subsistentie hebbende bij den Capitein Scot dienst genoomen had als matroos voor 7 ropijen 's maands, in wiens dienst hij als zoodanig nu wel een jaar lang was.' Declaration of crew, BL, IOR/R/9/21, 10.

10 Original: 'dat hij door de Maleijers van zijn plaats geligt en verkogt is geworden op Queda en dat hij zigzelve weder vrijgekogt hebbende voor 7 ropijen 's maands als matroos g'engageert had in den dienst van Capt: Scot'. Declaration of crew, BL, IOR/R/9/21, 10.

11 For an indication of the growth of intra-Asiatic shipping: Matthias van Rossum, *Werkers van de wereld: Globalisering, arbeid en interculturele ontmoetingen tussen Aziatische en Europese zeelieden in dienst van de VOC, 1600–1800* (Hilversum: Uitgeverij Verloren, 2014).

12 Ibid.

13 Jan Lucassen, 'A Multinational and its Labor Force: The Dutch East India Company, 1595–1795', *International Labor and Working-Class History* 66:2 (2004), pp. 12–39.

14 VOC Opvarenden database, version 6 – January 2012, *EASY DANS*, https://easy.dans.knaw.nl, persistent identifier: urn:nbn:nl:ui:13-pul9-xg (2012). Publicly available: http://vocopvarenden.nationaalarchief.nl.

15 VOC Opvarenden database (2012). Absent: 14,300; missing: 18,041; last reference (unknown): 28,968.

16 For this study, the VOC Opvarenden database (2012) has been linked to an enriched version of the list of spatial references created by Simon Hart as an archivist of the Amsterdam city archive in the 1950s. This list has been enriched by the author of this chapter with varieties of place names that are frequently mentioned in the VOC Opvarenden database (this concerned varieties with approximately more than sixty references). The spatial reference list of Hart is available through the website of Stadsarchief Amsterdam under the title 'Geografische verwijzingen notarieel en ondertrouw'. Linking this enriched version of the Hart list with the VOC Opvarenden database resulted in tracing 64 per cent of the places of origin of the 737,500 entries in the VOC Opvarenden. For the employees that deserted, 69 per cent of the places of origin were identified.

17 Robert Parthesius, *Dutch Ships in Tropical Waters: the Development of the Dutch East India Company (VOC) Shipping Network in Asia 1595–1660* (Amsterdam: Amsterdam University Press, 2007); Matthias van Rossum, 'De intra-Aziatische vaart: Schepen, "de Aziatische zeeman" en de ondergang van de VOC?', *Tijdschrift voor Sociale en Economische Geschiedenis* 8:3 (2011), pp. 32–69.

18 Jaap R. Bruijn, Femme S. Gaastra, Ivo Schöffer, *Dutch-Asiatic Shipping in the 17th and 18th Centuries* (The Hague: Martinus Nijhoff, 1979–87); Matthias van Rossum, 'A "Moorish world" within the Company. The VOC, Maritime Logistics and Subaltern Networks of Asian sailors', *Itinerario – International Journal on the History of European Expansion and Global Interaction* 36:3 (2012), pp. 39–60.

19 Van Rossum, *Werkers van de wereld*.

20 It is notable, however, that in the case of Batavia and Malacca it was possible that the workers performing this casual wage labour called *coeliewerk* could be free persons as well as slaves. On Ceylon, *coelie* services seem not to have referred to casual wage labour, but primarily to obligated labour services. J.A. van der Chijs, *Nederlandsch-Indisch Plakaatboek* (Batavia: Landsdrukkerij, 1885–1900), part V, p. 379.

21 Femme S. Gaastra, *De geschiedenis van de VOC* (Zutphen: Walburg Pers, 1991); Pepijn Brandon, 'Masters of War: State, Capital, and Military Enterprise in the Dutch Cycle of Accumulation (1600–1795)' (PhD thesis, Universiteit van Amsterdam, 2012).

22 This was not unusual in comparison to the Asian maritime labour market, following Matthias van Rossum, 'The Rise of the Asian Sailor? Inter-Asiatic Shipping, the Dutch East India Company and Maritime Labour Markets (1500–1800)', in S. Bhattacharya (ed.), *Towards a New History of Work* (New Delhi: Tulika Books, 2014), pp. 180–213.

23 Markus Vink, '"The World's Oldest Trade": Dutch Slavery and Slave Trade in the Indian Ocean', *Journal of World History* 14:2 (2003), pp. 131–77; Nigel Worden, *Slavery in Dutch South Africa* (Cambridge: Cambridge University Press, 1985); Matthias van Rossum, *Kleurrijke tragiek. De geschiedenis van Nederlandse slavernij in Azië onder de VOC* (Hilversum: Uitgeverij Verloren, 2015).

24 Matthias van Rossum, 'Radjas, Sailors and Slaves. Convict Workers and Resistance', paper and presentation at Labour History – a Return to Politics?

Tenth Conference of the Association of Indian Labour Historians (National Labour Institute, Delhi, 23 March 2014).

25 The 'dienstbaere Moren' in the *gemene werken* of Galle worked on average 102 days from September 1750 until September 1751. Sri Lanka National Archives (SLNA), VOC Archives, Record Group 1, 2758, nr. 22. In the period from September 1745 until September 1746, they only worked on average 77 days. SLNA 1, 5906.

26 Jairus Banaji, *Theory as History. Essays on Modes of Production and Exploitation* (Chicago: Haymarket Books, 2011).

27 Van Rossum, 'A Moorish world'.

28 Van Rossum, *Werkers van de wereld*.

29 The list of cases against runaway slaves and convicts accused with *fugie* is endless; there seems one exception in the case of Cornelis Hoogeboom from Amsterdam, who was not a convict or a slave, but a soldier. Nationaal Archief (NA), Archief van de VOC (VOC), 9412, case 18.

30 NA, VOC, 9733. This was explicitly done in the 'eisch en conclusie' against twenty-five deserters on 19 August 1760.

31 This becomes apparent for example in the cases NA, VOC, 9419, 3 and 21.

32 NA, VOC, 9414, 3; 9420, 14.

33 NA, VOC, 9408, 30.

34 These are the categories used in the database VOC Opvarenden, based on the so-called *Scheepssoldijboeken*.

35 Van der Chijs, *Nederlandsch-Indisch Plakaatboek*, I, pp. 214–16.

36 Van der Chijs, *Nederlandsch-Indisch Plakaatboek*, VI, p. 190; VII, p. 868.

37 NA, VOC, 9295, ff. 218–20.

38 NA, VOC, 9295, f. 237.

39 NA, VOC, 9468, 26. See for a more elaborate description of this case Van Rossum, *Werkers van wereld*.

40 Original: 'een dienaar van de compagnie en gevolgelijk ook een onderdaan van den Nederlandschen Staat'; 'het drossen van een Moors zeevarenden in dienst van de comp: voor so grove misdaad niet wierde geconsidereert'; 'over desertie niet met de lood, of andersints capitaal, maar eenelijk met een laarsing of andere domestique correctie'. NA VOC, 9468, 26.

41 Van der Chijs, *Nederlandsch-Indisch Plakaatboek*, VII, p. 418. This regulation was included in the new statutes of Batavia: Van der Chijs, *Nederlandsch-Indisch Plakaatboek*, IX, p. 207.

42 Machiel Bosman, *De polsslag van de stad. De Amsterdamse stadskroniek van Jacob Bicker Raije (1732–1772)* (Amsterdam: Athenaeum, 2009), p. 129. Original: 'veroordeeld om eerst in de Boeien met die vrouw te trouwen, dan binnenskamers gegegeseld te worden, en dan geboeid aan boord gebracht te worden om als matroos voor de hoofdofficier te varen.'

43 The percentage of workers with a *transportbrief*, but no *maandbrief* remained between 50 and 65 per cent in the period up to 1733, then rose in the period

1734–42 between 65 and 70 per cent, and fluctuated between 75 and 85 per cent in the period 1743–80. Source: VOC Opvarenden (2012).

44 One might argue that it is not the intermediary retrieving the *transportbrief* who has a stake in making sure that the recruit is actually on board during departure, but the buyer of the *transportbrief*, but this might underestimate the role of personal contacts and credibility in the buying and selling of the *transportbrieven*, or to rephrase this, boarding-house masters who did not prevent their recruits from fleeing before departure may have had a hard time selling their *transportbrieven* or might see their value dropping significantly.

45 Femme S. Gaastra, 'The Recruitment of Soldiers by the VOC in the 18th Century', in Wim Klooster (ed.), *Migration, Trade and Slavery in an Expanding World* (Leiden: KITLV Press, 2009), pp. 101–14.

46 Jaap R. Bruijn, 'De Personeelsbehoefte van de VOC overzee', *Bijdrage en Mededelingen betreffende de Geschiedenis der Nederlanden* 91:2 (1976), pp. 218–48.

47 Bosman, *De polsslag*, p. 154. Original: 'dat zij nu van het huis een keizerlijke vrijstad hadden gemaakt, en dat iedereen er naar believen in en uit mocht gaan'.

48 Bosman, *De polsslag*, pp. 196–7. Original: 'door honderden Jutten of Noren', 'hun maten', 'niet meer wilde overdragen of loslaten', 'zielverkopershuis op de Zeedijk geheel geplunderd'; 'Alles in huis was vernield, een porseleinkast met porselein omvergesmeten, een staande klok verpletterd, zelfs een papegaai en de kanaries waren vermoord', 'haar knechten of toezichthouders'; 'Ze hebben iedereen die daar opgesloten zat laten lopen en het huis uit gejaagd.'

49 See, for example, the case of Egbertus Gravers from Amsterdam. NA, VOC, 9375, 19. NA, VOC, 5912, f. 143. VOC Opvarenden: id-number 634924.

50 DAS voyage number: 1348. Dutch-Asiatic Shipping (DAS), 1602–1795, *EASY DANS*, https://easy.dans.knaw.nl, persistent identifier: urn:nbn:nl:ui:13-yng-6vb. Publicly available via: http://www.historici.nl/Onderzoek/Projecten/DAS. VOC Opvarenden: 1575734.

51 The ship *Huis te Zilverstein* was anchored before Portland between 6 and 29 March. DAS: 1393. VOC Opvarenden: 1578025.

52 DAS: 1655; 1656; 1657; 1660. VOC Opvarenden: 1606902; 1563086; 1563096; 1600766; 1601967; 1563097; 1631604; 1596562; 1563078; 1563098; 1603810; 1603214; 1607091; 1642927; 1645604; 1605768; 1639036; 1574552; 1633708; 1597314; 1598390; 1616366; 1618454; 1641658; 1644580; 1574247; 1604538; 1574249; 1597452; 1595666; 1574345; 1637724.

53 DAS: 1420. VOC Opvarenden: 1644186; 1616572; 1615918; 1624795.

54 Van der Chijs, *Nederlandsch-Indisch Plakaatboek*, VII, p. 787. Original: 'niet ontzien den dienst hunner betaals heeren te verlaaten en zigh in vreemden dienst te engageeren'; 'als alle plaatsen zynde, van waar de desertie naar vreemde natiën het frequentst en gemaklykst is.'

55 For evidence on the Coromandel coast and Surat, see: NA, VOC, 2966, 3025, 9733. For Bengal, see the paper of Titas Chakraborty presented at the session 'Leaving work across the world: Comparing desertion in early modern globalization, 1600–1800' at the ENIUGH Conference in Paris, September 2014.

56 Jelle van Lottum, *Across the North Sea: The Impact of the Dutch Republic on International Labour Migration, c. 1550–1850* (Amsterdam: Aksant, 2007); Van Rossum, *Werkers van de wereld*.
57 Van Rossum, *Werkers van de wereld*.
58 NA, VOC, 9375, 19.
59 NA, VOC, 9424, 48.
60 Van der Chijs, *Nederlandsch-Indisch Plakaatboek*, X, p. 895.
61 NA, Collectie Brugmans, 171, f. 99.
62 NA, Collectie Brugmans, 170. Letter from equipagemaster Blom, 30 October 1786.
63 NA, VOC, 9410, 18.
64 NA, VOC, 9420, 15
65 A.H. Bollemeijer, 'Demography of Batavia, 1689–1789', *EASY DANS*, https://easy.dans.knaw.nl, persistent identifier: urn:nbn:nl:ui:13-y0h-pdg (1989/2010).
66 NA, VOC, 9382, 9.
67 Van Rossum, *Werkers*, pp. 301–8.
68 NA, VOC, 9467, 13.
69 Phillip de Bertherand was recruited as a soldier in February 1753 in the Dutch Republic as 'Phielip Debertrand' from Luxemburg. NA, VOC, 13064.
70 Original: 'tusschen de posten Rijswijk en Noordwijk, bij off op het sogenaemde drosserspadt alwaer hij gev: verscheijde jongens welke daer passeerd heeft aengesogt om met hem alleen te gaen ten eijnde dat vuijle en boosaardig feijt te pleegen [. . .] almeede die jongens niet te kennen off te weten waer deselve thuijs hooren'.
71 NA, VOC, 9468, 26. For this case, see also Van Rossum, 'A Moorish world'.
72 NA, VOC, 9412, 16.
73 NA, VOC, 9411, 8.
74 NA, VOC, 9510, H, K.
75 NA, VOC, 9375, 23.
76 NA, VOC, 9515, 14.
77 NA, VOC, 9468, 23.
78 NA, VOC, 9355, 13.
79 NA, VOC, 9416, 59.
80 Van Rossum, *Kleurrijke tragiek*; Hendrik E. Niemeijer, *Batavia. Een koloniale samenleving in de 17de eeuw* (Amsterdam: Uitgeverij Balans, 2005).
81 NA, VOC, 9425, 123.
82 Niemeijer, *Batavia*, 200.
83 Matthias van Rossum, '"Amok!" Mutinies and Slaves on Dutch East Indiamen in the 1780's', *International Review of Social History* 58, Special Issue (2013), pp. 109–30.
84 Notably, the revolt on the *Slot ter Hooge* (slaves, 1783), *Java* (Chinese sailors and possibly slaves, 1783), and *Haasje* (slaves, 1790).

85 Arsip Nasional Republic Indonesia (ANRI), Dagregister van Batavia, 14 January 1715, 2542, ff. 32–3; 18 January 1715, 2542, f. 53; 19 January 1715, 2542, ff. 57–61. The Dagregisters are available online via www.sejarah-nusantara.anri.go.id/marginalia. Unfortunately, the scanned documents for these specific dates are in a very bad condition and very difficult to read.
86 Van Rossum, *Kleurrijke tragiek*.
87 Dan Sleigh and Piet Westra, *De opstand op het slavenschip Meermin* (Amsterdam: Uitgeverij Cossee, 2013).
88 Paul Truter, 'The Robben Island Rebellion of 1751: A Study of Convict Experience at the Cape of Good Hope', *Kronos: Journal of Cape History* 31 (2005), pp. 34–49; Van Rossum, 'Radjas'.
89 Van Rossum, *Werkers van de wereld*.

Between Worlds

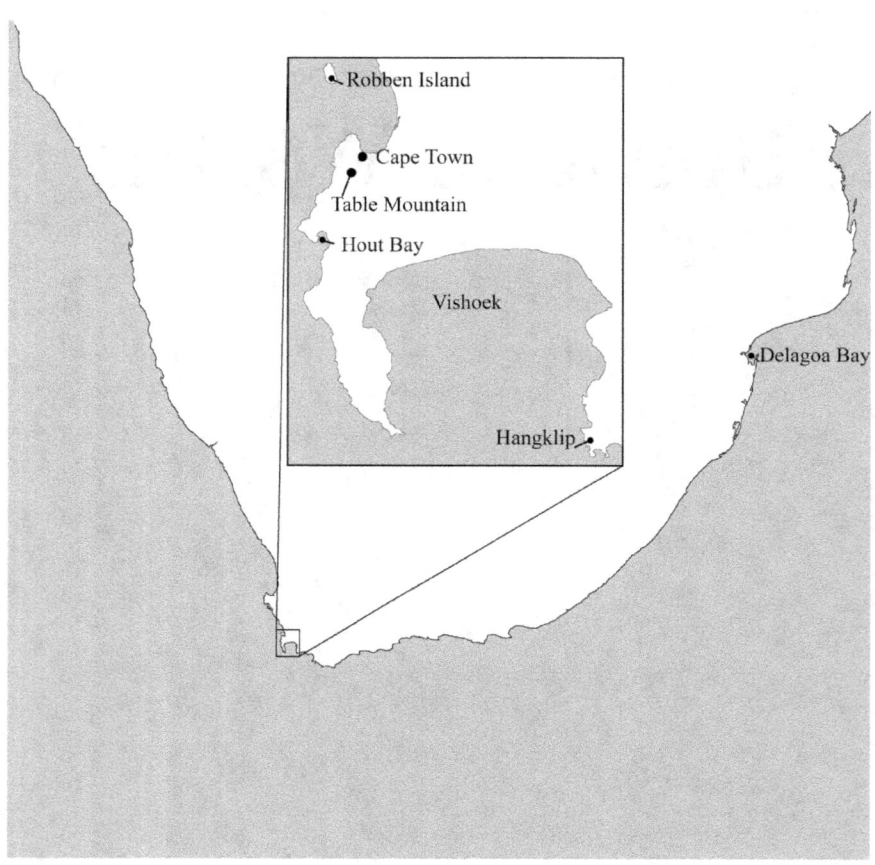

ILLUSTRATION 8 *Map of South Africa (Erik Odegard).*

7

Just Deserters:

Runaway Slaves from the VOC Cape, c. 1700–1800

Kate J. Ekama

An oath of blood

In late 1713 or early 1714, a group of enslaved men hatched a plan to run away from their respective masters. Knap een Deuntie, Tromp from Madagascar, Jeroen from 'the Malayan coast' and Thomas from Bengal were privately owned enslaved men who had been transported to the Cape, which was at that time under the control of the Dutch East India Company (VOC). It is unclear how the four men knew each other: they originated from different areas and belonged to different masters. Between them they decided to recruit some of their fellow slaves to join them in their escape beyond the Cape frontier, to the land of the Portuguese. They convinced Cupido from Batavia, Neptunis from Bima, Titus from the Cape, Joumat from Ternate, Januarij from Batavia, Jonas from Tranquebar and Pasqual from 'the Spanish West-Indies' to go with them. However, persuasion was sometimes insufficient. One of the enslaved men they tried to recruit – Anthonij from the Malabar coast – refused to join the band. Later, he claimed that he had been bound and abducted by Thomas, and thereby forced to go along with the runaways. Willingly or unwillingly, the enslaved men escaped to the agreed-upon rendezvous point. They took with them supplies for their journey: some of the group had stolen weapons and ammunition from their masters; Knap een Deuntie and Thomas had baked

260 *beschuit* (rusks) for provisions. Furthermore, in readying themselves for their escape, they committed to defend themselves should they be pursued and they swore an oath of loyalty to one another. They ate a piece of bread covered in blood to cement their allegiance. Thus prepared, they set out for the Piketberg with the intention of fleeing the colony entirely.

While on the run the enslaved men committed a number of serious crimes. Most likely in desperate need of sustenance, the group stole livestock from Khoikhoi *kraals* (corrals), including those of captains Prins, Couragie, Hanibal and Caesar. As was often the case, stock-theft and violence went hand in hand: on instruction from Tromp, a Khoikhoi woman was murdered and her daughter wounded by Titus and Cupido. It was at a Khoikhoi *kraal* that the runaways were tracked down by a VOC militia. As they had agreed, the group, probably numbering about eleven at that point, resisted arrest and a shoot-out ensued in which the soldier Jan Ghravesant and Khoikhoi man Jantie were killed. A number of the enslaved men, the instigator Tromp among them, took the opportunity to run away from the soldiers. At some point in the chaos of the encounter, Knap een Deuntie was shot dead, Anthonij gave himself up, Neptunis was taken prisoner and the enslaved man Balij escaped and was not recaptured. Tromp returned to his master. In the end, eleven enslaved men who had been part of the group were taken prisoner. They were all interrogated, sentenced and punished through the Cape Council of Justice.[1]

Like a flash of lightning illuminates a landscape, the legal proceedings against the eleven runaways provides information on the life and work of slaves as well as on patterns of desertion. In their interrogations, the recaptured runaways recounted, in different versions, why they ran away, their plans, and the course of their journey. The picture that emerges from the records is of an exclusively male, ethnically heterogeneous group led by Knap een Deuntie with Tromp as his second-in-command. Worden and Groenewald state:

> Although unusual in its scale and organisation, this episode was in one way typical of slave resistance in the VOC period. The slaves did not mount a rebellion against their owners, but rather sought to escape from them and from the colony. This was more characteristic of a slave society in its early stages, when slaves were all imported, and so aware of a world of freedom outside the Cape.[2]

While they were aware of that world, and had planned to escape to it, it is highly unlikely that any of the enslaved runaways in the group led by Knap een Deuntie and Tromp ever made it beyond the frontier. Knap een Deuntie himself was killed by the commando pursuing them. Eleven of his accomplices were taken prisoner and punished by the court. In the sentence Anthonij was treated leniently, an indication that his claims to have been abducted and not to have committed any crimes while on the run, were believed. His punishment was to watch the gruesome execution of Tromp, Cupido, Jeroen, Neptunis, Titus and

Thomas, as well as the beating of Joumat, Janaurij, Jonas and Pasqual, all of whom also had their Achilles tendon severed.[3] Of their number, two men were still at large at the time of sentencing and may have managed to escape entirely, namely Theunis and Balij. But being on the run was no easy task considering the hostile landscape, cold winters, and wild animals with which to contend, and most dangerous of all were the people runaways encountered – commandos, loyal slave herders, travelling burghers and the Khoi.

The story of Knap een Deuntie and Tromp et al. is not unique for the period of slavery at the Cape. The enslaved ran away from as early as the VOC began importing slaves. While the historiography of slavery at the Dutch Cape has grown since the 1980s and can now be described as a mature body of scholarship, much research remains to be done on desertion. In the sections which follow I will draw together some of the work on runaways which has already been done by historians of Cape slavery, and combine that with a new analysis of sentences and trial records to draw some conclusions regarding patterns of desertion during the eighteenth century. I will begin with an overview of the nature of slavery at the Cape under the VOC from the 1650s to the end of the eighteenth century. This will include some comments on the size and composition of the slave population at various times. In the second section criminal sentences will be analysed in order to quantify desertion – specifically, those recaptured. This leads to the conclusion that desertion was an overwhelmingly male phenomenon at the Cape. In the third section I argue that three types of running away can be seen in the criminal records of the Cape Council of Justice. Crimes committed combine with motives, destination and the accomplices slaves chose, to reveal three patterns: short-term absence; spontaneous individual desertion to escape punishment; and planned, collective desertion to flee beyond the frontier. The fourth section comprises a close analysis of a number of collective runaway dramas to elicit the characteristics of group desertion. In particular, I will consider the importance of persuasion and violence; group composition with regard to ownership and place of origin; the places where slaves could meet to hatch plans and put them into action; and finally creating group cohesion. The ethnic heterogeneity of the Cape slave population did not stop slaves from running away together. Slaves interacted with fellow slaves, convicts, soldiers and sailors in locations where they worked and socialized together which provided and created opportunities to make escape plans together too. In the fifth section I will consider the changing relationship between slaves at the Cape and the Khoi peoples whom they encountered. Over the eighteenth century there was a shift in the relationship which, simply put, can be seen as moving from sabotage to solidarity.

Characteristics of Cape slavery

From the outset, the Dutch East India Company officials involved in establishing the refreshment station at the Cape of Good Hope in 1652 realized their need for labour. To provision ships that called at the Cape en route to Asia required cultivation of quantities of fresh produce over and above that needed by the Cape population and garrison for sustenance. The VOC directors in the Republic (*Heren XVII*) had not envisaged the Cape as a slave society but the need for agricultural labourers to underpin burgher farming brought the question of slavery to the fore in the early years of the Cape settlement.[4] The local Khoi and San were not slave-owning communities and the Company chose not to enslave the local people; thus a slave society was created through importation.[5] The first shipments of slaves were landed at the Cape in 1658 when around 400 Angolan and Guinean slaves were disembarked. Desertion was a problem from the outset: a number of Angolan Company-owned slaves escaped in June 1658 and, despite the efforts of their pursuers, were never recaptured.[6] Desertion continued as long as there were slaves at the Cape. In fact, during the eighteenth century, the most common crime committed by slaves was running away.[7]

Initial slaving voyages sailed from the Cape up the west coast of Africa to source slaves. But the focus soon shifted eastwards, to the Indian Ocean where the VOC already had a well-established network of settlements and trading factories and insinuated itself into long-standing slave-trading networks in South and Southeast Asia.[8] It is well established that slaves at the Cape originated from a wide range of locations including Bengal, the Malabar and Coromandel coasts, Ceylon, the Indonesian archipelago, Mauritius, Madagascar and Mozambique. While shifts in sources of slaves for the Cape are difficult to pinpoint, it seems that the proportion of Asian slaves in the slave population shrank over the eighteenth century; African slaves imported from Mozambique and Madagascar made up the totals, with a small but growing proportion of Cape-born slaves.[9] The multiple provenance zones resulted in an ethnically heterogeneous slave population at the Cape. Historians have argued that this was one of the factors which precluded mass rebellion: there was no collective slave uprising at the Cape until the early nineteenth century. Rather, it has been argued, resistance was individual and was aimed at escaping the immediate situation of slavery rather than overthrowing the social order.[10]

This was perpetuated by continued importation, which was itself necessitated by high mortality rates and the fact that the Cape slave population was not self-reproducing.[11] The result was a small but growing group of locally born slaves and the continual presence of newcomers. Mainly due to importation, the slave population grew in the closing years of the seventeenth century, from about 300 enslaved men, women and children in 1687 to 891 in 1701. Over the course of the eighteenth century the population expanded into the thousands, numbering 14,747 in 1793.[12] Throughout this period, enslaved men significantly outnumbered enslaved women. According to Worden, it was during the 1790s, after more than a century of slavery at the Cape, that enslaved women first constituted more than 25 per cent of the adult slave population.[13] The imbalance in the sex-ratio was the result of the high demand for adult male slaves to meet the labour needs of burgher farmers and the Company.[14]

Slave labour was crucial to the Cape's economy. The enslaved laboured for private owners and for the VOC which was itself a slave-owner. In the arable region of the south-western Cape slaves laboured on wine and wheat farms; in pastoral zones and on the ever-shifting frontier slaves worked as shepherds and herders; on the farms and in the towns slaves also performed domestic service. In Cape Town in particular, the working of the port called for slave labour; skilled slaves worked as artisans; slaves tended their master's gardens and collected firewood among other tasks.[15]

Slave-holdings at the Cape were generally small. Records from 1750 indicate that 57 per cent of all burgher slave-owners owned between one and five slaves; 22 per cent owned six to ten slaves, and only 4.7 per cent owned more than twenty-five slaves.[16] Martin Melk, who owned one of the largest farms in the western Cape, owned over 100 slaves – an exceptionally large slave-holding in the eighteenth century.[17] In 1752, the VOC owned a total of 506 slaves. According to Armstrong, '[in] 1750 burgher slaves exceeded Company slaves by more than ten to one; in 1793 by almost thirty to one.'[18]

Both Company and privately owned slaves deserted their masters. Some of those who ran away succeeded in avoiding recapture for months or even years. In the early 1720s some runaways formed a maroon community which existed in the area of Hangklip on False Bay until 1737. Over the following decades of the eighteenth century and even into the nineteenth century slaves continued to use the area as a hideout.[19]

The most common crime

Desertion was the most common crime committed by slaves in the eighteenth century, as Heese has shown.[20] Yet, we know little about the number of slaves who fled by foot or by boat, the characteristics of desertion, when and how it took place, and how many were successful. Unsurprisingly, we know far more about those who were unsuccessful than those who were successful. Hundreds of slaves were recaptured and found guilty of desertion in the eighteenth century as the following analysis of sentences will show. But the criminal records provide access only to those who were unsuccessful in their bids to escape, that is, those who were recaptured. Because of this, quantifying desertion is no easy task. To date, no thorough quantitative analysis of recaptured slave runaways has been done for the Cape during the VOC period. Such an analysis would be necessary in order to ascertain how many enslaved runaways were recaptured, in specific years and how the number of recaptured changed over time in relation to other significant events and changes in the colony.

According to Bergemann's analysis of the criminal records of the 1730s (the criminal rolls and minutes) there were 169 cases of absconding, drosting and vagabondage as well as sixty-three counts of *aufugie*, together constituting 32 per cent of criminal cases in that decade. These were crimes generally associated with slaves, soldiers and sailors, as Bergmann points out.[21] But based on his data we cannot extract how many of those records relate to slaves specifically. His data do give an idea of the scale of desertion, which is the context in which slave desertion should be seen.

What follows is a quantitative analysis based on data drawn from the complete series of *sententien* (sentences) in the archive of the Cape Council of Justice.[22] Over 700 enslaved individuals were named in the sentences spanning the eighteenth century; those accused of desertion number over 400. There were certainly many more runaways in this period – both those recaptured and those who succeeded in evading the authorities. A sentence was not drawn up for every criminal case; thus we can be sure that there were far more runaways recaptured during the period than those named in the sentences but how many more we do not know for now.

There were 429 enslaved individuals against whom a sentence was passed for crimes including desertion during the eighteenth century. They are represented in Figure 7.1 which shows the number of individuals sentenced for desertion over the eighteenth century, distinguishing between slave men and women.

Considering the enduring imbalance in the sex-ratio of the enslaved population at the Cape, it is not surprising that the recaptured runaways named in sentences throughout the eighteenth century were predominantly male. According to the sentences, 412 men were found guilty of running away, constituting 96 per cent of the total; only seventeen women were sentenced for running away (4 per cent). While it is to be expected that

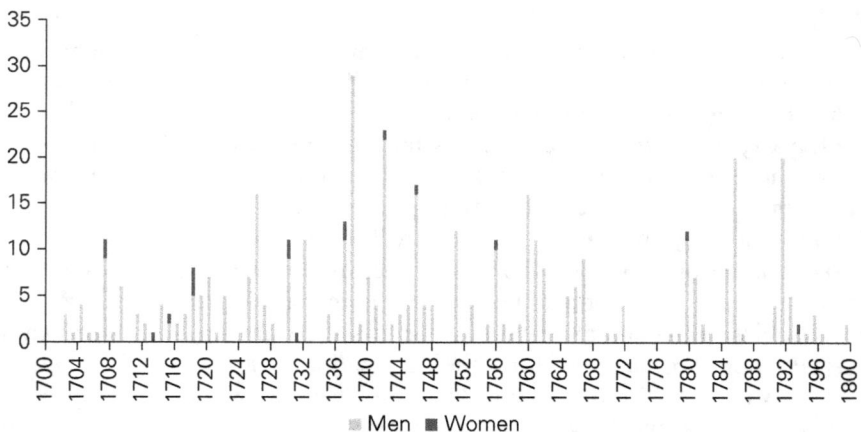

FIGURE 7.1 *Convicted runaways, Court of Justice Cape Town, 1700–1800*

Source: Council of Justice sentences against slaves in Hans F. Heese, *Reg en Onreg: Kaapse Regspraak in die Agtiende Eeu* (Bellville: West-Kaapianse Instituut vir Histories Navorsing, 1994).

male runaways were more numerous than female runaways, females are underrepresented in the data. Enslaved men constituted a far higher proportion of total runaways than can be explained by the imbalance in the sex-ratio. The difficulty of fleeing with children in tow may have been a factor that discouraged slave mothers from running away. Their position in the slave-owning household may be a second factor. The position of slave women within the slave-owning household has been the topic of much debate in the historiography of slave societies, the Cape included. The general line of argument goes that slave women were incorporated into the household in a position very different to slave men, primarily because enslaved women were entrusted with nursing and child rearing for the slave-owning family and in some instances entered into sexual relationships (willing or unwillingly) with the men of the house.[23] Familial bonds and position in the slave-owning household may begin to explain why fewer slave women than men ran away. We are left to conclude that desertion at the Cape was an overwhelmingly male phenomenon.

The slave population was not evenly distributed between town and countryside: the imbalance in the sex-ratio was probably not as extreme in Cape Town itself. It is likely that slave women constituted a higher proportion of the slave population in Cape Town because they were employed as domestic workers for Cape Town families and Company slave women resided in the Slave Lodge in the heart of the town.[24] A distinction should also be made between the arable districts and the pastoral areas. Working on the wine and wheat farms of the south-western Cape was a very different experience to working on the isolated sheep and cattle farms of the interior and shifting frontier. The details provided in the series of sentences do not allow a distinction to be made between urban and rural patterns of desertion but the type of household in which slaves lived and its location must have had an influence on the opportunities for running away which a slave could exploit. During the eighteenth century Cape Town grew significantly but it is unlikely that it ever offered urban runaways the same anonymity as a city like Batavia did.[25] Slaves from Cape Town needed to get to the edges of the town and beyond to limit the risk of being recognized and recaptured; they could not hide within the town itself.

Neither does the data in the sentences allow any analysis of when slaves ran away. Worden has suggested that it was more likely for slaves to desert during harvest season.[26] The season during which ships called in at the harbour presented slaves in Cape Town with a ready escape; Ross notes that not only did the majority of Company slaves who escaped between 1724 and 1747 do so in the first three months of the year, but 'what little information that there is seems to show that stowing away was the favourite way of casting off their bondage for those slaves who lived in Cape Town – or at the very least the most successful'.[27]

In this analysis the perpetrators of desertion have been differentiated to show the number of enslaved men and enslaved women who were named in the sentences for the crime of desertion. In the following section further differentiation will be made on the nature and duration of their desertion. This results in three patterns of running away during the eighteenth century.

Absence, desertion and escape: Identifying patterns at the Cape

In pursuit of runaways, I delved into the eighteenth-century criminal records of the Cape Council of Justice, led by three specific questions. The first of these questions was why – why did the enslaved run away? The obvious answer to this is to escape the condition of bondage in which they lived, which can be thought of as a bid for freedom. But the court records allow a closer look at some individuals' specific reasons for fleeing. For instance, Jeroen and Titus who joined Knap een Deuntie and Tromp's band of runaways in 1713–14 each stated that they had deserted because the *knecht* had turned against them.[28] Others in the same group claimed that they ran away because Jeroen, Thomas and others had promised to take them to a different country.[29] A second category of motivation was escape from punishment. A moment of crisis involving a crime precipitated flight.

The second guiding question regarded destination: where did those who ran away run to? At the heart of the choice was whether to remain in the colony or to flee it entirely. This question touches on the opportunities and constraints provided by the Cape landscape, as well as the vision of a wider world held by the slaves who sought to flee beyond the ever-expanding Cape frontier. Nigel Worden argues that during the eighteenth century slaves tried to escape from the settler environment. He identifies a 'slave geography':

> [A] landscape perceived and used by slaves in different ways from both that of their owners or that of the indigenous Khoi and San ... This landscape included the areas around and between settler farms, mountains in the heart of the colony, coastal and maritime environments as well as a vast and unknown terrestrial and maritime hinterland.[30]

According to Worden, it was only in the early nineteenth century that instead of escape, slave resistance took the form of attempted conquest of the settler environment.[31]

Within this 'slave geography', mountains played a central role as temporary refuges and meeting points.[32] For urban slaves working in Cape Town households, the port or gardens above the town, Table Mountain was easily accessible. As Worden writes, '[t]he mountain that symbolically and literally formed the core of the runaway slave's world was Table Mountain.'[33] Many slave men and women would have been familiar with the mountain geography and have spent some time on the mountainside themselves:

collecting wood was a task given to slave men, and slave women used the mountain streams for washing.[34] The Cape authorities were well aware of the presence of runaways on the mountain and were afraid of the links that could be established between slaves in the town and runaways on Table Mountain. According to Worden, Table Mountain was part of 'an underground runaway network that linked the urban and peri-urban core of the colony via Table Mountain to the wider Cape Peninsula and beyond'.[35] One of the places to which Table Mountain was connected via these networks was Hangklip, the site of the only maroon community known to exist at the Cape during the eighteenth century.[36]

The final question concerned accomplices – were slaves more likely to run away alone or in groups? If they ran away collectively, who did the enslaved choose to run away with? Of particular interest is what brought the individuals together and to what extent networks and contacts were revealed in the interrogations of recaptured runaways. Given the ethnically diverse slave population at the Cape in the period under examination, the role of ethnicity or place of origin is important to consider: specifically, whether or not it was more likely for slaves of the same ethnic background to band together and form somewhat ethnically homogeneous groups.

In answering the why, where to and who with questions outlined above, patterns emerge in which motives, destination and company combine in three different ways. I have found it fruitful to differentiate between three different types of running away, each of which consists of a cluster of characteristics. The first is *absence*: an enslaved man (or woman) ran away from his master temporarily, was not gone for more than a few days, most likely remained close-by his master's house or farm, and then returned or was returned to his master. During this temporary absence the enslaved man most likely missed work but did not commit any further crimes. Absence was dealt with within the slave-owning household, that is within the sphere of the master's power not the court's. Punishment was most likely a beating, performed in front of the other slaves by the slave owner, *knecht* or one of the slaves. It was in the master's interest to deal with absence himself because handing his slave over to the court meant relinquishing his power over his property and having to accept the sentence meted out by the judge. The punishment could deny him the slave's labour for a period of years or deprive him of his asset permanently if the slave was sentenced to a life of hard labour, banishment or capital punishment.[37]

It is likely that absence was common but because it was dealt with within the slave-owning household it is difficult to trace in the Company's court records.[38] There are incidental mentions of absence when the same slave later committed a crime for which he faced legal proceedings. An example should illustrate this point: Anthonij from Goa had been punished for being absent from Beatrix Verweij's farm. He claimed to have been given permission to go to collect some of his things from another farm. Having done that, Anthonij then went to the farm he had lived on before being sold to Verweij.

His intention was to visit the slave woman who was his 'wife'. But after Anthonij had been away two nights Verweij's *knecht* found him and took him back to her farm where he was punished. Either he did not have permission to be absent as he claimed, or he was away too long, or he was punished for going to the second farm for which he had not been given permission. The only reason this first absence was recorded was that Anthonij left Verweij's farm again eight days later, once again to go and see his 'wife'. His 'heart ached' when he saw her with another man, and he stabbed her in the abdomen, then ran away and tried to commit suicide in order to escape punishment.[39] Because of the stabbing and subsequent flight and suicide attempt, the first absence and punishment came to light.[40]

As Matthias van Rossum indicates in his chapter, differentiating between absence and desertion is not always straightforward. Conceptually, the difference lies in time-frame: absence is temporary and short term whereas desertion is intended to be permanent. As van Rossum rightly points out, punishment of slaves was divided between the household where the slave master exercised a right to punish slaves known as 'domestic correction' while the legal authorities would sentence slaves in criminal matters. Absence fell into the first category – masters punished their slaves for short-term absence when they returned or were returned to the household. From the criminal records of the Cape it becomes clear that desertion went hand in hand with other crimes and was punished by the courts.

Thus the second and third types of running away involved crimes other than the desertion itself and for that reason were dealt with in the Company's court. While runaways each had their own stories, their motives, destination and chosen accomplices combined with crime in distinct ways. The second type of desertion was collective, planned desertion by which the enslaved attempted to flee the colony entirely. In preparing for their flight the enslaved involved in collective desertion were likely to commit minor crimes such as theft: they stole weapons and food from their masters to take with them. Major crimes including murder and stock-theft were committed while on the run as the enslaved were not only desperate to prevent being betrayed by those with whom they crossed paths, but were also in dire need of provisions. The story of Knap een Deuntie, Tromp and their band of runaways which was recounted in the introduction to this chapter is an excellent example of desertion of this type.

The third type of running away was individual, spontaneous escape which was usually sparked by a moment of crisis – often a crime – from which the enslaved fled in fear of punishment. According to Worden, '[m]any desertions followed punishment'.[41] Because flight was unplanned, the runaway often did not venture too far from the slave-owning household. While this may have allowed continued access to provisions through theft or helpful slave contacts, it came with the high risk of recapture. From a time-period point of view, whether this kind of escape should be classified as absence or desertion is unclear and most likely varied from one slave to another.

The lines dividing these three types of running away are certainly blurry. Fluidity and contingency come to the fore in cases of runaways as key elements. Groups formed in an ad hoc manner as individuals who had run away out of fear of punishment or were absenting themselves banded together. These groups were formed and re-formed, thus one type of running away could become another, depending on the circumstances. The presence of runaways on the outskirts of Cape Town, in the mountains and at Hangklip meant that groups could form on the run. These ad hoc groups of runaways were always fluid: new deserters joined their ranks, some were captured, some returned to their master, some were killed, and groups split up.[42] The same was true of groups of slaves who chose to desert together. While the categories are not watertight by any means, they do help to distinguish patterns.

Group desertion

It might be assumed that slaves of the same background would be more likely to run away together, facilitated by a common language and perhaps the common goal of returning to their place of origin by land or by sea. It is clear from the court records that groups of runaways, however, were not only made up of individuals of different provenance, but also of those who were owned by different masters, confirming that opportunities for slaves to plan escapes certainly existed both in the town and farmlands. Using detailed case studies from the legal proceedings, the formation of and dynamics within groups of runaway slaves will be analysed.

Persuasion and violence

The Bugi slave September was not a runaway himself, but assisted runaways and had in fact planned to escape to the Xhosa with the gang he had been supplying with food and medical attention. September had agreed to recruit more Bugi slaves to join them on their escape. But it never came to that because the gang and a number of slaves who had assisted the runaways were killed by a commando and taken prisoner respectively.[43] Like September, other slaves agreed to recruit their fellows to join in escape plans. In some cases this was done by runaways who ventured back to Cape Town or the farms they had fled in order to persuade others to join them. In the group of slaves who stole a boat and sailed as far as Onrus, the plan was initially agreed upon between Isack and Baatjoe from Sambawa. As they had planned, when Baatjoe went into Cape Town he spoke to the slave man Damon from Batavia who not only agreed to go with them but promised that he would convince more slaves to join their journey up the coast.[44]

Similarly, enticing fellow slaves to run away was an important part of the escape plan executed by Knap een Deuntie and Tromp, as recounted at the beginning of this chapter. But as that same case makes clear, recruiting possible runaways did not always go smoothly – some slaves just said no, refusing to join the gangs of deserters. The danger of a slave who knew but was not part of escape plans informing on his fellows was very real, and perhaps led Thomas to abduct Anthonij and force him to join Tromp's group.[45]

A number of cases also highlight the tension between slaves who had run away from their masters but returned to raid farms on the one hand, and the loyal slaves who remained on the farm on the other hand. The loyal slaves in fact resisted the raiders, choosing instead to protect their master's property against the runaways. This dynamic came to the fore in the testimony of Scipio from 'the Coast' regarding an attack on his owner's farm carried out by a group of runaways led by Aaron from Bengal, who belonged to the same owner, widow Ten Damme.[46]

For about six months in 1725–6 a gang of more than twenty runaway slaves, led by Aaron and April from Sumbawa, raided farms in the Blaauwberg, Tygerberg and Koeberg areas surrounding Cape Town. One night the slaves targeted widow Ten Damme's farm and in particular, the *knecht* Adam van Dijk who was staying in the house on the farm, with a number of the widow's slaves, including Scipio. Perhaps to the attackers' surprise, they received no help from the slaves inside the house, despite the fact that they clearly knew each other and belonged to the same owner. In fact, talking to the *knecht*, Scipio reportedly described the attackers as 'not good people'.[47] Both sides were armed, and a gunfight ensued. Adam van Dijk managed to escape into the night and while some of the gang pursued him, much to Aaron's disappointment they could not catch him. Scipio and the other slaves in the Ten Damme house at Brakke Fontein feared for their lives, worried that the gang would murder them. They were spared; the runaways were focused on the *knecht*, and after he got away the gang stole all of van Dijk's possessions as well as food and firearms from the house. They tried to persuade Scipio and the other slaves on the Ten Damme farm to join them in their flight, but Scipio and the others refused. What is so fascinating about Scipio's account is the clear picture we see of two groups of slaves – one loyal to their owner and ready to protect her property alongside the *knecht,* and one gang of runaways, some of whom belonged to the same owner, who had been at large for some time already, were armed and dangerous and adding to their list of crimes. Scipio did not clearly articulate a reason for not joining the gang of runaways but that he felt no affinity with them is clear. Not only did he think of them as bad people – at least that is what he told the authorities – but he refused to join them when he had an easy opportunity to run away.[48]

The lack of sense of solidarity among slaves evident in Scipio's account as well as the kidnapping of Anthonij recounted above is further reinforced by the frequency with which slaves helped to capture runaways and informed their masters of deserters in the vicinity.[49] The common situation of bondage and oppression seems not to have been enough to foster bonds between slaves. Ties between slave runaways were created in other ways, which will be explored later in the context of group cohesion.

Group composition: Origins and owners

Pinpointing the composition of a group of runaways at any given moment is very difficult because fluidity and contingency played important roles in life on the run and because slaves who ran away together were not necessarily recaptured together. From a close analysis of seven groups of runaways some comments will be made here on the composition of the groups regarding the place of origin of the slaves named and their owners. I will base the analysis on these two factors in order to test whether slaves of the same provenance or owner were more likely to desert together than slaves of diverse backgrounds and ownership.

Slave toponyms were widely used at the Cape and are often the only indication of where a slave was from. The researcher always needs to bear in mind that such toponyms were not always accurate, and in some cases may indicate a port through which the slave was transported or had previously resided, rather than his place of origin. As already noted, the slave population at the Cape was ethnically heterogeneous. Slave-holdings were generally small, both in towns and on the farms, and the likelihood of a unit of slaves all being of the same origin was very small.[50]

Of the sample of seven groups, place of origin is a significant factor in two of them. In 1751 a group of ten slave deserters was recaptured. Their leader, Tallone, was a Bugis convict who was serving out his sentence at the Cape. The runaway group was made up of men all of whom were imported from Southeast Asia. Of the ten slave men involved, five were 'from Bugis', and one each from Bali, Macassar, Padang, Sumbawa and Mandar. Only two of the slave men were owned by the same man: the Bugis slave Jephta and the Balinese Baatjoe were owned by Hermanus Hermans. All the other slaves had different owners.[51] In this group, place of origin appears significant – the leader and 50 per cent of his slave followers were 'from Bugis'.

Another group in which Bugis background played a significant role was the Smuts family murderers and their accomplices. Of the slaves sentenced in 1760 some were found guilty of desertion (and murder), the rest of aiding deserters. The case documents name twenty-seven slave men involved in the case in some way or other. The origins of nineteen of the slave men involved were recorded: thirteen of the slaves were imported from Southeast Asia and of those, by far the majority were 'from Bugis' (69 per cent). One of the slaves found guilty of aiding the absconders was September 'from Bugis'. He was seen not only as a traditional healer but also as a leader of Bugis slaves at the Cape. He had some knowledge of traditional medicine and was able to write. The fact that he was one of the nine Bugis and had agreed to convince more Bugis slaves to join the runaways speaks to the important role of place of origin in this runaway drama.[52] Within the group of twenty-seven slaves named, there was also a clear subgroup of slaves owned by widow Heuning – eight in total. They had been providing fugitives with assistance and had agreed to join the runaways but had not yet done so. Among the others there were no more than two slaves belonging to each owner.[53]

A clear instance of the importance of common ownership is the Company slaves who were sentenced in 1735. Four slave men were recaptured and convicted. One of them, Kinsa from Madagascar, revealed that they had been part of a large group of runaways living on Table Mountain. At one point, the group numbered fifteen and they were all, like Kinsa, Company-owned slaves. Of the four recaptured, no toponym was given for two, and of the other two Kinsa was from Madagascar and Claas was Cape-born. Kinsa gave no insight into the origins of the other group members who had not been recaptured, but it is highly unlikely that the whole group was Malagasy and locally born. That all fifteen slaves in the group Kinsa spoke of were owned by the Company indicates that ownership may have been an important factor in this specific runaway group.[54]

The importance of ownership is also present in the band of eleven runaways led by Tromp from Madagascar that was recaptured in 1714. Four men were owned by Nicollas Oortmans, three by Johannes Swellengrebel, two belonged to widow Diepenauw, and two to Christoffel Esterhuijs. Looking at their toponyms we see they originated from South and Southeast Asia, Madagascar, the Cape and one man from the Spanish West Indies. No more than two of the eleven men had the same toponym. Again, common ownership was a more important factor in the composition of this group than place of origin.[55]

In 1786 a group of six slave runaways was recaptured. The men belonged to six different owners and were recorded with six different toponyms.[56] Clearly something other than common origin or a single owner united this group.

From this sample of cases it can be concluded that common origin was not a defining feature of groups of slave runaways. The ethnic heterogeneity of the Cape slave population did not preclude cooperation between slaves in bids to desert their masters. Neither does a single owner seem to be a factor on which groups formed. But ownership did have an impact on the opportunities slaves had to meet fellow slaves, it influenced the location and type of their work and, because of those two factors, it shaped at least in part the kinds of opportunities slaves could create and exploit for running away.

Meeting places

Slaves of the same owner had opportunities to speak together and hatch plans, whether it was in a Cape Town house or working on the farms or cattle posts in the surrounding areas. But slaves created and were presented with opportunities to meet slaves belonging to other owners. In terms of degree of mobility and relative freedom, a distinction should be made between Cape Town and its hinterland – slaves in Cape Town itself had a different range of opportunities for interacting with fellow slaves and free people which must have affected opportunities to and characteristics of escape. Ross states: 'The diversity of occupations [in Cape Town] and the normal relationships of the town allowed a great amount of contact between slave and free, in the pub as well as in the workplace.'[57] As already discussed, differentiating between urban and rural patterns of desertion at the Cape is problematic. But what is clear is that slaves were not restricted to working within the slave-owning household, nor were they limited to labouring only for their master. This shaped opportunities for desertion.

Slaves could perform labour outside of the slave-owning household. For instance, some slaves worked in their masters' gardens in and around Cape Town.[58] Others, such as Aron from Madagascar, were sent out onto the slopes of Table Mountain to collect wood. Table Mountain was an important meeting point where slaves could meet other slaves as well as slave runaways. When Aron was sentenced in 1737, he was found guilty of two crimes – aiding runaways, and running away himself. The two crimes took place years apart. In his confession Aron described in detail his encounter with Leander Boegies, leader of the Hangklip maroon community. At the time Aron was owned by widow Admiraal and he went out to search for wood on Table Mountain along with fellow slave Januarij. Januarij had clearly been in contact with Leander before – he not only knew that Leander was in the area that day, on Table Mountain, but had also received some money from him to use to buy flint-stones. Januarij passed the task and the coins on to Aron who purchased the flint as soon as they went down the mountain. The following day Januarij and Aron met up with Leander to hand over the six flint-stones which had been bought for him. At their encounter Leander was accompanied by two other slave runaways and had firearms with him, clearly ready to defend himself when necessary. Aron's confession included no further references to contact with Leander or the maroons.

Years later, in early 1736 by which time Aron was in his late twenties, he absconded from his owner, then Paul Jourdan. His confession did not include his motive, but he was accompanied by slaves from Rio de la Goa. They headed for the beach and made their way around False Bay to the Gordon's Bay area, then known as Vishoek. They stayed there for a while, with other runaways. But Aron decided to leave the group because he saw some of the runaway slaves eating snakes. On his journey he encountered other runaways, including one slave man he recognized from having met on Table Mountain with Leander Boegies years before. After a few days Aron was on the move again, and made his way back to the Cape. It is not clear whether he returned to his owner or if he was caught, but he was turned over to the authorities. He was found guilty of desertion and aiding deserters, and sentenced on 28 March 1737.[59]

The practice of hiring out slaves allowed slaves of different owners to meet while they worked together.[60] Isack and Baatjoe from Sambouwa who featured in a plan to escape to the Xhosa by boat met while working as coal burners in Hout Bay. Isack was owned by Isack de Villiers but had been hired out to Christiaan Victor, Baatjoe's owner.[61] Wine and wheat farmers at the Cape hired additional slave labour during peak periods, and some slave artisans were also hired out. Worden notes that slaves were also loaned out to others, especially to the slave-owner's family members. Furthermore, on some occasions the VOC 'ordered' privately owned slaves to labour on the Company's works.[62]

It was not only through their labour that slaves interacted with others: despite the fact that it was against the law for slaves to meet in taverns and on the streets of Cape Town, they certainly did. These were two of the places where slaves were recruited as runaways and where recruits met up to plan their escapes. The men who sailed to Onrus provide the perfect example: Baatjoe recruited Damon out in the streets of Cape Town, and the designated meeting point for the runaways was the tavern run by Jan Holst. The nine men met in the tavern and remained there until evening, then one by one proceeded from the tavern to the flagman's house where they had agreed to congregate again. From their second meeting point they made their way to Hout Bay together and the rest of their unsuccessful escape unfolded.[63] In the towns slaves gambled and drank with fellow slaves, soldiers and sailors as is clear in the numerous ordinances against such behaviour.[64] Worden states that 'cross-racial socialising was well-established in the tavern culture of early Cape Town, where Asian and African slaves, free blacks and Chinese traders and exiles associated with soldiers and sailors'.[65] A picture emerges of the urban world of the slaves, interacting with each other and free people, with a degree of mobility and range of actions. In such circumstances slaves had opportunities to hatch escape plans with individuals of different owners and from diverse backgrounds.

In some cases slaves also ran away with non-slaves, such as the group led by the convict Tallone discussed above. Nigel Penn has written about the *droster* gangs, some of which were composed of slaves and Europeans who banded together while on the run.[66] He argues that after 1740 such groups became less common: 'the expansion of the colony would seem to have had a transformative effect on the composition of *droster* gangs'.[67] Runaway groups were far less likely to include Europeans, who could easily find work on the frontier farms.[68]

Creating cohesion

The band of runaways led by Tromp from Madagascar was a heterogeneous group in terms of both place of origin and owner, and the men ranged in age from twenty to forty years old. Forming strong bonds between them was important to the group, as their actions demonstrate. Early on in their escape they took steps to cement the bonds between them. As already mentioned in the introduction to this chapter, the men swore allegiance to each other by eating blood-soaked bread. In his interrogation, Thomas from Bengal was asked specifically whether or not he also partook of the blood oath: 'If the prisoner also ate there ... a piece of bread covered in blood and took an oath of allegiance to each other in order to do the Dutch every harm and never to return to them?'[69]

Forging strong bonds between the group of runaways was important to another band, consisting of six runaways each of whom originated from a different location and was owned by a different person. No indication is given in the records of how the six men knew each other or how they planned their escape, but plan they most certainly did. The runaways August from the Cape, Andries (Calcutta), Jonas (Batavia), Damon (a Buginese), Saripa (Mandar) and Welkom (Ternate) undertook their journey to the land of the Xhosa only after very careful and creative planning. August and Jonas had already had one failed runaway attempt in which they took a forged letter claiming that they had their owner's permission to travel to the interior, but along the way they lost it and were recaptured.[70] For their second escape attempt August and Jonas and their four accomplices acquired another forged permission letter, in duplicate this time; they acquired charms and powders which they believed would protect them from all evil, including recapture; and they stole weapons for further protection. Once thus prepared the men swore loyalty to one another, promising to die together 'which allegiance sworn by them here (i.e. at the Cape) was subsequently confirmed by them with the oath of loyalty as often as they could obtain wine on their way'.[71] The men were bonded in their common beliefs as well as by their oaths to one another.

Analysis of the sample of seven groups of runaways indicates that groups did not cohere around a single commonality – place of origin or a common owner. Slaves of different ethnicities, owned by different people, banded together to plan their escapes. The ethnic heterogeneity of the Cape slave population did not create divisions between slaves that could not be overcome. While it may have influenced interaction between slaves and therefore alliances for desertion, it was not the deciding feature of group composition. The places at which slaves met – locations of labour and socializing – can be identified as significant determinants in how groups of runaways were formed and escape plans put into action.

From sabotage to solidarity: Encounters between runaways and the Khoi

Over the course of the eighteenth century the relationship between the enslaved population at the Cape and the local Khoi and San peoples changed. This was in no small measure due to the incorporation of the Khoi into the Company's labour system.

Slaves on the run encountered local Khoi and San peoples who, the slaves may have hoped, would accept them into their autonomous communities. The VOC tried hard to avert this: 'the company', Penn writes, 'worked hard to ensure that the neighbouring Khoikhoi would return colonial property [namely, runaway slaves]'.[72] The Chariguriqua became known as a community willing to welcome runaways. The Company made them suffer for it – commandos were sent to the Chariguriqua under the guise of trade but intent on recapturing runaways whom they harboured. In case the Chariguriqua were not compliant, the commando was instructed to take one of their leaders or some women and children as hostages and return with them to the Castle.[73]

Slaves were most certainly not assured of assistance and accommodation from Khoi they encountered.[74] Penn argues that already by 1700 the Khoi were 'refugees from the colony' who were likely to view runaways as intruders and destroyers of their way of life.[75] There was no sense of a common enemy to unite slaves and Khoi; violence and animosity characterized encounters between them. Khoi workers were loyal to their masters, reporting suspected runaways and sightings of deserters, and taking part in commando raids sent against them. In particular, Khoi men familiar with the Cape landscape were used as trackers for such expeditions.[76]

Over the course of the eighteenth century the position of the Khoi at the Cape changed as they were incorporated into the Company labour system in a position not unlike the slaves, and in some cases even worse.[77] During the same period the frontier of the colony was expanding which was detrimental to the Khoi and meant that fugitive slaves had to flee further to reach the sparsely inhabited areas beyond Company control. Areas which were at the frontier, or even beyond in the early eighteenth century, became part of the colony over the century. As these changes took place, the violent nature of runaway-Khoi encounters diminished. By the early nineteenth century, Khoi workers supported and were involved in the attempted overthrow of the colony led by Cape Town slave Louis of Mauritius. Worden characterizes the 1808 uprising as 'a significant change of slave tactic, a deliberate bid to capture and overturn core colonial space rather than to escape from it'.[78] That Khoi supported the uprising is evidence of how the relationship between them and slaves had changed since the early eighteenth century: Worden argues that 'class solidarity was replacing the earlier conflicts between slave runaways and Khoi herders'.[79]

Conclusion

Slaves ran away for a variety of reasons, to diverse destinations, both singly and in groups of differing composition. But through the specificity of individual cases patterns emerge. The first conclusion that can be drawn is that during the eighteenth century slave desertion was an overwhelmingly male phenomenon. The imbalance in the sex-ratio – which was heavily skewed towards the male – is only part of the explanation for this occurrence. A further factor to consider may be the position of enslaved women in the slave-owning household as distinct from the position of enslaved men. On the other hand, perhaps the slave women who ran away were more successful at remaining on the run resulting in fewer slave women being recaptured, but it is unlikely that sources exist to explore this line of reasoning.

I argued that patterns in motives, destinations and accomplices are intricately linked. Three types of running away can be discerned. The first category was absence, which was dealt with by the master outside of the Company's legal system. It is therefore difficult to trace in the legal sources. The second type was planned, collective desertion. Slave runaways prepared for their escape, often had a specific destination in mind, recruited other slaves to join them, and committed minor crimes of theft in preparation for their journey. Groups of slaves were far more likely to commit major crimes of stock-theft, assault and/or murder in order to get supplies and remain hidden while on the run. The third type was slaves who fled to avoid punishment and did so spontaneously and alone. Because their flight was unplanned, they were more likely to remain within the colony where they could steal food to sustain themselves. These categories are useful to see how motives, destination and accomplices congealed in overarching patterns in combination with crimes but the categorizations are blurred by the way that groups formed and re-formed while on the run.

An analysis of a small sample of groups of runaways seems to indicate that the diverse origins of slaves at the Cape did not hinder cooperation when it came to running away and remaining on the run. Groups of slaves of diverse origins existed. While ethnicity may have influenced slave interactions it was not the defining feature of groups of runaways – neither in the sense that it was the foundation on which groups were based nor that it hindered cooperation among slaves. With this in mind, the contacts that slaves formed with their fellow slaves as well as free people were very important. Slaves at the Cape certainly had the opportunity to interact with slaves belonging to other owners in locations where they laboured and socialized. Social contacts could be the foundation of escape attempts. Locations including Table Mountain and taverns among others facilitated such contacts.

While slaves did act together in deserting their masters they were not assured of assistance from fellow slaves, nor from the Khoi and San. Encounters between runaway slaves and the Khoi changed over time from violence and hostility – due to the twin factors of agreements to return runaways and a sense that runaways threatened their way of life – to solidarity in the 1808 uprising. Future research on desertion could fruitfully be directed to discerning whether or not a similar development can be seen among the slave population. The court records attest to the fact that slave runaways were betrayed by fellow slaves and that when gangs of runaways attacked homes and farms they encountered fierce resistance from loyal slaves who protected their masters' property. Whether or not slaves were less likely to be betrayed by fellow slaves towards the end of eighteenth century than in the early years remains to be seen.

The spectres who hover in the background of this analysis are those individuals who – like Tromp van Madagascar's fellow runaways Theunis and Balij, and Hangklip maroon leader Leander Bugis – successfully evaded recapture. How did these runaways survive on the run? Did any of them successfully reach the Xhosa peoples beyond the frontier? How many individuals successfully escaped slavery? We cannot currently answer these questions, but of the existence of successful runaways we can be sure.

Notes

1 Nigel Worden and Gerald Groenewald, *Trials of Slavery: Selected Documents Concerning Slaves from the Criminal Records of the Council of Justice at the Cape of Good Hope, 1705–1794* (Cape Town: Van Riebeeck Society for the Publication of South African Historical Documents, 2005), pp. 21–42.

2 Ibid., p. 21.

3 Ibid., pp. 31–2.

4 Nigel Worden, *Slavery in Dutch South Africa* (Cambridge: Cambridge University Press, 1985), pp. 6–7. On the introduction of slavery at the Cape see also: Victor de Kock, *Those in Bondage: An Account of the Life of the Slave at the Cape in the Days of the Dutch East India Company* (London: George Allen & Unwin, 1950); James C. Armstrong, 'The Slaves, 1652–1795', in Richard Elphick and Herman Giliomee (eds), *The Shaping of South African Society,1652–1820* (Cape Town: Longman, 1979); Robert Ross, *Cape of Torments: Slavery and Resistance in South Africa* (London: Routledge & Kegan Paul, 1983); Karel Schoeman, *Early Slavery at the Cape of Good Hope, 1652–1717* (Pretoria: Protea Book House, 2007).

5 According to Worden, Jan van Riebeeck proposed enslaving the Khoi in 1654 but the Heren XVII rejected the idea because enslavement of indigenous populations was forbidden. Worden, *Slavery in Dutch South Africa*, p. 7.

6 Schoeman, *Early Slavery*, pp. 56–64.

7 Hans F. Heese, *Reg en Onreg: Kaapse Regspraak in die Agtiende Eeu* (Bellville: West-Kaaplanse Instituut vir Historiese Navorsing, 1994), p. 23.

8 See Markus Vink, '"The World's Oldest Trade": Dutch Slavery and Slave Trade in the Indian Ocean in the Seventeenth Century', *Journal of World History* 14:2 (2003), pp. 137–46.

9 Worden, *Slavery in Dutch South Africa*, pp. 46–8. See also Armstrong, 'The Slaves', pp. 76–84.

10 This argument is well established in the literature. See Ross, *Cape of Torments*, pp. 3–5; Nigel Worden, 'The Environment and Indian Ocean Slavery', workshop organized at the Indian Ocean Studies Center, McGill University, Montreal, April 2011.

11 Worden, *Slavery in Dutch South Africa*, p. 52.
12 Ibid., Table 5.1, p. 53.
13 Ross, *Cape of Torments*, p. 16, p. 46; Worden, *Slavery in Dutch South Africa*, p. 52.
14 Worden, *Slavery in Dutch South Africa*, p. 52.
15 Robert Ross, 'The Occupations of Slaves in Eighteenth-Century Cape Town', *Studies in the History of Cape Town* 2 (1980), pp. 1–14.
16 Armstrong, 'The Slaves', pp. 96–8.
17 Worden, *Slavery in Dutch South Africa*, pp. 57–8.
18 Armstrong, 'The Slaves', p. 86.
19 Robert Ross's research on the composition and dynamics of the slave runaway groups at Hangklip remains the most thorough account of the maroons. According to Ross there was no continuity between the maroon community of the 1720s to 1730s and those who lived at Hangklip around the turn of the century. He argues convincingly that the area remained a favourite for runaways throughout the eighteenth century and into the nineteenth. Ross, *Cape of Torments*, pp. 54–72, pp. 122–4.
20 Heese, *Reg en Onreg*, p. 23.
21 Karl J. Bergemann, 'Council of (in)Justice: Crime, Status, Punishment and the Decision-Makers in the 1730s Cape Justice system' (unpublished MA thesis, University of Cape Town department of Historical Studies, 2011), Crime frequency table p. 12, pp. 13–14.
22 Heese published a list of the individuals named in sentences in the appendix to *Reg en Onreg*. I first extracted all the sentences against slaves and then selected only those in which desertion was among the crimes listed and put these into a database. This forms the basis of the quantitative analysis in the section. A significant drawback of the series is that sentences were not drawn up in every case. Neither historians nor legal scholars who have used the sentences have yet discerned the rationale behind it; it remains unclear why certain cases have sentences and others do not.
23 Shell has argued that 'slave women were not only brought into the bosom of the family, so to speak, but also actually became in a literal sense the bosom of the settler family'. Robert Shell, *Children of Bondage: A Social History of the Slave Society at the Cape of Good Hope, 1652–1838* (Hanover: University Press of New England, 1994), p. 304. It should be noted that Shell's arguments regarding patriarchy and paternalism at the Cape have been disputed by Robert Ross as well as Patricia van der Spuy.
24 Worden, *Slavery in Dutch South Africa*, pp. 53–4.
25 Eric A. Jones, 'Fugitive Women: Slavery and Social Change in Early Modern Southeast Asia', *Journal of Southesat Asian Studies* 38:2 (2007), p. 217.
26 Worden, *Slavery in Dutch South Africa*, p. 126.
27 Ross, *Cape of Torments*, p. 76. The slaves Jan from the Cape and Jacob from the Cape each succeeded in reaching the Dutch Republic but when they returned to the Cape in Company employ, were arrested and found guilty of desertion. Worden and Groenewald, *Trials of Slavery*, pp. 285–8, pp. 302–5.

28 *Knechten* were hired by farmers as overseers. Usually, they were in direct authority over slaves. *Knechten* were usually European men who were or had been in Company employ, especially soldiers. Worden and Groenewald, *Trials of Slavery*, p. XIII. Jeroen's motivation was recorded in the sentence against all eleven of the recaptured runaways. Worden and Groenewald, *Trials of Slavery*, p. 39.

29 Ibid., p. 40.

30 Worden, 'The Environment and Slave Resistance', p. 1.

31 Ibid., pp. 1, 18.

32 Ibid., pp. 7–10.

33 Ibid., p. 7.

34 Ibid., p. 8.

35 Ibid., pp. 9–10.

36 Ross, *Cape of Torments*, pp. 54–72.

37 Worden, *Slavery in Dutch South Africa*, p. 127.

38 Heese makes the same point. Heese, *Reg en Onreg*, p. 83.

39 Worden and Groenewald, *Trials of Slavery*, pp. 83–95. Anthonij was sentenced to stand beneath the gallows with a rope around his neck. He was then beaten, branded, put in chains for two years and returned to his mistress, Verweij.

40 Another example of absence coming to light because of other crimes was an accusation of murder by a slave against his owner in which the slave claimed that one of his fellow slaves was severely beaten as punishment for being absent, leading to the slave's death. Ibid., pp. 65–72. Worden notes that there were cases of slaves being flogged to death once recaptured and one slave who claimed he would rather be shot than recaptured. Worden, *Slavery in Dutch South Africa*, p. 127.

41 Worden, *Slavery in Dutch South Africa*, p. 127.

42 For example, the case against Achilles 'from the West Coast' et al. in 1760 reveals these dynamics. Worden and Groenewald, *Trials of Slavery*, pp. 355–84.

43 Ibid. September 'from Boegies' was one of the men who assisted the gang of runaways who murdered Michiel Smuts and his family in their Cape Town home in 1760. It is a complex case with rich and voluminous records. See also Ross, *Cape of Torments*, pp. 19–20.

44 Worden and Groenewald, *Trials of Slavery*, pp. 250–63.

45 An example of this is Jan from Ceylon who did not tell his fellow slaves on the farm that he planned to run away with a gang of deserters, specifically because he feared they would inform his master and so betray him. Heese, *Reg en Onreg*, p. 78.

46 Ibid., pp. 75–7. Worden and Groenewald, *Trials of Slavery*, p. 101.

47 Worden and Groenewald, *Trials of Slavery*, p. 105.

48 Ibid., pp. 101–6.

49 There are many examples of this, one of which was the Achilles 'from the West Coast' gang – infamous for the Smuts family murders – who were ratted on by slaves. Ibid., pp. 355–84.

50 Worden, *Slavery in Dutch South Africa*, p. 3, p. 93. Martin Melk, who owned one of the largest farms in the western Cape, owned over 100 slaves, which was exceptional in the eighteenth-century Cape. Armstrong's analysis of the size of burgher slave-holdings in 1750 shows that only a small group of slave-owners owned more than twenty-five slaves, precisely 4.7 per cent of all slave-owners. Far more common was owning between one and five slaves (57 per cent) and six to ten slaves (22 per cent). Armstrong, 'The Slaves', pp. 96–8.

51 Worden and Groenewald, *Trials of Slavery*, p. 288.

52 Ibid., p. 355.

53 Ibid.

54 Ibid., p. 119.

55 Ibid., pp. 21–42.

56 Ibid., pp. 537–56.

57 Ross, 'The Occupations of Slaves', p. 12.

58 Worden and Groenewald, *Trials of Slavery*, pp. 133–9.

59 Ibid., pp. 139–43.

60 On hiring additional slave and Khoi labourers on wheat and wine farms see Worden, *Slavery in Dutch South Africa*, pp. 20–1.

61 Worden and Groenewald, *Trials of Slavery*, pp. 250–63.

62 Worden, *Slavery in Dutch South Africa*, pp. 25–6, 87–8. In Colombo, the VOC hired slaves from private owners. Kate J. Ekama, 'Slavery in Dutch Colombo: A Social History' (unpublished MA thesis, Leiden University Institute for History, 2012), pp. 10–11.

63 Worden and Groenewald, *Trials of Slavery*, pp. 250–63.

64 K. M. Jeffreys, *Kaapse Argiefstukke: Kaapse Plakkaatboek, 1652–1707*, Vol. 1 (Cape Town: Cape Times Limited, 1944), pp. 46 (6/8 Desember 1658 – Verbod teen dobbelspel), 107–8 (11/12 Desember 1669 – Verbod tten die verkoop van sterke drank . . .), 227 (2 Januarie 1687 – Generaal Plakkaat). Ordinances such as these were reissued during the Company period at the Cape.

65 Nigel Worden, 'Strangers Ashore: Sailor Identity and Social Conflict in Mid-18th Century Cape Town', *Kronos* 33 (2007), p. 81.

66 Nigel Penn, *Rogues, Rebels and Runaways: Eighteenth-Century Cape Characters* (Cape Town: David Philip Publishers, 1999), pp. 73–99.

67 Ibid., p. 91.

68 Ibid., pp. 91–2.

69 Worden and Groenewald, *Trials of Slavery*, p. 35 [Interrogation of Thomas, Article 21].

70 Ibid., pp. 537–56.

71 Ibid., p. 550.

72 Penn, *Rogues, Rebels and Runaways*, pp. 74–5.

73 Ibid., p. 75.

74 On slave–Khoi relations see also Ross, *Cape of Torments*, pp. 38–53.

75 Penn, *Rogues, Rebels and Runaways*, p. 75.
76 The recapture of August from the Cape and others who were sentenced in 1786 involved Khoi, most likely as trackers. See Worden and Groenewald, *Trials of Slavery*, p. 554 n. 17.
77 Richard Elphick, 'The Khoisan to c. 1770', in Richard Elphick and Herman Giliomee (eds), *The Shaping of South African Society, 1652–1820* (Cape Town: Longman, 1979), pp. 33–5; Robert Ross, *Beyond the Pale: Essays on the History of Colonial South Africa* (Hanover: Wesleyan University Press, 1993), p. 166.
78 Worden, 'The Environment and Slave Resistance', p. 15.
79 Ibid., p. 16.

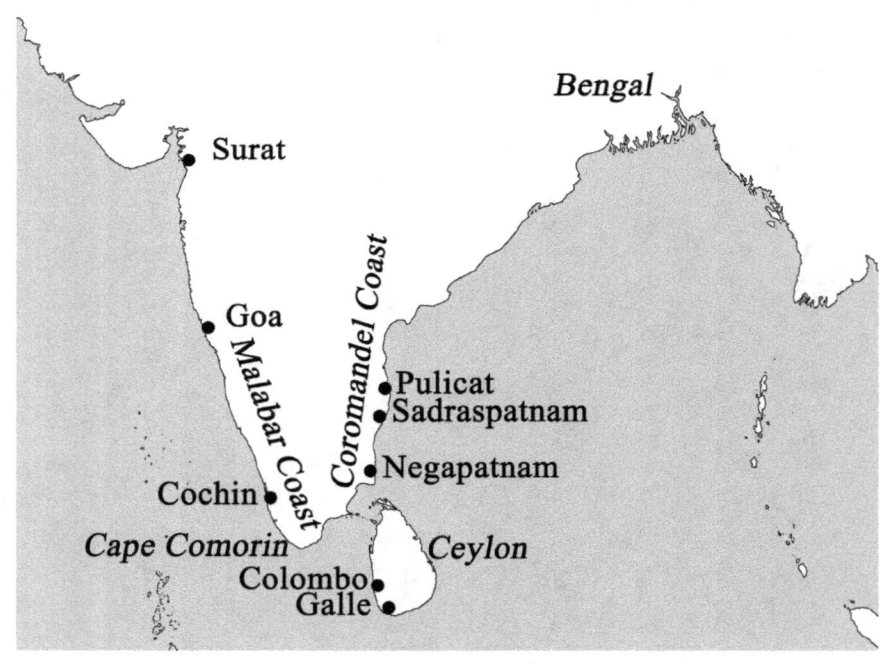

ILLUSTRATION 9 *Map of South Asia (Erik Odegard)*.

8

From Contracts to Labour Camps?

Desertion and Control in South Asia

Matthias van Rossum

Open countries, closed forts

'The country here is open and our men, who cannot always be kept locked up, can run away as easily as in any other place in India when they have a day off.' In his memorandum of April 1781, governor Adriaan Moens analysed the problem of desertion at the Malabar coast. Instructing his successor, he complained that 'desertion is an evil, which it seems impossible to put a stop to in this place'.[1]

Just as desertion was central to the concerns of the elites of trading companies around the world, the topic has not escaped the attention of historians who have dealt with the history of European expansion and Euro-Asian interactions in South Asia. Although the phenomenon has not yet been fully scrutinized, various historians have noted that desertion was widespread and had an important impact. According to Gijs Kruijtzer, 'desertion was especially prevalent in South Asia'. He explains this with the fact that 'VOC settlements and trading posts were often close to English, French, Danish and Portuguese establishments' and to the 'large demand for European military labour and expertise from the Indian courts'.[2] In her study of Cochin, Anjana Singh states that 'the problem of desertion was acute'. She remarked that 'many European newcomers in Fort Cochin were replacements for the ones who had deserted'.[3]

Desertion was not prevented by ethnic or national loyalties. On the VOC fort in Cannanore, Binu John Mailaparambil concludes that the recruitment of soldiers 'from various European nationalities', especially Germans, 'created trouble as there was a risk that these soldiers might abscond to other European settlements nearby'. This was only partly related to the multi-national character of the workforce of early modern trading companies. Mailaparambil notes that there 'were also instances of desertions by Dutch soldiers'.[4] In his extensive history of the Arabian Seas, Barendse makes a stronger statement, claiming that there was no loyalty towards the VOC, especially among its foreign workers. 'Of the twenty-three soldiers fleeing the VOC's garrisons in Malabar in 1751', he explains, 'not a single one was Dutch.'[5]

The response of the VOC has been assessed in different ways. Barendse emphasizes the draconian character of the punishments. He refers to the historian of VOC law J.G. Schmitz, who employed the characterization 'medieval barbaric sentences'.[6] Barendse refers to the case of corporal Albrecht Taughtenbein from Siegen (Germany) who deserted from the Company in Ceylon and was sentenced in Cochin to be 'lashed with the cord until death, and then hung on the gallows on the public execution place' 'to serve as an example for others'. Other deserters were hanged or branded, publicly lashed and put to labour in chains on the public works.[7] As we have seen in other contributions in this volume, such sentences were common in trials against deserters. Mailaparambil contextualizes this by explaining that since desertion was a criminal offence 'these renegades had severe punishments meted out to them'.[8] Singh argued, however, that the severe labour shortages meant that 'from time to time' 'a general pardon for all deserters from the Malabar Command was granted'.[9]

The VOC was not the only European power facing the issue of desertion. The Portuguese were continually hit by waves of desertion in their settlements, especially Goa. According to Barendse, some sixty men deserted from the fleet from Lisbon, while being anchored before Goa in 1759 – this was a desertion rate of 14 per cent upon arrival of the fleet. The East India Company faced severe losses through desertion as well, but it also made use of high desertion rates among competitors, employing the many deserters from the Dutch and Portuguese settlements. It is reported that in the second half of the eighteenth century, the EIC even sent 'a professional recruiter, a freebooter named Joachim Friederich Müller, to Goa who would receive a premium for any Portuguese soldiers he enticed fleeing the flag of Aviz; the British ships were already stationed at Vengurla to whisk them away'.[10]

Neither severe punishments nor general pardons could 'stem the tide of desertions in Kerala' and, it can be added, in the rest of South Asia. As Barendse notes, 'a great many voted with their feed [sic] and escaped'.[11] Faced with continuous waves of desertion, companies were forced to develop practices to counter desertion that were more refined than public punishment or pardons alone. This chapter will explore the dynamics of control that came into being in South Asia in response to the widespread desertions. In order to do so, it will first study the dynamics of desertion, both individual and collective forms, and its socio-economic and political context. After this, it will study the measures that were employed as well the effects of these mechanisms of control.

Desertion in South Asia

The region of South Asia held a central position in the early modern global dynamics of desertion. A short overview of the region, although from a somewhat Dutch imperial perspective, might help to see the structural character of desertion in this region. In Surat, one of South Asia's main port cities, European trading companies lost many workers to desertion, especially soldiers and sailors. In the years between April 1757 and May 1758, for example, in total thirty-two employees deserted from the factory and the ships of the Dutch East India Company. Reportedly, they all found employment with 'foreign nations', 'except for the sailor Pieter Davidsz, who went to the Moors'.[12] In April 1759 it was again reported that at least thirty-two employees of the Company had deserted from the factory and from four ships anchored there, mostly soldiers, some sailors and petty officers.[13] From April 1759 until the end of April 1760, in total 103 VOC workers deserted at Surat, consisting of eighty soldiers, twenty sailors, a trumpeter, an artisan and the petty officer in charge of provisions.[14] From April 1760 until mid-June 1761 only nine employees deserted, consisting of five soldiers, one corporal, one sailor, one assistant and one smith.[15]

As Surat was only a small trading port, only a dozen merchants and other VOC personnel were stationed there. The number of deserters must be considered as very high. This can be partly explained by the fact that many of the deserters fled from the VOC ships that sailed to Surat regularly from Batavia and from or via other settlements. In the years 1757–58 and 1758–59, some seven to eight VOC ships visited Surat yearly. Taking into account the number of personnel on these ships, the desertion rate seems to have been around 5 per cent.[16] For the period 1759–60, the desertion rate was much higher, possibly even between 15 and 30 per cent.[17]

European trading companies faced similar waves of desertion in Bengal. As a region of economic importance, there was a large demand for labour, making it easy for European workers to find employment outside the service of European trading companies. Simultaneously, European trading companies heavily competed each other in their search for personnel, systematically hiring deserters from competitors. For the VOC, Bengal – as well as Surat – was one of the main places where the Company lost its workers. The period in which the VOC operated a direct shipping connection from the Dutch Republic to Bengal, roughly between 1754 and 1780, provides an interesting perspective. Workers arriving on ships from Europe were much more likely to desert in Bengal than the workers arriving in Batavia and Ceylon, the two main destinations for VOC ships sailing from the Dutch Republic. Desertion rates in Bengal – within the first six months after arrival – varied from 2 to 5 per cent, with regularly lower and also higher desertion rates, ranging from 1 to even 10 per cent. In Batavia and Ceylon, desertion rates among newly arriving workers within their first half-year in Asia, were much lower, ranging between 0.2 and 1 per cent.

TABLE 8.1 *Desertion rates of European workers, within first six months after arrival (1755–75)*

Year	Batavia	Bengal	Ceylon
1755	0.1%	2.1%	0.1%
1756	0.3%	2.0%	0.0%
1757	0.5%	2.2%	0.4%
1758	0.4%	4.9%	0.8%
1759	1.0%		0.2%
1760	0.4%	0.0%	0.0%
1761	0.7%	1.8%	0.6%
1762	0.6%	0.9%	0.2%
1763	0.8%	4.9%	0.0%
1764	0.6%	0.8%	0.4%
1765	0.6%	0.4%	0.8%
1766	0.3%	4.0%	0.0%
1767	0.3%	3.9%	0.3%
1768	0.5%	2.0%	0.2%
1769	0.6%	3.8%	0.0%
1770	0.5%	9.8%	0.2%
1771	0.5%	2.2%	0.0%
1772	0.4%	0.9%	0.2%
1773	0.2%	2.7%	0.2%
1774	0.3%	1.1%	0.2%
1775	0.6%	3.7%	0.2%

Source: VOC Opvarenden (2012).

It was not only European workers who deserted in these regions. In Bengal, for example, Indian sailors also were reported to desert. More often than in Batavia, desertion by Indian sailors in Bengal took the form of a collective act. In 1698, a whole crew of Indian sailors, probably from the region itself, deserted here from the VOC ship *Susanna*. This may have been related to treatment or payment issues. A year later, the same crew was reported to have forced their unpaid wages from the VOC ship *Haas*, while it had run aground in the Chittagong river.[18]

Desertion by European and Asian workers, at least in the case of the VOC, was not less in the southern parts of South Asia – the Malabar and Coromandel coasts and Ceylon. In 1759, desertion from the settlements on the Coromandel coast amounted to twenty-nine European and Asian workers in total. Most of them ran from the ship *Lycochton* while it was anchored before Bimilipatnam (ten); the rest were stationed in the settlements and forts of Bimilipatnam (three), Nagapatnam (eight), Pulicat (four), Sadraspatnam (two) and Jaggernaijkpoeram (two). Again, soldiers were in the majority as eleven European and three Malayan or Javanese soldiers deserted. Sailors were a good second (seven), followed by tambours (two), a cook's mate, a corporal and a quartermaster.[19] The *Oosterling* or Asian soldiers were stationed at Bimilipatnam. They deserted together or shortly after one another. Laban from Malacca deserted on 10 May, Samat from Batavia and Madi from Malacca deserted on the 10 June.

Most of the Coromandel deserters not categorized as 'Asians' came from varying places in Europe. Some of them, however, were actually locals, being Company servants from European or Eurasian descent from the various settlements on the coast. In Pulicat, for example, three of the four deserters came from the VOC settlement Nagapatnam, located on the Coromandel coast, just a few hundred miles south. The soldier Dominicus Jansz of Nagapatnam deserted on 1 March, followed by Pieter Thierij de Saintvannel from Rhenis on 8 March. Tambour Fredrik Amoor from Nagapatnam deserted on the 17th of the same month. His fellow-tambour Michiel Jansz from Nagapatnam only left on 2 October.[20]

Some of the deserters had a long history of leaving and entering the service of the Company. The sailor Hans Paullusse van der Tak from 'Scharloh' (Germany), for example, was noted to have deserted from Sadraspatnam already on 6 December 1758. Hans apparently went inland from Sadraspatnam, probably along the Palar river as he was held up at the British fort at Chingleput. 'On the condition of the Agreement', he was returned on 22 January by the commander of the fort together with two deserters who had deserted in previous years or were not from settlements on the Coromandel coast.[21] Hans managed to desert again on 18 March 1759. In October of the same year, Hans apparently 'returned by his own initiative, amongst a few foreign deserters'. On 23 January 1760, he deserted from Sadraspatnam for the third time.[22]

Company workers often deserted individually, or in small groups of two to five runaways. Only occasionally did they desert in larger groups. Although

VOC personnel did not hesitate to escape from urban working environments, the military posts outside urban settlements especially provided opportunities to desert. These posts seem to have been more favourable to group-wise desertion. From the post at Cape Comorin, for example, nine of the ten deserters in 1742 seem to have deserted with someone else. The soldiers Ustatius Benedictus de Lanoij from 'Annas' and Jan Jacob Christiaansz from Gelhausen fled on 2 August. The sailor Evert van der Heijden from Hoorn and the quartermaster Willem Terwel from Zutphen fled on 27 September. Somewhat earlier, on 19 July, a group of five mainly German and French solders deserted.[23] From 'the camp at Climanoer', two Dutch gunners deserted in late March. The camp 'at Totocatte' was hit by an even larger wave of desertion. First, the soldier Jan Roedolf Goedknegt from 'Hogerswe' left on 3 April. The next day, three soldiers deserted: Jan Christiaan Schoghart from Luneburg, Fredrik Lots from Coblenz and Judocus van Mellefilloost from Gent. On the 8 April, the deserters were joined by a group of five German and Dutch soldiers. Early May, a group of six German, Dutch and French soldiers fled from the 'pagger [post] Zeeburg at Paroe'.[24]

Local Asian workers were not afraid to desert either, sometimes in even bigger numbers than European or non-local Asian workers. 'With regard to the Lascorins', governor Van Gollenesse accounted in his memorandum on the Malabar coast in 1741, 'some 300 of them deserted during the last campaign, and many of them took the Company's muskets with them.' These local soldiers, often converted to Catholicism, were subjects of the Company. At least a number of them were arrested and 'thrown into prison'. Most deserters were granted a pardon, due to the need for military labour. An exception was made for 'the leader and those who took with them the Company's muskets', who were brought before the Court of Justice, 'in order to make an example for the future'.[25]

For Ceylon the rich historical data provides interesting insights into differences between different groups of workers, desertion patterns and other dynamics. The corvée labour system in place in the VOC-controlled areas of coastal Ceylon produced pressures and constraints on labour that – although with completely different dynamics – produced similar criminalization of labour relations for contract and slave labour (see Chapter 6 on labour and desertion under the Dutch East India Company). The local workers who were obligated to perform such corvée duties, such as the 'Moors' and 'Chittijs' of Galle, Matura and Belligam, regularly remained absent or fled.[26] In 1750 and 1751, for example, the workers that had 'run away' made up some 4 per cent of the 236 'Moors', who were obligated to perform *oeliam* services in Matura, consisting mainly of transport work and Company services. This did not include the workers unable to work, amounting to another 3 per cent of the corvée workers.[27]

Remaining absent from work also served as part of collective strategies of negotiation and representation of interests. In September 1699, it was reported in the Council of Coromandel in Negapatnam that 'part of the *patnams*, referring to the inhabitants of villages, 'had withdrawn themselves from the service of the Honourable Company and had hidden themselves here and there in the outer city'.[28] The conflict arose after four local inhabitants, named Thomelan, Bartholome, Antonij and Patilo, were convicted of theft and exiled to the Cape of Good Hope. The leaders of local communities, as well as 'several women, had very compellingly requested' to recall the verdict of exile. This seems to have been a method of collective bargaining, flirting with the threat of the absence of even larger numbers of workers.

Discussing the matter, the members of the council considered 'whether, in case the mentioned request was declined, it should be feared that the rest of the patnams would also disappear' – 'they feared this unanimously'.[29] The 'beach master' Gerrit de Veer reported that 'he had only been able to find people for four *chialengen*' (local boats), resulting in 'very slow' unloading and loading of the ships. The problems arising in the unloading of the four VOC ships, with two more ships to be expected, were considered more important than the principle that 'the delinquents were not to be relieved from their banishment'. The collective absence of the local village workers was successful: the four convicts were released.[30]

Deserters' afterlife

The local workers of the *patnams* withdrew from work, but probably returned to their homes and work after their demands had been met. Most European and Asian workers, however, did not try to return after escaping Company working environments. Many of the deserters remained fugitive. The widespread patterns of desertion and the options available to the runaways were related to a number of the socio-economic characteristics of the region.

South Asia was densely populated and relatively urbanized, but simultaneously offered extensive rural areas or wild terrains with sometimes rather favourable natural conditions. Several agricultural and manufacturing industries marked South Asia as an economically important region with, for example, saltpetre, opium and silk coming from Bengal and Surat, pepper from Malabar, textiles from Coromandel and cinnamon from Ceylon. South Asian merchants traded throughout and beyond the region, maintaining connections with Persia, China and the Indonesian archipelago. European trading companies, competing for trade and influence, maintained numerous trading factories, military posts and settlements. European (and Eurasian) private traders became increasingly important, with British protected private ('country') traders almost entirely dominating intra-Asiatic trade towards the end of the eighteenth century. In combination with the vast armies and various projects of South Asian rulers, this created a world with competing authorities, a large demand for (skilled) labour, at least some degree of mobility (although future research should explore that further) and opportunities to run away and hide.

It was not uncommon for runaways to seek employment elsewhere. European deserters often tried to find work at other European trading Companies. The VOC employees at Coromandel were mentioned to run to 'the English, French, Danish or other Nations on this Coast of Coromandel'. It was also possible to find work with Asian employers. The soldiers Jacob Floderase from Rijnen (probably Rheine) and Johannes Bijer from Bergin deserted from Jaggernaikpuram (present-day Kakinada) on 1 June. Two weeks later, it was reported they were hiding in 'Peddapoer under protection of the prince Annandarasoe who was reigning there'.[31] For most of the deserters, there were no reports on what happened to them after their desertion.

In the late eighteenth century, Adriaan Moens mentioned that the English increasingly attracted runaways from the Dutch East India Company. Local rulers at the Malabar coast seem to have been important in earlier decades, but in his memorandum of 1781 Moens stated:

> The king of Cochin does not take them into his service any longer and I do not believe the king of Travancore keeps our deserters, except it may be some individual who has special skill or can be of special use. If he kept a good number of our deserters, we should certainly know of it. So our deserters go as a rule to the English at Anjengo, Tellichery or Mahe. But what is astonishing is that there have even been occasional desertions to the Nabob, although it is sufficiently known among the men how badly his Europeans are treated and paid.[32]

Singh notes that 'there were many opportunities for them to make a living outside the fort walls, independent of the VOC and these were especially attractive to the men in the military wing of the Company'.[33] Employment with private traders in local or intra-Asiatic shipping may have been attractive especially for sailors. Soldiers and other workers could often find employment by finding work with other European trading companies or by 'entering the service of Indian kings and nobles became Muslim and established families'. Kruijtzer notes that 'cities like Hyderabad had special streets for their European military personnel as early as the seventeenth century' and that these runaways 'may have been among the more successful migrants with respect to progeny'.[34]

Contracts, administration, punishment

The measures aimed at limiting desertion are often to be found in either fierce punishment or forgiving attitudes towards runaways that are willing to return to their work. And indeed, these extremes were important practices in attempts to control potentially very mobile workforces. The VOC, for example, made it common practice to sentence absent runaway contract workers to hard punishments. The deserters of the Coromandel coast in 1759, for example, were sentenced during their absence to severe beatings through the practice of *spitsroeden* and to ten years of forced labour in the rope factory on the island of Edam, the convict island near Batavia.[35]

At the same time, workers willing to return to work, especially in situations involving large-scale desertion or labour scarcity, were sometimes pardoned. Together with ensuring more reasonable working conditions, such pardons could be important answers formulated by employers to the challenges of desertion. In his memorandum, Moens claimed that he made sure 'that the men here are not fleeced or done out of their due' in order to make sure this would not encourage desertion. These claims on 'good' or 'reasonable' working conditions were often sustained or strengthened by discourse or identities that were intentionally fostered by employers to maintain morale. Moens explained that he 'had the good fortune' that:

> some deserters have written from the English, French or from the Nabob, on promise or in the hope of pardon, of hearing them tell their comrades that the great cry of better pay with other nations is all *bosh*, for it ends in their only getting half of what is announced, and also that they had everywhere been treated badly and nowhere so well as when in the service of the Honourable Company.[36]

The interplay between the threat of harsh punishments and the (often) actual pardoning attitude towards former deserters was only part of the story. Underlying the everyday dynamics of control, labour and mobility were several crucial mechanisms that were more refined than the two extremes of draconian punishment and welcoming pardons. A range of regulations and mechanisms created ways through which control was exercised over Company workers, increasing incentives to remain in Company service, or tying them down to working environments and Company territories.

Part of these mechanisms focused on exercising control through the payment of wages. European contract workers were paid their wages only after return in Europe. During their contract period in Asia, they were only able to receive advances up to six months of the wages earned every year.[37] These advances were paid half in cash and half in kind. The Company tried to ensure itself against the desertion of (Asian) contract workers through similar payment arrangements. For Javanese sailors, it was suggested limiting the monthly advances to only half their wages, but this idea was discarded on the grounds that this would actually stimulate desertion instead of decreasing it. Early in the 1780s, the VOC recruited eleven Ambonese sailors on the condition that 'they, one for another, had to agree to bail for each other, in order to pay for the damages for the Company, in case of death or desertion'.[38] The Chinese officer that recruited Chinese sailors for the VOC in the second half of the 1780s was made responsible for similar repayments in the case of 'death or absence' of the sailors.[39]

The administration of the Company was important in supporting wage payments as well as related measures of control. The administration of the workforce, of course, was crucial, providing insight into which workers should be present in specific workplaces. Workers who went missing were immediately looked for. A small note, signed in the Castle of Batavia on 29 February 1736, provides some insight into the relation between administration and control. The note referred to Egbertus Gravers from Amsterdam, a sailmaker, who had been transferred on 5 January 1735 from the ship *Meijnden* to the equipage wharf. 'Thereafter people have been searching for this man, because he was not to be found on the wharf or elsewhere, while his account still ran in the Batavian books.' This resulted in a reference in the so-called *drossersrolle* – the list with names of employees who were in hiding or who had deserted. When Gravers was later found hiding on the *chialoup*, *De Deka*, he was accused of 'continuous attempts at desertion'.[40]

Despite these measures through administration and payment, desertion of both European and Asian sailors remained a serious challenge. Other forms of control were created, often more physical and direct, to reinforce the binding regimes for workers in both contract and other labour relations. Hierarchy and direct relations of command in working environments played a crucial part in everyday life. From the early seventeenth century onwards, bosses and 'other overseers' of the working environments of the Company, for example, were ordered to make sure that 'her servants, slaves and coolies were present and working immediately after the clanging of the bells, which means from six to eleven in the morning and from one to six in the afternoon'. The overseers were ordered to see that their workers 'would maintain their work without stopping'.[41]

Confining and dividing

The effect of these hierarchies in working environments was strengthened through restrictions that bound workers to their job, criminalizing mobility and labour offences. VOC ordinances made a clear distinction between the 'bonded' period of service and the period of 'freedom' that began once the contract ended. In 1764, referring to Asian 'sailors or soldiers released from their service' in Batavia, it was noted that 'most natives who gained their freedom are unable to pay for the costs of their letter of freedom' – the licence was literally referred to as a *vrijbrief*. In order to make sure former employees were in possession of this letter, distinguishing them from workers still in the service of the Company, it was decided to provide sailors and soldiers with a less expensive letter at the end of their service.[42] A similar arrangement was in place for European workers, who were repatriated to

Europe after their contract ended, unless they applied for the status of *vrijburger* (free burgher) for which they needed a written licence from the Company, recorded in the so-called *vrijboeken*.[43]

These regulations concerning letters and passes were not without effect in everyday life outside working environments. At the gates of Company settlements and at the *boom*, the toll and water gate, travellers, slaves, *vrijburgers*, Company workers and others where checked by the soldiers of the guard. Whereas slaves were to have 'passes' in order to be able to work outside the city, 'free' persons were to have letters or passes to prove their freedom. Slaves could be locked up when they wanted to go in or out of the city without a pass or whenever they were suspected of being absent without permission or other things.[44] In turn, Europeans and Asians outside of Company service needed passes to get around and even to get certain work. In 1759, it was decided in Batavia that 'private and foreign' captains were only allowed to recruit sailors who 'could prove their freedom and provide a letter of consent from their chief'. The *sjabandaar* was ordered to keep an administration account and to 'let no other hired people pass the *boom* [water gate] than those who have met aforementioned requirements'.[45]

The control over its workforce was never complete, but the impact of the combination of legal and physical control was significant. This was not only the case for slaves, but also for contract workers. Contract workers themselves compared their position in the service of the Company to that of more profound relations of coercion. Sometimes they even made the comparison to slavery to describe their life and work under the Company. A German *Valet-Lied*, a song celebrating the departure from Batavia and the return to Europe, mentioned: 'Setzt alle eur Seegel bey, Wir sind nun loss der Sclaverey' – 'Hoist the Sails, We are now free from Slavery'.[46]

The German Company servant Elias Hesse may have preserved this song in his published travel account, because he himself found there were important comparisons between slavery and the contract labour of sailors in his seventeenth century: 'Nichts kan man wohl einer Sclaverey füglicher vergleichen als das Schiffs-Leben, wenn man der Schiffer und derselbigern Anhang Gnade Leben muss' – 'Nothing could one compare better to Slavery than Life aboard a Ship, when one has to Live at the Grace of the Shipper and his Followers.'[47] On the punishments sailors and soldiers had to endure in the service of the Company at sea and on land, Hesse stated that they 'in solcher langwirigen Sclaverey gar crepiren' – 'in such lengthy Slavery perished completely'.[48] He was not alone in referring to the concepts of slavery and service in relation to contracted wage labour. Even the storehousekeeper of Surat, Heinrich Hüsserl, wrote after deserting the VOC and taking service with the EIC: 'I hold myself to be a slave to no one: only a servant of the Honourable Company.'[49]

Another crucial element may have added to this discourse comparing the position of contract workers to that of slaves and other coerced workers. As offences in the domain of labour and mobility were criminalized, the means through which disobedience was dealt with could take on extreme forms. This was visible in the legal prosecution. Except for the highest classes of employees, such as Heinrich Hüsserl, all types of lower workers could expect severe and cruel punishments, with additional extreme levels of cruelties for slaves. Even more crucial, however, may have been the visible and sometimes extremely fierce methods that were used to guard and recover workers.

Divide and rule was an important mechanism within these methods; not only between different (groups of) workers, but also between local populations and the (mainly migrant) workforce of European trading companies. The first approach, playing off different groups of workers, was based on both divisions between different occupations, such as soldiers and sailors, and also different ethnicities. Soldiers were placed as guards and gates, on ships and near other workplaces. Sometimes these methods were more explicit. In the middle of the eighteenth century, for example, the EIC and VOC became so cautious that they did 'not risk even a single European soldier or sailor to walk the streets without giving him some native soldiers along to watch over him'.[50] Employing local soldiers to watch over European workers in public spaces combined the factors of occupation and ethnicity to create division and control among the workforce.

The VOC was also familiar with even cruder methods of repressing desertion. Moens explained in his memorandum how European (and perhaps non-local Asian) workers were effectively isolated on Company territories. Company workers were forbidden to go beyond a certain distance alone and a reward of ten rupees was promised to everyone who brought in workers who had wandered off. Moens stated that this reward was paid '*de facto* to the native who catches a sailor or a soldier at a certain fixed distance; which reward is taken out of his pay. The people know what the distance is, and if the men go out of bounds, they are caught by the natives, who look out greedily for a chance.'[51]

Moens described the system in more detail as follows:

> So, as soon as one of the men is found absent at roll-call or otherwise, or is suspected of having deserted, it should immediately be reported and not be postponed till the next morning. For the administrator can then, before the gates are closed, let it be known to the people outside that a sailor or soldier is absent, and the news spreads among the Malabaris like wild-fire. The people at once go in search, even if it is late at night, just as if they were going a-hunting; it has happened that a crowd of people went out and brought the absentee back in a few hours, and divided the money amongst themselves. The offering of this reward results in a good many being brought back, who would have gone astray through drunkenness or desert if they had not been caught.[52]

Moens advised his successor in 1781 that 'this system should be rigorously maintained', claiming that he knew 'of no better remedy against desertion than to continue the present system'. Even workers who are 'caught out of bounds sober and from all the circumstances apparently without intention to abscond' should not be dealt with by a pardon, but should 'be made to pay the reward' as 'he knows what the bounds are and, being sober, does wilfully what he knows he must not do'. This was crucial to keep 'the zeal and diligence of the Malabar people, who keep a look-out for deserters for the reward's sake'. Moens was careful to ensure that this zeal would not 'cool, and at last be altogether extinguished'.[53]

This practice was described for the Malabar coast, but it is not unlikely that it was employed around other Company settlements too. The methods of the VOC resemble many of the practices used in eighteenth-century Prussia (described in Chapter 2 by van der Linden). In later periods, similar methods were used in colonial settings to retrieve runaway convicts. The British effectively organized local populations against convicts at the Andaman islands, resulting in a system of 'runaway-hunting' targeting deserting convicts.[54] Around the plantations of Assam rewards were given to local communities bringing back deserters.[55] Similar practices were in use in the Dutch East Indies around the mines of Sumatra at the beginning of the twentieth century. As a result, the contracted migrants and colonial convict workers employed in the mines could be killed by local populations when they ran away.[56]

Conclusion

The divide and rule policies exercised by the VOC and by later colonial authorities must have had an important impact on the relations between European and non-local Asian workers on the one hand and local Asian communities on the other. The visibility of difference on which some of these more explicit mechanisms of control relied, especially the use of native guards and the systems of runaway-hunting, must have increased racialization and tensions between groups. At the same time, the large-scale desertions in economically thriving regions such as South Asia seem to indicate that it was actually possible to run, hide, wander around and find new work with European trading companies, local rulers and elsewhere.

Although draconian punishments and strikingly welcoming pardons have received most attention in the historiography on desertion for South Asia, it is crucial to emphasize that the practices employed against desertion were more complex and refined. The mechanisms of control and discipline that were created, adapted or reinforced in response to the continual flow of desertions focused on regulating labour relations as well as social dynamics. Systems of passes, gates and guards formalized social control and regulated access to and from corporate and public spaces.

These physical and practical regulatory regimes built upon elements of coercion and control that were an integral part of labour relations, especially in the case of corvée labourers, slaves and contract workers. In this sense, desertion and its countermeasures were intimately linked with the transformation of urban and work environments into increasingly closed and controlled spaces. As a result, already in these early modern global situations, one could argue that there are indications that the control exercised through contracts and other coercive elements in labour relations was reinforced by developments creating what one could perhaps see as resembling forms of labour camps.

Notes

1. 'Memorandum on the Administration of Malabar by the right Worshipful Adriaan Moens, 18th april 1781' in A. Galletti et al. (eds), *The Dutch in Malabar: Selections from the Records of the Madras Government: Dutch Records No. 13* (New Delhi: Usha, 1984), pp. 212–13.
2. Gijs Kruijtzer, 'European Migration in the Dutch Sphere', in G. Oostindie (ed.), *Dutch Colonialism, Migration and Cultural Heritage: Past and Present* (Leiden: KITLV Press, 2008), pp. 97–154, pp. 102–3.
3. Anjana Singh, *Fort Cochin in Kerala, 1750–1830: The Social Condition of a Dutch Community in an Indian Milieu* (Leiden: Brill, 2010), p. 121.
4. Binu John Mailaparambil, *Lords of the Sea: the Ali Rajas of Cannanore and the political economy of Malabar* (Leiden: Brill, 2012), p. 86.
5. Rene J. Barendse, *Arabian Seas, 1700–1763* (Leiden: Brill, 2009), p. 577.
6. J.G. Schmitz, 'Rechtshistorische bijdrage tot de kennis van het materiële en formele strafrecht van toepassing op de dienaren van de VOC, voornamelijk betrekking hebbende op het delict van desertie' (PhD thesis, Universiteit Utrecht, 1938); Barendse, *Arabian Seas*, p. 579.
7. Barendse, *Arabian Seas*, p. 579.
8. Mailaparambil, *Lords of the Sea*, p. 86.
9. Singh, *Fort Cochin*, p. 121.
10. Barendse, *Arabian Seas*, pp. 578–9.
11. Barendse, *Arabian Seas*, p. 579; Kruijtzer, 'European Migration', pp. 102–3.
12. Nationaal Archief (NA), Archief van de VOC (VOC), 11327.
13. NA, VOC, 2966.
14. NA, VOC, 3025.
15. NA, VOC, 11330.
16. The number of ships visiting Surat can be derived from the Boekhouder Generaal-Batavia Database, available at http://bgb.huygens.knaw.nl/bgb/. From the Generale Zeemonsterrollen Database, available at http://dutchshipsandsailors.nl/, it can be estimated that on average some eighty-five workers were on board ships sailing (from Batavia) to regions such as Surat, Bengal, Ceylon and Persia. The average is based on 342 ships in the database, excluding small local vessels referred to as *pantjalang*, *hoeker* or

chialoup (leading to an exact average of 83.1). For the local personnel in Surat, the number of forty workers is assumed.

17 Only four ships can be traced to have visited Surat, leading to an estimate of 27 per cent; calculating the desertion rate with the yearly average of eight ships would lead to 14 per cent. Barendse mentioned that 'the Dutch complained in 1760 they lost their entire garrison'. Barendse, *Arabian Seas*, p. 578.

18 W.Ph. Coolhaas, J. van Goor, J.E. Schooneveld-Oosterling and H.K. s'Jacob (eds), *Generale Missiven van Gouverneurs-Generaal en Raden aan Heren XVII der Verenigde Oostindische Compagnie* (The Hague: Martinus Nijhoff, 1960–2007), part VI, p. 126.

19 NA, VOC, 9733.

20 NA, VOC, 9733.

21 NA, VOC, 9733. As reported from Sadraspatnam to Nagapatnam. Original: 'om ze op voorwaarde van 't Cartel weder over te geeven'.

22 NA, VOC, 9733. Original: 'onder eenige vreemde deserteurs, van zelfs weeder terug gekoomen'.

23 NA, VOC, 2580, Malabar, 740.

24 NA, VOC, 2580, Malabar, 740.

25 Galletti, *The Dutch in Malabar*, pp. 88–91.

26 Sri Lanka National Archives (SLNA), VOC Archives, Record Group 1, 2758, 2766, 5906.

27 SLNA 1, 2758, 19.

28 NA, VOC, 8313, Coromandel, 176–81. Original: 'een gedeelte der patnams haar om voorsz: oorsaek den dienst van d' E: Comp: ontrocken en haar hier en daar inde buite stad verscholen hadden'.

29 Original: 'off het niet te bedugten soude wesen wanneeer men gem:te versoek quam aff te slaan dat de rest der patnams haer ook tsoek soude maken twelck eenparigh te bevreesen geoordeelt zijnde'.

30 NA, VOC, 8313, Coromandel, 176–81.

31 NA, VOC, 9733. Original: 'naar Peddapoer, onder bescherminge van den aldaar thans huishoudende prins Annandarasoe'.

32 Galletti, *The Dutch in Malabar*, pp. 88–91.

33 Singh, *Fort Cochin*, p. 121.

34 Kruijtzer, 'European Migration', pp. 102–3.

35 NA, VOC, 9733.

36 Galletti, *The Dutch in Malabar*, pp. 88–91.

37 Matthias van Rossum, *Werkers van de wereld. Globalisering, arbeid en interculturele ontmoetingen tussen Aziatische en Europese zeelieden in dienst van de VOC, 1600–1800* (Hilversum: Uitgeverij Verloren, 2014), pp. 231–2. Before 1658, most workers were allowed even less in the way of overseas advances.

38 J.A. van der Chijs, *Nederlandsch-Indisch Plakaatboek* (Batavia: Landsdrukkerij, 1885–1900), part X, p. 478.

39 Van der Chijs, *Nederlandsch-Indisch Plakaatboek*, X, p. 982.
40 NA, VOC, 9375, 19.
41 Van der Chijs, *Nederlandsch-Indisch Plakaatboek*, II, p. 473.
42 Van der Chijs, *Nederlandsch-Indisch Plakaatboek*, VII, pp. 786–7.
43 See, for example, NA, VOC, 12646. Transcriptions provided by *Tracing History Trust*.
44 Niemeijer, *Batavia*, p. 200; Matthias van Rossum, *Kleurrijke tragiek. De geschiedenis van Nederlandse slavernij in Azië onder de VOC* (Hilversum: Uitgeverij Verloren, 2015). See, for example, the case of Ontong of Palembang, locked in a trunk for two days and nights at the Moorish Guard in the Chinese campong after being suspected of being absent from house without leave. VOC, NA, 9467, case 15.
45 Van der Chijs, *Nederlandsch-Indisch Plakaatboek*, VII, p. 225. Original: 'hun vrijdom konden bewijzen en een permissiebriefje van hun hoofd overleggen'; 'geene andere gehuurde menschen de Boom te laten passeereen, dan die aan de voorsz. Requisiten volkomen voldaan hebben'.
46 Elias Hesse, *Gold-bergwerke in Sumatra 1680–1683*, in S.P. L'Honoré Naber (ed.), *Reisebeschreibungen von Deutschen Beambten und Kriegsleuten im Dienst der Niederländischen West- und Ost-Indischen Kompagnien 1602–1797*, X (The Hague: Martinus Nijhoff, 1931) pp. 117–21.
47 Hesse, *Gold-bergwerke in Sumatra*, p. 22.
48 Hesse, *Gold-bergwerke in Sumatra*, p. 23.
49 Barendse, *Arabian Seas*, p. 578.
50 Ibid. NA, VOC, 2765, f. 15.
51 Galletti, *The Dutch in Malabar*, pp. 212–13.
52 Ibid.
53 Ibid.
54 S. Sen, *Savagery and Colonialism in the Indian Ocean. Power, pleasure and the Andaman islanders* (Abingdon: Routledge, 2010).
55 Rana Behal, *One Hundred Years of Servitude: Political Economy of Tea Plantations in Colonial Assam* (Delhi: Tulika, 2014).
56 *Koloniaal tijdschrift*, 5:2 (1916) 1663.

SELECTED BIBLIOGRAPHY

Agostini, T., '"Deserted His Majesty's Service": Military Runaways, the British-American Press, and the Problem of Desertion during the Seven Years' War', *Journal of Social History* 40:4 (2007), pp. 957–85.
Allen, R., 'A Serious and Alarming Daily Evil: Marronage and its Legacy in Mauritius and the Colonial Plantation World', *Slavery and Abolition* 25:2 (2004), pp. 1–17.
Anderson, C., *Subaltern Lives: Biographies of Colonialism in the Indian Ocean World, 1790–1920* (Cambridge: Cambridge University Press, 2012).
Anderson, R.N., 'The Quilimbo of Palmares: A New Overview of a Maroon State in Seventeenth-Century Brazil', *Journal of Latin American Studies* 28:3 (October 1996), pp. 545–66.
Armstrong, J.C., 'The Slaves, 1652–1795', in R. Elphick and H. Giliomee (eds), *The Shaping of South African Society, 1652–1820* (Cape Town: Longman, 1979).
Balachandran, G., *Globalizing Labour: Indian Seafarers and World Shipping, c. 1870–1945* (Delhi: Oxford University Press, 2012).
Barendse, R.J., *Arabian Seas, 1700–1763* (Leiden: Brill, 2009).
Bearman, P.S., 'Desertion as Localism: Army Unit Solidarity and Group Norms in the U.S. Civil War', *Social Forces* 70:2 (December 1991), pp. 321–42.
Behal, R.P., *One Hundred Years of Servitude: Political Economy of Tea Plantations in Colonial Assam* (Delhi: Tulika, 2014).
Biernacki, R., *The Fabrication of Labour: Germany and Britain, 1640–1914* (Berkeley: University of California Press, 1997).
Brandon, P., 'Accounting for Power: Bookkeeping and the Rationalization of Dutch Naval Administration', in J. Fynn-Paul (ed.), *War, Entrepreneurs, and the State in Europe and the Mediterranean* (Leiden and Boston: Brill, 2014).
Brandon, P., *War, Capital, and the Dutch State (1588–1795)* (Leiden and Boston: Brill, 2015).
Brass, T. and M. van der Linden (eds), *Free and Unfree Labour: The Debate Continues* (Bern: Peter Lang, 1997).
Bröckling, U. and M. Sikora (eds), *Armeen und ihre Deserteure: Vernachlässigte Kapitel einer Militärgeschichte der Neuzeit* (Göttingen: Vandenhoeck & Ruprecht, 1998).
Burschel, P., *Söldner im Nordwestdeutschland des 16. und 17. Jahrhunderts: Sozialgeschichtlichen Studien* (Göttingen: Vandenhoeck & Ruprecht, 1994).
Bush, M. (ed.), *Serfdom and Slavery: Studies in Legal Bondage* (London: Longman 1996).
Campbell, M., *The Maroons of Jamaica 1655–1796: A History of Resistance, Collaboration and Betrayal* (Trenton: African World Press, 1990).

Childs, J., *Armies and Warfare in Europe 1648–1789* (Manchester: Manchester University Press, 1982).
Chowdhury-Zilly, A.N., *The Vagrant Peasant: Agrarian Distress and Desertion in Bengal, 1770 to 1830* (Wiesbaden: Franz Steiner Verlag, 1982).
Christopher, E., *Slave Ships and Their Captive Cargoes, 1730–1807* (Cambridge: Cambridge University Press, 2006).
Coclanis, P.A. (ed.), *The Atlantic Economy during the Seventeenth and Eighteenth Centuries: Organization, Operation, Practice, and Personnel* (Columbia, SC: University of South Carolina Press, 2005).
Cooper, F., *Decolonization and African Society: The Labor Question in French and British Africa* (Cambridge: Cambridge University Press, 1996).
Cooper, F., T. Holt and R. Scott, *Beyond Slavery: Explorations of Race, Labor, and Citizenship in Postemancipation Societies* (Chapel Hill: University of North Carolina Press, 2000).
Craven, P. and D. Hay, 'The Criminalization of Free Labour: Masters and Servants in Comparative Perspective', *Slavery and Abolition* 15:2 (1994), pp. 71–101.
De Vliegher, R., 'Desertie bij Oostendse Oost-Indiëvaarders', in J. Parmentier and S. Spanoghe (eds), *Orbis in Orbem: Liber amicorum John Everaert* (Ghent: Academia Press, 2001).
De Vries, J. and A. van der Woude, *Nederland 1500–1815: De eerste ronde van moderne economische groei* (Amsterdam: Balans, 2005).
Dekker, R., 'Labour Conflicts and Working-Class Culture in Early Modern Holland', *International Review of Social History* 35 (1990), pp. 377–420.
Den Heijer, H., *Goud, ivoor en slaven: Scheepvaart en handel van de Tweede Westindische Compagnie op Afrika, 1674–1740* (Leiden: Walburg Pers, 1997).
Dorreboom, M.L., *'Gelijk hij gecondemneert word mits deezen': Militaire strafrechtspleging bij het krijgsvolk te lande, 1700–1795* (Amsterdam: Cabeljauwpers, 2000).
Dutta, M., 'Disciplining the Madras Army During the Early Years of the English East India Company's Dominance in South India', *Socialnių mokslų studijos/ Societal Studies* 4:3 (2012), pp. 887–99.
Eibach, J., *Frankfurter Verhöre: Städtische Lebenswelten und Kriminalität im 18. Jahrhundert* (Paderborn: Schöningh, 2003).
Ekama, K.J., 'Slavery in Dutch Colombo: A Social History' (unpublished MA thesis, Leiden University Institute for History, 2012).
Fatah-Black, K., 'Orangism, Patriotism, and Slavery in Curaçao, 1795–1796', *International Review of Social History* 58:21 (2013), pp. 1–26.
Fatah-Black, K., 'Suriname and the Atlantic World, 1650–1800' (Dissertation, Leiden University 2013).
Fisher, M.H., 'Working Across the Seas: Indian Maritime Laborers in India, Britain, and in Between, 1600–1857', in R. Behal and M. van der Linden (eds), *Coolies, Capital and Colonialism: Studies in Indian Labor History, International Review of Social History Supplements* (Cambridge: Cambridge University Press, 2006).
Forrest, A., *Conscripts and Deserters: The Army and French Society during the Revolution and Empire* (Oxford: Oxford University Press, 1989).
Gaastra, F.S., 'The Recruitment of Soldiers by the VOC in the 18th Century', in W. Klooster (ed.), *Migration, Trade and Slavery in an Expanding World* (Leiden: KITLV Press, 2009).

Galenson, D.W., *White Servitude in Colonial America: an Economic Analysis* (Cambridge: Cambridge University Press, 1981).

Galenson, D.W., 'The Rise of Free Labor: Economic Change and the Enforcement of Service Contracts in England, 1351–1875', in J.A. James and M. Thomas (eds), *Capitalism in Context: Essays on Economic Development and Cultural Change in Honor of R.M. Hartwell* (Chicago and London: University of Chicago Press, 1994).

Gaspar, D.B., 'Runaways in Seventeenth-Century Antigua', *Boletín de Estudios Latinoamericanos y del Caribe* 26 (1979), pp. 3–13.

Glassman, J., 'The Bondsman's New Clothes: The Contradictory Consciousness of Slave Resistance on the Swahili Coast', *Journal of African History* 32:2 (1991), pp. 303–9.

Glete, J., *War and State in Early Modern Europe: Spain, the Dutch Republic and Sweden as fiscal-military states, 1500–1660* (London: Routledge, 2002).

Groen, P. (ed.), *De Tachtigjarige Oorlog. Van Opstand naar geregelde oorlog 1568–1648* (Amsterdam: Boom, 2013).

Hall, G., *Social Control in Slave Plantation Societies: A Comparison of St. Domingue and Cuba* (Baltimore and London: The Johns Hopkins University Press, 1971).

Hall, N.A.T., 'Maritime Maroons: "Grand Marronage" from the Danish West Indies', *William and Mary Quarterly*, Third Series, 42:4 (1985), pp. 476–98.

Hirschmann, A.O., *Exit, Voice, and Loyalty: Responses to Decline in Firms, Organizations, and States* (Cambridge, MA: Harvard University Press, 1970).

Hondius, D., 'Access to the Netherlands of Enslaved and Free Black Africans: Exploring Legal and Social Historical Practices in the Sixteenth–Nineteenth Centuries', *Slavery & Abolition* 33:3 (2011), pp. 377–95.

Jagdew, E., *Vrede te midden van oorlog in Suriname: Inheemsen, Europeanen, Marrons en vredesverdragen, 1667–1863* (Paramaribo: Anton de Kom Universiteit, 2014).

Jones, E.A., 'Fugitive Women: Slavery and Social Change in Early Modern Southeast Asia', *Journal of Southeast Asian Studies* 38:2 (2007), pp. 215–45.

Jordaan, H., H. den Heijer and V. Enthoven (eds), *Geweld in de West: een militaire geschiedenis van de Nederlandse Atlantische wereld, 1600–1800* (Leiden: Brill, 2013).

Kars, M., 'Policing and Transgressing Borders: Soldiers and Cross-Cultural Relations in the Berbice Slave Rebellion, 1763–1764', *New West Indian Guide/ Nieuwe West-Indische Gids* 83:3 (2009), pp. 191–217.

Ketting, H., *Leven, werk en rebellie aan boord van Oost-Indiëvaarders (1595–1650)* (Amsterdam: Aksant, 2005).

Klein, M., *Breaking the Chains: Slavery, Bondage and Emancipation in Modern Africa and Asia* (Madison: The University of Wisconsin Press, 1993).

Kock, V. de, *Those in Bondage: An Account of the Life of the Slave at the Cape in the Days of the Dutch East India Company* (London: George Allen & Unwin, 1950).

Kruijtzer, G., 'European Migration in the Dutch Sphere', in G. Oostindie (ed.), *Dutch Colonialism, Migration and Cultural Heritage: Past and Present* (Leiden: KITLV Press, 2008).

Lalla, B., *Defining Jamaican Fiction: Marronage and the Discourse of Survival* (Tuscaloosa: University of Alabama Press, 1996).

Lichtenstein, A. and C. De Vito, 'Writing a Global History of Convict Labour', *International Review of Social History* 58:2 (August 2013), pp. 285–325.

Linebaugh, P. and M. Rediker, *The Many-Headed Hydra: Sailors, Slaves, Commoners, and the Hidden History of the Revolutionary Atlantic* (London: Verso, 2000).

Lohnstein, M., *De militie van de sociëteit c.q. directie van Suriname in de achttiende eeuw* (unpublished manuscript, 1984).

Lucassen, J., 'A Multinational and its Labor Force: The Dutch East India Company, 1595–1795', *International Labor and Working-Class History* 66:2 (2004), pp. 12–39.

Morgan, P.D., *Arming Slaves: From Classical Times to the Modern Age* (Yale: Yale University Press, 2006).

Oostindie, G. and J.V. Roitman (eds), *Dutch Atlantic Connections, 1680–1800* (Leiden: Brill, 2014).

Parker, G., *The Military Revolution: Military Innovation and the Rise of the West, 1500–1800*, 2nd edn (Cambridge: Cambridge University Press, 1996).

Parrott, D., *The Business of War: Military Enterprise and Military Revolution in Early Modern Europe* (Cambridge: Cambridge University Press, 2012).

Parthesius, R., *Dutch Ships in Tropical Waters: The Development of the Dutch East India Company (VOC) Shipping Network in Asia 1595–1660* (Amsterdam: Amsterdam University Press, 2007).

Peers, D.M., 'Sepoys, Soldiers and the Lash: Race, Caste and Army Discipline in India, 1820–50', *The Journal of Imperial and Commonwealth History* 23:2 (1995), pp. 211–47.

Penn, N., *Rogues, Rebels and Runaways: Eighteenth-Century Cape Characters* (Cape Town: David Philip Publishers, 1999).

Penn, N., 'Great Escapes: Deserting Soldiers during Noodt's Cape Governorship, 1727–1729', *South African Historical Journal* 59:1 (2007), pp. 171–203.

Price, R. (ed.), *Maroon Societies: Rebel Slave Communities in the Americas* (Baltimore: Johns Hopkins University Press, 1996).

Pröve, R., 'Zum Verhältnis von Militär und Gesellschaft im Spiegel gewaltsamer Rekrutierungen (1648–1789)', *Zeitschrift für historische Forschung* 22 (1995), pp. 191–223.

Rediker, M., *Between the Devil and the Deep Blue Sea: Merchant Seamen, Pirates, and the Anglo-American Maritime World, 1700–1750* (Cambridge: Cambridge University Press, 1987).

Ross, R., 'The Occupations of Slaves in Eighteenth-Century Cape Town', *Studies in the History of Cape Town* 2 (1980), pp. 1–14.

Ross, R., *Cape of Torments: Slavery and Resistance in South Africa* (London: Routledge & Kegan Paul, 1983).

Rupert, L.M., *Creolization and Contraband: Curaçao in the Early Modern Atlantic World* (Athens, GA: University of Georgia Press, 2012).

Sanborn, J.A., *Drafting the Russian Nation: Military Conscription, Total War, and Mass Politics, 1905–1925* (DeKalb: Northern Illinois University Press, 2003).

Schoeman, K., *Early Slavery at the Cape of Good Hope, 1652–1717* (Pretoria: Protea Book House, 2007).

Scott, J., *Weapons of the Weak: Everyday Forms of Peasant Resistance* (New Haven: Yale University Press, 1985).
Sen, S., *Savagery and Colonialism in the Indian Ocean: Power, Pleasure and the Andaman Islanders* (Abingdon: Routledge, 2010).
Shell, R., *Children of Bondage: A Social History of the Slave Society at the Cape of Good Hope, 1652–1838* (Hanover: University Press of New England, 1994).
Sikora, M., *Disziplin und Desertion: Strukturprobleme militärischer Organisation im 18. Jahrhundert* (Berlin: Duncker und Humbolt, 1996).
Singh, A., *Fort Cochin in Kerala, 1750–1830: The Social Condition of a Dutch Community in an Indian Milieu* (Leiden: Brill, 2010).
Stanziani, A., 'Beyond Colonialism: Servants, Wage Earners and Indentured Migrants in Rural France and on Reunion Island (c. 1750–1900)', *Labor History* 54:1 (2013), pp. 64–87.
Stanziani, A., 'Local Bondage in Global Economies: Servants, Wage-Earners, and Indentured Migrants in Nineteenth-century France, Great Britain and the Mascarene Islands', *Modern Asian Studies* 1 (2013), pp. 1–34.
Stanziani, A., *Bondage: Labor and Rights in Eurasia from the Sixteenth to the Early Twentieth Centuries* (New York: Berghahn Books, 2014).
Stanziani, A., *Sailors, Slaves, and Immigrants in the Indian Ocean World, 1750–1914* (New York: Palgrave, 2014).
Steinfeld, R., *The Invention of Free Labor: The Employment Relation in English and American Law and Culture, 1350–1870* (Chapel Hill: University of North Carolina Press, 1991).
Swart, E., *Krijgsvolk: Militaire professionalisering en het ontstaan van het Staatse leger, 1568–1590* (Amsterdam: Amsterdam University Press, 2006).
Tallett, F., *War and Society in Early-Modern Europe, 1495–1715* (London and New York: Routledge, 1992).
Thoden van Velzen, H.U.E. and W. Hoogbergen, *Een zwarte vrijstaat in Suriname: De Okaanse samenleving in de 18^e eeuw* (Leiden: KITLV, 2011).
Thompson, A., *Flight to Freedom: African Runaways and Maroons in the Americas* (Kingston: University of the West Indies Press, 2006).
Thomson, J.E., *Mercenaries, Pirates and Sovereigns: State-building and Extraterritorial Violence in Early Modern Europe* (Princeton: Princeton University Press, 1994).
Tomlins, C., *Freedom Bound: Law, Labor, and Civic Identity in Colonizing British America, 1580–1865* (Cambridge: Cambridge University Press, 2010).
Van der Linden, M., *Workers of the World: Essays toward a Global Labor History* (Leiden: Brill, 2008).
Van der Putte, R., 'Surinaamse "Wegloopers" van de Jaren 1767–1802', *OSO: Tijdschrift voor Surinamistiek* 24:2 (2005), pp. 276–88.
Van Nimwegen, O., *'Deser landen crijchsvolck': Het Staatse leger en de militaire revoluties 1588–1688* (Amsterdam: Bakker, 2006).
Van Rossum, M., '"Amok!" Mutinies and Slaves on Dutch East Indiamen in the 1780s', *International Review of Social History* 58, Special Issue (2013), pp. 109–30.
Van Rossum, M., 'The Rise of the Asian Sailor? Inter-Asiatic Shipping, the Dutch East India Company and Maritime Labour Markets (1500–1800)', in S. Bhattacharya (ed.), *Towards a New History of Work* (New Delhi: Tulika Books, 2014).

Van Rossum, M., *Werkers van de wereld: Globalisering, arbeid en interculturele ontmoetingen tussen Aziatische en Europese zeelieden in dienst van de VOC, 1600–1800* (Hilversum: Verloren, 2014).

Van Rossum, M., *Kleurrijke tragiek: De geschiedenis van Nederlandse slavernij in Azië onder de VOC* (Hilversum: Uitgeverij Verloren, 2015).

Vink, M., '"The World's Oldest Trade": Dutch Slavery and Slave Trade in the Indian Ocean in the Seventeenth Century', *Journal of World History* 14:2 (2003), pp. 131–77.

Wilson, P.H., 'The German "Soldier Trade" of the Seventeenth and Eighteenth Centuries: A Reassessment', *The International History Review* 18:4 (1996), pp. 757–92.

Winter, M., '"Der Untertan auf Posten": Deserteursverfolgung an der brandenburgisch-mecklenburgischen Grenze im 18. Jahrhundert', *Militär und Gesellschaft in der Frühen Neuzeit* 10 (2006), pp. 139–80.

Wokeck, M.S., *Trade in Strangers: The Beginnings of Mass Migration to North America* (University Park, PA: Pennsylvania State University Press, 1999).

Worden, N., 'Strangers Ashore: Sailor Identity and Social Conflict in Mid-18th Century Cape Town', *Kronos* 33 (2007), pp. 72–83.

Worden, N. and G. Groenewald, *Trials of Slavery: Selected Documents Concerning Slaves from the Criminal Records of the Council of Justice at the Cape of Good Hope, 1705–1794* (Cape Town: Van Riebeeck Society for the Publication of South African Historical Documents, 2005).

Zemon Davis, N., 'Judges, Masters, Diviners: Slaves' Experience of Criminal Justice in Colonial Suriname', *Law and History Review* 29:4 (2011), pp. 925–84.

Zürcher, E.J. (ed.), *Fighting for a Living: A Comparative History of Military Labour 1500–2000* (Amsterdam: Amsterdam University Press, 2014).

INDEX OF PLACES

Ambon 9, 195
Amsterdam 75, 90n.17, 100, 119, 132, 139–41, 143–5, 155n.29, 156n.49, 196

Bali 148–50, 173
Banda 136
Batavia 9–10, 130–3, 135–6, 144–52, 153n.8, 154n.20, 155n.41, 161, 167, 171, 177, 189–91, 195–7, 200n.16
Bengal 9, 128, 136, 142, 144, 148, 161, 164, 172, 177, 189–91, 193, 200n.16
Berbice 98, 107, 111–12
Bimilipatnam 191
Brazil 9, 20, 32, 98, 102–3, 117
Breda 87

Cannanore 188
Cape Comorin 192
Cape of Good Hope 9–10, 132, 141–2, 144, 149–50, 161–84, 193 (see also Cape Town)
Cape Town 10, 165–8, 171–2, 174–6, 178
Cape Verde 141–2
Caribbean 39, 98, 101, 103
Ceylon 132–4, 142, 151, 154n.20, 164, 182n.45, 188, 190–3, 200n.16
China 7, 31, 132, 193
Chingleput 191
Cochin 187–8, 194
Colombo 132, 183n.62
Coromandel 142, 156n.55, 164, 191–5
Curacao 98, 103, 105, 107, 113, 116

Demerara 98, 116
Dinant 49, 66n.2

Dutch Republic 6, 9, 74–6, 84, 88, 102, 112, 130–3, 137, 141–4, 151, 157n.69, 181n.27, 189–90

Edam, island 132, 137, 150, 195
Elmina 98, 108
England 17–18, 20–1, 26, 75, 141 (see also Great Britain)
Essequibo 98

Fort Amsterdam 104, 111, 113–14
Fort Zeelandia 104
France 17, 19–20, 26, 50, 76
Frankfurt am Main 49–72

Galle 155n.25, 192
Goa 9, 169, 188
Göttingen 56
Great Britain 19, 21–3, 25–6, 103 (see also England)
Guiana 98, 112, 115

Hamburg 113, 119
Heidelberg 59, 61

India 18, 21, 31, 33, 35, 38, 132–3, 153n.8, 187–202

Java 128, 132–4, 144–5, 151

Luik 50, 74, 80, 84–5, 89

Macassar 173
Madagascar 21, 150, 161, 164, 174–6, 180
Malabar 142, 161, 164, 187–202
Malacca 127–8, 142, 153n.8, 154n.20, 191
Middelburg 100–2, 109, 118

Nagapatnam 191–2
Namur 80–1
Nürnberg 49, 59

Onrust, island 145–7

Paramaribo 116
Pulicat 191

Rio de la Goa 175
Riouw 128
Robben Island 150
Rotterdam 119

Sadraspatnam 191
St Eustatius 98, 103–4

Semarang 145, 147
Spain 20, 77
Strassbourg 50, 59
Sumbawa 172
Surat 9, 142, 146, 156n.55, 189, 193, 197, 200n.16, 201n.17
Suriname 9, 20, 37–8, 76, 88, 92n.30, 98, 100, 103–7, 112–14, 116

Utrecht 141

Veere 118, 136
Vlissingen 118

Zeeland 11, 100–2, 109, 113

SUBJECT INDEX

accommodation *including* lodging 10, 20, 40, 60, 65, 116, 167

bonus *including* bounty, *handgeld* 7, 40, 50, 53–6, 58–9, 65, 68n.16, 86
bounty *see* bonus

capitalism 12, 16, 32, 78, 130
career 4, 11, 19, 61, 66, 74, 84–6, 88, 93n.52, 100, 115–16, 134, 142–3
clothing 20, 39–40, 138
coercion 4–5, 10, 12, 16–17, 22, 25–7, 37, 50, 52, 54–5, 59, 98–9, 130, 134–5, 140, 145, 149, 197, 199–200
competition 4, 17, 22, 24–6, 50–2, 54–6, 59, 61, 65, 75, 78, 104, 112–14, 117, 129, 188–9, 193
conscription 15–17, 32
conspiracy *see* plot
contract 4–11, 18–24, 33, 35, 52–4, 58–9, 63–4, 74–8, 82–9, 98–101, 103, 130–6, 144, 146–52, 192–200
control 4–7, 10–12, 16, 22–6, 33–4, 39, 51–2, 59–61, 64–5, 76, 78, 114–18, 129–32, 139–40, 144, 148–52, 161, 178, 189, 195–200
convicts *including* convict labour, prisoners 8, 15–17, 21, 34, 38, 41n.6, 44n.43, 49–50, 52–3, 115, 121n.7, 130, 132, 134–7, 148–51, 155n.29, 162–3, 171, 173, 176–7, 193, 195, 199
cooperation *including* collaboration, solidarity, support 9, 21, 40, 59–60, 63, 107, 112–13, 163, 172, 174, 177–9
corvee labour 5–7, 9–10, 43n.24, 132, 134, 151, 192, 200
Court of Justice (*see also* law)
  Court of Aldermans 136
  Court of Justice 8, 25, 44n.43, 49, 50, 52, 58–9, 61–2, 65, 80–4, 88, 128, 135–7, 140, 145–9, 162, 166, 169–70, 192
  records of 38, 58, 61, 65, 70n.45, 166, 168, 171, 179

death *see* mortality rate; punishment, death penalty
debt 11, 19, 58, 106, 108, 114–16, 118, 123n.56, 134, 137–9
desertion rate 8–11, 19, 22, 50, 57, 99–100, 102–6, 117, 131, 137–8, 140, 142–4, 188–90, 201n.17
discipline *including* drills 4–5, 25, 34, 50, 52, 58, 60–1, 74–5, 78–9, 82–3, 88, 97, 107, 115, 130, 132, 199

East India Company
  Compagnies des Indes (CdI) 17
  East India Company (EIC) 31, 188, 197–8
  Verenigde Oostindische Compagnie (VOC) 7–9, 54, 127–200
extradition, extradition treaties 57–8, 64, 112, 115, 135

factories *including* sugar, rope and trade factories 4–5, 24–5, 132, 137, 150, 152, 164, 189, 193, 195

food 10, 20, 34, 60, 65, 108–9, 140, 150, 152, 170–2, 179
forts 4–5, 10, 12, 79, 98–9, 104, 106, 108, 111, 113–15, 117, 143, 188, 191, 194
free labour 4, 11, 15, 20–3, 76, 134

globalization 4–6, 12, 129–31, 151, 189, 200

handgeld see bounty
household
    (domestic) servants and 8, 16, 19, 23, 25
    slaves and 136, 147, 167–70, 175, 179

impressment 17, 52, 58, 63–4, 81–3, 88, 103
indenture 8, 15–16, 18–22, 33, 76 (*see also* servants)
intermediaries
    intermediary (in general) *including* broker 3, 9–10, 91n.17, 109, 138–9, 156n.44,
    recruiter 3, 10, 51–6, 58–9, 61, 64–5, 134, 137–40, 146, 150, 152, 156n.44, 188
    translator 3

labour market *see* market
law
    criminal law 17, 75, 130, 134, 136, 176, 188
    domestic law 8, 11, 136–7, 155n.40, 169–70
    labour laws 5, 18, 21, 23–5, 61, 74–6, 130, 134, 188
    military law 61–2, 65, 78–9, 88
    poor and vagrancy laws 17, 21, 23, 25
licenses *see* passes
lodgings *see* accommodation

maltreatment *see* treatment
markets 4, 9–12, 15–19, 23–6, 30, 49–51, 53, 55, 59, 61, 63, 65, 75, 78, 99, 103–4, 130, 147, 151, 154n.22

maroon
    absence, temporary 8, 135–7, 144, 147–8, 151, 163, 169, 170, 179, 182n.40, 193 (*see also petit marronage*)
    communities 3–4, 8–9, 15, 20, 32, 37, 39, 98, 104, 106–7, 111–13, 116, 150–1, 165, 169, 175, 180, 181n.19
    petit marronage 8, 105–7 (*see also* temporary absence)
    states 32
    towns 20
    wars 98
Middelburgsche Commercie Compagnie (MCC) 7, 11, 100–2, 109, 118
migration 4–5, 8, 12, 15–16, 20–2, 26, 33, 51, 75–6, 194, 198–9
mines 5, 12, 34, 98, 199
mortality rate 100, 164
mutinies 4, 35, 102–3, 107–9, 111–12, 116, 150

navy *including* admiralty 7–8, 16–18, 32, 107, 115–16, 123n.56, 139
negotiation 36, 52–4, 60, 63, 65, 77–9, 84–6, 98, 108, 117, 150, 192

oaths
    military, oath at recruitment 53–4, 58
    runaways, oath of loyalty by *including* round robin 10, 111, 115, 161–2, 177 (*see also* petitions)

passes *including* license, passport, permit, *vrijbrief* 12, 39, 44n.45, 61, 63, 65, 69n.43, 77, 79, 84–7, 92nn.31–2, 93n.54, 127–8, 197–9
payment 11, 21, 34–6, 40, 51, 53–4, 57, 59–60, 65, 78, 82–3, 86, 88, 103, 108, 116, 130, 136–9, 145, 191, 195–6, 196–9
permit *see* passes

petitions 10, 43n.26, 63
planned escape *see* plot
plantations 4–5, 12, 20–2, 33–5, 37–40, 76, 98–9, 104–12, 115–17, 199
plots 9, 38, 44n.43, 106–8, 111, 113–15, 162–3, 170–1, 177, 179, 182n.45 (*see also* oaths)
press-gang *see* impressment
prison 16, 34, 38, 42n.18, 140, 192
prisoner *see* convict
prisoner of war 19, 23, 49, 151
provisioning *including* supplies 21–2, 38–9, 57, 64, 103, 105, 108, 113, 138, 145, 162, 161, 164, 170–1, 179, 189
punishment
 death penalty 11, 36, 61–3, 65, 73, 77–88, 105, 115, 136–7, 188 (*see also* discipline)
 gauntlet, running the 11, 62–3, 65, 73, 81–2, 87
 hunting of runaways 12, 38, 115, 198–9
 imprisonment 23–4, 50, 58, 136, 177
 punishment (in general) 11–12, 19–22, 25, 31, 34–6, 40, 51, 57–8, 61–5, 73, 75, 77–8, 81–5, 87–9, 98–9, 106, 109, 113, 115, 118, 132–7, 142, 144, 146–7, 162–3, 168–71, 179, 188, 194–5, 197–9
 shame, shaming 62, 78

recruitment 3, 6, 10, 16–18, 37, 40, 50–9, 61, 63–5, 68nn.13–15, 70n.45, 74–5, 77, 80–1, 83–4, 86, 88–9, 99, 101–4, 118, 129–32, 134, 137–40, 142–6, 148–52, 161, 171–2, 176, 179, 188, 195–7 (*see also* intermediaries)
revolt
 by convicts 150
 by slaves 32, 38, 98–9, 106, 111–12, 150. 157n.84, 164, 178–9
 by sailors 150, 157n.84
 by soldiers 121n.8
 by workers in general 6, 38, 43n.24, 134, 151
round robin *see* oaths, runaways

servant 7, 15–16, 18, 19, 21–5, 50, 55, 74, 76, 79, 82, 88, 128, 136, 140, 191, 196–7 (*see also* household)
smuggling 16–17, 56, 100, 116, 129, 134
supplies *see* provisioning

temporary absence 8–9, 76, 79, 87, 105, 135–7, 144, 151, 169–70
trading companies 4, 6, 50, 52, 129–30, 135, 137, 143, 152, 187–9, 193–4, 198–9 (*see also* *individual companies*)
treatment *including* maltreatment 10–11, 21, 58, 60, 70n.54, 74–6, 78, 83, 134, 142, 145, 191

uprising *see* revolt

Verenigde Oostindische Compagnie (VOC) *see* East India Company
Vrijbrief see passes

West Indische Compagnie (WIC) 7, 98, 103–4, 108, 117
women 7–8, 34, 55, 99, 147–8, 162, 164, 166–70, 178–9, 181n.23, 193

www.ingramcontent.com/pod-product-compliance
Lightning Source LLC
Chambersburg PA
CBHW050138240426
43673CB00043B/1720